ISBN 978-1-330-10293-0
PIBN 10026428

This book is a reproduction of an important historical work. Forgotten Books uses
state-of-the-art technology to digitally reconstruct the work, preserving the original format
whilst repairing imperfections present in the aged copy. In rare cases, an imperfection in
the original, such as a blemish or missing page, may be replicated in our edition. We do,
however, repair the vast majority of imperfections successfully; any imperfections that
remain are intentionally left to preserve the state of such historical works.

1 MONTH OF
FREE
READING

at

www.ForgottenBooks.com

By purchasing this book you are eligible for one month membership to ForgottenBooks.com, giving you unlimited access to our entire collection of over 700,000 titles via our web site and mobile apps.

To claim your free month visit:

www.forgottenbooks.com/free26428

English
Français
Deutsche
Italiano
Español
Português

www.forgottenbooks.com

Mythology Photography **Fiction**
Fishing Christianity **Art** Cooking
Essays Buddhism Freemasonry
Medicine **Biology** Music **Ancient
Egypt** Evolution Carpentry Physics
Dance Geology **Mathematics** Fitness
Shakespeare **Folklore** Yoga Marketing
Confidence Immortality Biographies
Poetry **Psychology** Witchcraft
Electronics Chemistry History **Law**
Accounting **Philosophy** Anthropology
Alchemy Drama Quantum Mechanics
Atheism Sexual Health **Ancient History**
Entrepreneurship Languages Sport
Paleontology Needlework Islam
Metaphysics Investment Archaeology
Parenting Statistics Criminology
Motivational

YEDO AND PEKING.

A NARRATIVE

OF

A JOURNEY TO THE CAPITALS

OF

JAPAN AND CHINA.

WITH NOTICES OF

THE NATURAL PRODUCTIONS, AGRICULTURE, HORTICULTURE, AND TRADE OF
THOSE COUNTRIES, AND OTHER THINGS MET WITH BY THE WAY.

BY ROBERT FORTUNE,

HONORARY MEMBER OF THE AGRI-HORT. SOCIETY OF INDIA.

WITH MAP AND ILLUSTRATIONS

LONDON:
JOHN MURRAY, ALBEMARLE STREET.
1863.

N: PRINTED BY W. CLOWES AND SONS, STAMFORD STREET,
AND CHARING CROSS.

PREFACE.

THE Empire of Japan has been all but closed to the inhabitants of other nations for more than two hundred years. Except a few Dutch and Chinese, who were kept almost like prisoners at Nagasaki, no foreigners have been allowed to reside or trade in the country since about the year 1636. A great and unexpected change has now taken place; Japan has not only opened some of her ports to foreign trade, but has also sent her Ambassadors to visit many of the principal Courts of Europe and America.

The news of the success which attended the English and French forces in the earlier part of the late war with China was quickly wafted across the "Eastern Sea" to Yedo, and, doubtless, had no little effect in inducing the Tycoon and his Ministers (in an evil hour for them) to open their country to foreign intercourse. It is to be hoped that this re-entry into the great family of nations will not bring on those dissensions and wars which marked the period between 1560 and

1636, when the experiment was last tried; for it is well known that, ever since foreigners were expelled from Japan, " the land has had peace."

This change of policy on the part of the Japanese Government gave me an opportunity which I had long desired of visiting the country. I was well aware that Japan was remarkable for the beauty of its scenery, and that it was rich in many species of trees, and other vegetable productions of an ornamental and useful kind, unknown in Europe. With the view of making collections of these and other objects of natural history and works of art, I took my departure for the " far East" in the summer of 1860, and reached Japan in the month of October of that year.

The story of my wanderings is now presented to the reader, with the hope that it may add somewhat to the knowledge already acquired concerning this strange people and their very beautiful land. I have confined my descriptions in a great measure to what came under my own observation. The manners and customs of the people are painted as they appeared to me in their everyday life. The natural productions of the country, whether of commercial importance to other nations, or " pleasant to the eye, and good for food," I have very fully described; and

I have endeavoured to show that its export trade is capable of being greatly increased, particularly in those staple articles of tea and silk, which have now become almost necessaries of life amongst ourselves.

The Agriculture of the country was carefully examined; and, as it is in many respects somewhat remarkable, a full description of it has been given in the following pages. I have also ventured to make a few observations on our political relations with this extraordinary people, which may be of some interest at the present time.

Most of the illustrations were kindly sketched for me by Dr. Dickson of China. I am also indebted to my fellow-passenger, Dr. Barton, for some views in the Inland Sea, and for that of Castle Island, Cape Gotto.

When I had finished my work in Japan, the Chinese war had been brought to a successful termination, and I was enabled to visit the new ports of Chefoo and Tien-tsin, on the Gulf of Pe-chele, and also the capital city of Peking itself, and the mountains which lie beyond it. In the concluding chapters of the work I have sought to give a faithful description of this part of my travels over a country which, until the last war, was almost as little known to Europeans as Japan itself. Mr. Wyndham, of H.M. Legation in Peking, furnished me with the sketch of the curious " *White-barked Pine*" of that country.

Having thus given an outline of what may be expected in this narrative of my journey to the capitals of Zipangu and Cathay, I have only to solicit the kindness and indulgence of my readers, trusting that they will overlook the many faults of my imperfect performance.

THE AUTHOR.

London, February, 1863.

CONTENTS.

CHAPTER I.

CHAPTER II.

CHAPTER III.

CONTENTS.

CHAPTER IV.

CHAPTER V.

CHAPTER VI.

CHAPTER VII.

CHAPTER VIII.

CHAPTER IX.

CHAPTER X.

CHAPTER XI.

CHAPTER XII.

CHAPTER XIII.

CHAPTER XIV.

CHAPTER XV.

CHAPTER XVI.

CHAPTER XVII.

CHAPTER XVIII.

CHAPTER XIX.

CHAPTER XX.

LIST OF ILLUSTRATIONS.

YEDO AND PEKING.

View of Castle Island, Cape Gotto

CHAPTER I.

First view of Japan — Curious islands — Papenberg — Massacre of Christians — Visit from the officials — Harbour of Nagasaki — Desima of old — Desima of the present day — Japanese factory — Town of Nagasaki — Tea-houses — Salamanders — Buddhist temples — Large camphor-trees — Tombs — Mimic processions — Dr. Siebold's residence — Excursions — Epunga — Natural productions — Scenery — Trade of Nagasaki — Its capabilities as a Sanatarium.

At daylight on the 12th of October, 1860, the swift little barque 'Marmora,' in which I was a passenger from China, was rapidly approaching the coast of Japan—a country at the ends of the earth, and well named by its inhabitants "the

Kingdom of the Origin of the Sun." When I came on deck in the morning the far-famed shores of *Zipangu* lay spread before my wondering eyes for the first time. Having heard and read so many stories of this strange land—of its stormy coasts, on which many a goodly vessel had been wrecked; of its fearful earthquakes, which were said to have thrown up, in a single night, mountains many thousands of feet above the level of the sea; of its luxuriant vegetation, full of strange and beautiful forms; of its curious inhabitants; and last, but not least, of its salamanders!—I had long looked upon Japan much in the same light as the Romans regarded our own isles in the days of the ancient Britons.

My first view of these shores, however, did a good deal towards dispelling this delusion. It was a lovely morning. The sun rose from behind the eastern mountains without a cloud to obscure his rays. The Gotto islands and Cape Gotto were passed to the north of us, and with a fair wind and smooth sea we were rapidly approaching the large island of Kiu-siu, on which the town of Nagasaki is situated. The land is hilly and mountainous, and in many instances it rises perpendicularly from the sea. These perpendicular rocky cliffs have a very curious appearance as one sails along. There are also a number of queer-looking detached little islands dotted about; and one almost wonders how they got there, as they seem to have no connexion with any other

land near them. Some of them are crowned with
a scraggy pine-tree or two, and look exactly like
those bits of rockwork which are constantly met
with in the gardens of China and Japan. No
doubt these rocky islands have suggested the idea
worked out in gardens, and they have been well
imitated. Others of these rocks look in the distance like ships under full sail, and in one instance
I observed a pair of them exactly like fishing-
junks, which are generally met with in pairs.
Nearer the shore the islands are richly clothed
with trees and brushwood, resembling those pretty
"Pulos" which are seen in the Eastern Archi-
pelago. The highest hills on this part of the
mainland of Kiu-siu are about 1500 feet above
the level of the sea; but hills of every height,
from 300 to 1500 feet, and of all forms, were exposed to our view as we approached the entrance
to the harbour of Nagasaki. Many of these hills
were terraced nearly to their summits, and at this
season these terraces were green with the young
crops of wheat and barley.

The pretty little island of Papenberg stands as
if it were a sentinel guarding the harbour of
Nagasaki. Pretty it certainly is, and yet it is
associated with scenes of persecution, cruelty, and
bloodshed of the most horrible description. "If
history spoke true," says Captain Sherard Osborn,
" deeds horrid enough for it to have been for ever
blighted by God's wrath have been perpetrated
there during the persecutions of the Christians in

the seventeenth century. It was the Golgotha of
the many martyrs to the Roman Catholic faith. '
There, by day and by night, its steep cliffs had
rung with the agonized shrieks of strong men, or
. the wail of women and children, launched to rest,
after torture, in the deep waters around the island.
If Jesuit records are to be believed, the fortitude
and virtue exhibited by their Japanese converts
in those sad hours of affliction have not been excelled in any part of the world since religion gave
another plea to man to destroy his fellow-creature ;
and may it not be that the beauty with which
Nature now adorns that rock of sorrows is her halo
of glory around a spot rendered holy by the suf-
ferings, doubtless, of many that were brave and
good ? "   As we passed the island we gazed with
awe and pity on its perpendicular side, from
which these Christians were cast headlong into
the sea.

As soon as our ship rounded Papenberg the
harbour and town of Nagasaki came full into view.
On each side of this entrance to the bay there are
numerous batteries, apparently full of guns. On
Papenberg itself, as well as on every little island
and headland, fortifications were observed as we
sailed along. There is also a flagstaff and tele-
graph station on one of the hills ; and the moment
a ship is seen approaching, a signal is made and
passed on to Nagasaki. We were not molested
by either guard-boat or customhouse officer, but
allowed to sail quietly in to our anchorage. Here

we were boarded by sundry officials, who immediately began to put all sorts of questions regarding the ship, her cargo and passengers; and the
information obtained was all committed to paper.
The commanding officer was then informed that
two of these gentry would be left on board, and
he was requested to give them shelter and accommodation in the cabin.

The harbour of Nagasaki is one of the most
beautiful in the world. It is about a mile in
width, and threé or four in length. When you
are inside it appears to be completely land-locked,
and has all the appearance of an inland lake.
The hills around it are some 1500 feet in height,
and their surface is divided and broken up by long
ridges and deep glens or valleys which extend
far up towards the summits. These ridges and
glens are for the most part richly wooded, while
all the more fertile spots are terraced and under
cultivation. The whole scene presents a quiet
and charming picture of Nature's handiwork inter-
mingled with the labour of man.

On the south side of the harbour there has been
a portion of land set apart for the subjects of
foreign nations whose Governments have lately
made treaties with Japan. The various Consuls,
most of whom are also merchants, reside at present in small houses or temples on the sides of
the hill behind the settlement. It is an interesting sight to see the flags of several Western
nations—English, French, American, and Por-

tuguese—flying at this distance from home. A
great portion of the land set apart for the
foreign settlement was in the course of being
reclaimed from the sea, and ere long a town of
considerable size will rise on the shores of this
beautiful bay.

The island of Desima—dear old Desima, where
the Dutch have traded and dreamed so long—lies
a little further up the bay, and looks in the distance like a small fort or breastwork in front of
Nagasaki.* In these days, when Japan has to
a great extent been opened to foreigners, it is
amusing to read the account of the restrictions
which were placed upon the movements of the
Dutch during the period when all the trade of
Japan was their own. The little island was only
separated from Nagasaki by a narrow canal
spanned by a stone bridge, but the dwellers on
either side were prevented from seeing each other
by means of a high wall. The bridge was closed
by a gate, beside which was a guardhouse occupied
by police and soldiers; and no one was allowed to
quit the island on any pretence without the permission of the Governor. Japanese were not
allowed to visit the Dutch without permission, excepting those who were appointed to inspect their
dwelling-place, and then only at certain hours.
The Japanese servants of the Factory were obliged
to leave the island at sunset, and to report them-

* It is about 600 feet in length, and 240 in width.

selves at the guardhouse to prove that they had really left the Factory. The only individuals exempt from leaving the island at sunset were women who had forfeited the first claim of their sex to respect or esteem, and no female of good character was permitted on any pretence to set foot upon Desima. A placard set up near the bridge-gate announced this in the plainest and coarsest terms.

When any member of the Factory wished to visit the town of Nagasaki, or the country in its vicinity, for a little recreation or amusement, he was obliged to send in a petition to the Governor twenty-four hours beforehand. Leave was usually granted, providing the captive was accompanied by a certain number of officials, police-officers, and a compradore. These again had their servants and friends, so that the attendants and hangers-on of one unfortunate pleasure-seeker usually amounted to some twenty or thirty persons, all of whom he was bound to entertain.

On entering the town of Nagasaki the pleasure-party was soon surrounded and followed by all the boys and idlers within reach, who shouted "Holanda! Holanda!" or "Holanda Capitain!" in the Dutchman's ears, and rendered his walk anything but an agreeable one. The excursion into the surrounding country must, however, have fully repaid the unfortunate captive for the dis-agreeables of the town. The scenery amongst the hills is of the most charming description, and must have been fully appreciated by men who were cooped up on a little mud-bank like the island of Desima.

Such was the state of affairs only three or four years ago. At the time of my visit in the autumn of 1860 all this had undergone a wonderful change —certainly wonderful for Japan. The old bridge which connects the island with the town of Nagasaki is still there, and presents a venerable and somewhat ruinous aspect; the guardhouse is now empty, the gate has been removed, a part of the wall has been thrown down, and the Dutch are no longer the prisoners they once were. Like other foreigners, they can now visit the town when they choose, and roam about the surrounding country to any distance within twenty-five or thirty miles, without any interference from the Japanese.

In my wanderings in Desima I stumbled upon a large rough piece of rock, on which were carved the words "Kæmpfer" and "Thunberg." No other eulogy was necessary. It is pleasing to note that the modern Dutch reverence the names of these men of science who have done so much to make us acquainted with the people and natural productions of Japan.

Opposite Desima, and on the other side of the bay, the Japanese have a large factory in active operation. The machinery has been imported from Europe, and the superintendents are Dutch. The Japanese workmen appear to be most expert hands at moulding and casting, and in the general management of steam machinery. In this respect they are far in advance of their neighbours the Chinese. Indeed, to adopt everything foreign which they suppose to be useful, however different it may be from what they possess themselves, and to make themselves masters of the mode of working it, is a marked feature in the character of the Japanese people.

Nagasaki, or Nangasaki, as it is sometimes called, is situated on the northern shores of the bay, and is supposed to contain about 70,000 inhabitants. It is about a mile in length, and three-quarters of a mile in width, and fills up the space of ground between the shores of the bay and the hills which surround it. The streets are wide and clean, compared with those in Chinese towns; but as a general rule the shops are poor, and contain few articles of much value. Substances used as food, eggshell porcelain, lacquer ware of an inferior kind, and modern bronzes, are plentiful' and comparatively cheap. Although the houses of the common people have a poor and mean appearance, there are some of considerable pretensions. Curiously enough, the largest and most notable buildings in the town, if we except the palace of the Governor, are what are called tea-houses—places of amusement, where the entertainments are not such as accord with our ideas of morality. They seem at the present day much in the same condition in which Kæmpfer found them nearly two hundred years ago.

"The handsomest buildings," says Kæmpfer, "belonging to the townspeople, are two streets all occupied by courtesans. The girls in these establishments, which abound throughout Japan, are purchased of their parents when very young. The price varies in proportion to their beauty and the number of years agreed for, which is, generally speaking, ten or twenty, more or less. They are very commodiously lodged in handsome apartments, and great care is taken to teach them to dance, sing, play upon musical instruments, to write letters, and in all other respects to make them as agreeable as possible. The older ones instruct the young ones, and these in their turn serve the older ones as their waiting-maids. Those who make considerable improvement, and for their beauty and agreeable behaviour are oftener sent for, to the great advantage of their masters, are also better accommodated in clothes and lodging, all at the expense of their lovers, who must pay so much the dearer for their favours. . . . . One of the sorriest must watch the house overnight, in a small room near the door, free to all comers upon the payment of one *mase*. Others are sentenced to keep the watch by way of punishment for their misbehaviour.

"After having served their time, if they are married, they pass among the common people for honest women, the guilt of their past lives being by no means laid to their charge, but to that of their parents or relations who sold them in their infancy for so scandalous a way of getting a livelihood, before they were able to choose a more honest one. Besides, as they are generally well bred, that makes it less difficult for them to get husbands. The keepers of these houses, on the contrary, though possessed of never so plentiful estates, are for ever denied admittance into honest company."

The houses of the high officials, wealthy merchants, or retired gentlemen, though generally small, and only of one or two stories in height, are comfortable and cleanly dwelling-places. One marked feature of the people, both high and low, is a love for flowers. Almost every house which has any pretension to respectability has a flower-garden in the rear, oftentimes indeed small, but neatly arranged; this adds greatly to the comfort and happiness of the family. As the lower parts of the Japanese houses and shops are open both before and behind, I had peeps of these pretty little gardens as I passed along the streets; and wherever I observed one better than the rest I did not fail to pay it a visit. Everywhere the inhabitants received me most politely, and permitted me to examine their pet flowers and dwarf trees. Many of these places are exceedingly small, some not much larger than a good-sized dining-room; but the surface is rendered varied and pleasing by means of little mounds of turf, on which are planted dwarf trees kept clipped into fancy forms, and by miniature lakes, in which

gold and silver fish and tortoises disport themselves. It is quite refreshing to the eye to look
out from the houses upon these gardens. The
plants generally met with in them were the following :—*Cycas revoluta*, Azaleas, the pretty little
dwarf variegated bamboo introduced by me into
England from China, Pines, Junipers, Taxus, Podocarpus, *Rhapis flabelliformis*, and some ferns.
These gardens may be called the gardens of the
respectable working classes.

Japanese gentlemen in Nagasaki, whose wealth
enables them to follow out their favourite pursuits more extensively, have another class of
gardens. These, although small according to our
ideas, are still considerably larger than those of
the working classes; many of them are about a
quarter of an acre in extent. They are generally
turfed over; and, like the smaller ones, they are
laid out with an undulating surface, some parts
being formed into little mounds, while others are
converted into lakes. In several of these places
I met with azaleas of extraordinary size—much
larger than I have ever seen in China, or in any
other part of the world, the London exhibitions
not excepted. One I measured was no less than
40 feet in circumference! These plants are kept
neatly nipped and clipped into a fine round form,
perfectly flat upon the top, and look like dining-
room tables. They must be gorgeous objects
when in flower. *Farfugium grande*, and many
other variegated plants still undescribed, were

met with in these gardens, in addition to those I have named as being favourites with the lower orders.

One old gentleman to whom I was introduced by my friend Mr. Mackenzie—Mr. Matotski—has a nice collection of pot-plants arranged on stages, much in the same way as we arrange them in our greenhouses in England. Amongst them I noted small plants of the beautiful *Sciadopitys verticillata*, several *Retinosporas*, some with variegated leaves; *Thujopsis dolabrata*, and variegated examples of laurel, bamboo, orontium, and *Hoya Matotskii*—a name given by some Dutch botanist in honour of the old gentleman, and of which he was not a little proud. Mr. Matotski is a fine mild-looking Japanese, rather beyond the middle age. He has a collection of birds, such as gold and silver pheasants; and in his library are some illustrated botanical books, which he shows with great pride to his visitors. He presented me with a few rare plants from his collection, and offered to procure me some others, of which he had no duplicates in his own garden.

In the course of my rambles I came upon some tubs containing living salamanders for sale, and in the same quarter I observed some striking and beautiful kinds of fowls. These were rather above the ordinary size, but were remarkable for their fine plumage. The tail-feathers were long and gracefully curved, and fine silky ones hung down on each side of the hinder part of the back. Bantams were also plentiful, and bold independent-looking little fellows they appeared to be.

Three streams of water, spanned by numerous bridges, run down from the hills through the town; but at the time of my visit they were nearly dry. Besides supplying the town with water, they are used in summer for purposes of irrigation, and for driving water-mills.

A Chinese town of this size and importance would have had walls and fortifications, but there is nothing of the kind at Nagasaki; indeed, such a mode of defence does not seem to be common in Japan. The streets have gates thrown across them at certain places, and these are always closed at night; and, in the case of any disturbance, during the day, should occasion require it.

Behind the town, on the hill-side, there are many large Buddhist temples and gardens. These are placed in the best situations; the view over the town, the bay, and the distant hills is most charming, and well repays the visitor for the toil of the ascent. Camphor-trees of a great size were common about these temples. They were apparently of great age, and were the finest examples of this tree that had come under my observation. The *Pinus Chinense*, or *P. Massoniana*, was also common, and attains a great size. Higher up, the hill-sides were covered with many thousands of tombstones, marking the tombs of generations who have long since passed away. This large cemetery forms a prominent object in the landscape, and presents a striking and curious appearance to the stranger who looks upon it for the first time.

One day, during my walks in Nagasaki, I had an opportunity of seeing some extraordinary processions. The first one I saw consisted of a number of men dressed up as Chinamen, who were supporting a huge dragon, and making it wriggle about in an extraordinary manner. Another procession consisted of little children, some so small that they could hardly walk, who were dressed in the Dutch military costume—cocked hats, tailed-coats with epaulets, dress swords, and everything in the first style, closely resembling Mynheer on gala-days, when the trade of Japan was all his own, and Desima—dear little prison—his abiding place. In this procession, Dutch fraus and frauleins were duly represented, and truth compels me to say that they were never shown off to more advantage. The procession was accompanied by a band, dressed up also in an appropriate manner: they had European instruments, and played European music. The day was fine; thousands of people lined the streets, flags were hung from every window, and altogether the scene was most amusing. I followed the procession through the principal streets, and then up to a large temple situated on the hill-side above the town. Here the infantine troop was put through various military manœuvres, which were executed in a most creditable manner. I was amused at the gravity with which everything was done—each child looked as if it was in sober earnest, and scarcely a smile played on one of the many little faces that were taking part in this mimic representation of the good Dutchmen. The exercises having been gone through, the band struck up a lively air, and the little actors marched away to their homes.

On the side of a hill, a few miles out of Nagasaki, and amongst the most beautiful scenery, lives the veteran naturalist, Dr. Von Siebold. His house is some distance away from that of any other European; and his delight seems to be in his garden, his library, and the Japanese country people who are his friends. As I had determined to pay him a visit during my stay in Nagasaki, I chose a fine day, and set out in the direction of his residence after breakfast.

My road led me through the heart of the town. The streets, as I have already remarked, were wide and clean, and contrasted most favourably with towns of equal size in China. The common necessaries of life seemed to be abundant everywhere. Amongst fruits I observed the *Diospyros kaki*, pears, oranges, Salisburia nuts, chesnuts, water melons, acorns, &c. The vegetables consisted of carrots, onions, nelumbium roots, turnips, lily-roots, ginger, *Arum esculentum*, yams, sweet potatoes, and a root called "gobbo," apparently a species of Arctium.

After passing through the town the road led me up a beautiful rice valley, terraced in all directions and watered abundantly by the streams which flow from the mountains. On each side of the valley the hills are richly wooded, partially with trees and partially with brushwood. The trees I observed were *Pinus Massoniana, Cryptomeria, Retinospora,* camphor, oaks, camellias, &c. The view from one side, looking down upon and over the valley, and resting on the opposite hill, is rich indeed, and I almost envied Dr. Siebold his residence, which is situated on the left-hand side going up the valley. I found him at home, and he received me most kindly. His house is a good one for Japan, and his workshop or library, to which he introduced me, contains works of all countries on his favourite pursuits connected with natural history. But it was to the garden that my attention was more particularly drawn.

On a level with the house and around it are small nurseries for the reception and propagation of new plants, and for preparing them for transportation to Europe. Here I noted examples of most of the plants figured and described in Dr. Siebold's great work, the 'Flora Japonica,' so well known to all lovers of oriental plants; and several new things hitherto undescribed. A new *Aucuba* with white blotches on the leaves was striking; there was also the male variety of the old *A. japonica,* numerous fine Conifers, such as *Thujopsis dolabrata, Sciadopitys verticillata, Retinospora pisifera* and *R. obtusa,* and many other objects of interest. Plants with variegated foliage were numerous, and many of them were very beautiful. Amongst the latter I may mention Thujas, Eleagnus, Junipers, bamboos, Podocarpus, Camellias, Euryas, &c.

On the hill-side above the house Dr. Siebold is clearing away the brushwood in order to extend his collections and to obtain suitable situations for the different species to thrive in. For example, he will have elevation for such plants as require it, shade and dampness for others, and so on. Long may he live to delight himself and others with his enlightened pursuits!

Dr. Siebold speaks the Japanese language like a native, and appears to be a great favourite with the people around him, amongst whom he has great influence. "Doctor," said I to him on taking my leave, "you appear to be quite a prince amongst the people in this part of Japan." He smiled. and said he liked the Japanese, and he believed the regard was mutual; and with a slight cast of sarcasm in his countenance, continued : "It is not necessary for me to carry a revolver in my belt, like the good people in Desima and Nagasaki."

During my stay in Nagasaki at this time I was greatly indebted to Mr. Evans, of the well-known house of Messrs. Dent and Co., of China. Mr. Webb, the head of that house in Shanghae, kindly furnished me with letters of introduction and credit; so that even "at the ends of the earth" I found myself quite at home. Mr. Evans introduced me to a number of native gentlemen whose gardens were rich in the botanical productions of Japan; and I am glad to take this opportunity of stating, that to him and to Mr. Mackenzie I am indebted for many important additions to my collections. Everywhere we were received with the most marked politeness by the Japanese—a politeness which I am vain enough to think we did not abuse in the slightest degree.

I have already stated that according to treaty foreigners are now allowed to visit the country in the vicinity of the ports that have been opened to trade. The distance allowed is ten *ri*, or from twenty-five to thirty miles. I was not slow to avail myself of this liberty in order to examine the natural products and agriculture of the country. Day by day excursions were made, either on foot or on horseback. One of these was to a place called Epunga, a kind of picnic station amongst the hills, about four or five miles from the town. The summer agricultural productions of the country through which I passed were much like those in the province of Chekiang in China—that is, rice and *Arum esculentum* on the low lands, and sweet potatoes, buckwheat (*Polygonum tataricum*), maize, &c., on the dry hilly soil. In winter, wheat, barley, and rape are produced on the dry lands, and the rice-lands are generally allowed to lie fallow.

On the hill-sides I observed the Japan wax-tree (*Rhus succedaneum*) cultivated extensively.

It occupies the same position on these hills as
the Chinese tallow-tree (*Stillingia sebifera*) does
in Chekiang. It grows to about the same size,
and, curiously enough, it produces the same effect
upon the autumnal landscape by its leaves changing from green into a deep blood-red colour as
they ripen before falling off. Some camphor-trees
(*Laurus camphora*) of enormous size were observed
about the temples on the outskirts of Nagasaki,
and *Cryptomeria japonica* was a very common tree
on all the hill-sides. The latter is often used as
a fence round gardens, and a very pretty one it
makes. When I first saw it used for this purpose,
it struck me that something of the same kind
might be done with it at home, now that it is
so common in every nursery. The Japanese manage it much in the same way as we do our yew
hedges; and when kept regularly clipped it is not
only exceedingly pretty, but it also is so dense
that nothing can get through it. The tea-plant
is also common on these hill-sides, but the great
tea country of Japan is 200 or 300 miles further
to the northward, near the famous Miaco, where
the Spiritual Emperor resides.

At this season the tea was just coming into
flower, so that I was enabled to procure specimens for the herbarium. It is no doubt identical
with the China plant, and may have been introduced from China; although, as the productions of
the two countries are very similar in character, it
may be indigenous. In its mode of growth and

habits it resembles the plant in cultivation about Canton, commonly called *Thea bohea.*

Epunga, to which I was bound while making these observations, was reached in due course. I found the proprietor had a nice little private garden, and also a nursery in which he propagated and cultivated plants for sale. On the premises there was a building, apparently for the use of foreigners, which was only opened when any foreigner came out from Nagasaki for a day's pleasure. Like many other places of the kind, its walls were defaced with the writing of the great men who had visited it, and who took this means of immortalising themselves. Doggrel lines, some of them scarcely fit to meet the eye, were observed in many places written in Dutch, German, or Russian. Our own countrymen had not been there long enough to visit the place and leave their marks; doubtless these will be found also in good time.

The nursery garden at Epunga was found to contain a large collection of Japanese plants— some of which were new to me—and others of great rarity and interest. Several species were purchased for my collection, and duly brought in to the town the next day.

Having finished my examination of the nursery, I started, in company with some other gentlemen, on an expedition to the top of a hill some 1500 feet above the level of the sea, and celebrated for the fine and extensive view to be obtained from its summit. It was a glorious autumnal day, such a day as one rarely sees in our own changeable climate. The sky was cloudless, so that when we reached the top our view on all sides was bounded only by the horizon. Looking to the south-east, far below us we saw the town of Nagasaki, with the beautiful bay in its front. On its smooth waters were the ships of several nations at anchor, besides a number of boats and junks of native build, and rather picturesque in their way. Turning round and looking to the north-west, the eye rested on many hundreds of little hills having a conical form, and covered to their summits with trees and brushwood. Behind them were mountains, apparently 2000 or 3000 feet in height, and a deep bay looking like an inland sea. Amongst the hills there were many beautiful and fertile valleys, now yellow with the ripening rice crops; and numerous villages and farmhouses gave life to the scene, which was one of extraordinary beauty and interest.

On our way home we visited a little garden belonging to an interpreter to the Japanese Government. Here again I noticed some azaleas remarkable for their great size, and an extraordinary specimen of a dwarfed fir-tree. Its lower branches were trained horizontally some twenty feet in length; all the leaves and branchlets were tied down and clipped, so that the whole was as flat as a board. The upper branches were trained to form circles one above another like so many little tables, and the whole plant had a most curious appearance. A man was at work upon it at the time, and I believe it keeps him constantly employed every day throughout the year !

Since the opening of the port of Nagasaki to other nations besides the Chinese and Dutch, its trade has been greatly enlarged. The harbour is now gay with the ships of all nations, and a brisk trade has sprung up between Japan and China— a trade which the quiet old Dutchmen never seemed to have dreamed of. Large quantities of seaweed, salt fish, and sundry other articles are exported to China ; while the Chinese import medicine of various kinds, Sapan wood, and many other kinds of dyes. The exports to Europe are chiefly tea, vegetable wax (the produce of the Rhus already noticed), and copper, which is found in large quantities in the Japanese islands. At present there is little demand for our English manufactures, but that may spring up in time. Although Nagasaki may never become a place of very great importance as regards trade, it will no doubt prove one of the most healthy stations in the East ; and may one day become most valuable as a sanatarium for our troops in that quarter of the globe.

CHAPTER II.

We leave Nagasaki — Van Dieman's Strait — Gale of wind — Vrics's
Island — View of Fusi-yama — Bay of Yedo — Yokuhama — Its
value as a port for trade — Foreign houses — Native town —
Shops — Bronzes, ivory carvings, and curiosities — Lacquer ware —
Porcelain — Rock-crystal balls — Toys — Books and maps — Menagerie — The Gan-ke-ro — Surrounding country — Its geological
formation.

LEAVING Nagasaki and its beautiful scenery at
daylight on the 19th of October, we proceeded
on our voyage to the port of Kanagawa, near
Yedo, the capital of Japan, and distant from
Nagasaki about 700 miles. When outside the
harbour of Nagasaki the mariner has two courses
open to him : he may either go northward, and
pass through the inland sea which divides the
islands of Nipon and Kiu-siu, or he may take a
southerly course and go through Van Dieman's
Strait, and thus out into the waters of the Pacific
Ocean. Sailing vessels generally choose the latter,
as being the safer and more expeditious way of
reaching their destination, and this was the ' Marmora's' course in the present instance. Luckily
we had a fair wind all the way from Nagasaki
until we got through the strait. Near the entrance
to the strait there are some small islands known to

mariners as the " Retribution Rocks." They are
only a few feet above the water, and are rather
dangerous neighbours in a dark night, or during
those heavy gales for which this coast is so unfa-
vourably known.   On our left we observed the
mainland of Kiu-siu, stretching far away to the
eastward, and ending in a Cape named " Cape
Chichakoff."   A high conical-shaped mountain
named " Horner Peak," 2345 feet in height, and
not unlike Fusi-yama in miniature, was also passed
on our left.   It forms an excellent landmark to
the navigator of these seas.   Between " Horner
Peak" and the Cape there is a deep bay jutting
inland for 30 or 40 miles, and having at its head
an important city named Kagosima, where the
Prince of Satsuma has his head-quarters.   On the
south side of the strait we observed several large
islands, one of which is named Iwo-sima, or Sul-
phur Island.   This is an active volcano, and smoke
and flames are continually rising, not from its summit in the usual way, but from many parts of its
sides.   The whole mountain seems on fire, and
has a very curious appearance when seen during
the night.

   The coast of Japan is remarkable for the suddenness with which gales of wind come on, and we
were now destined to have our turn.   It was a
beautiful evening when we were nearly abreast of
Cape Chichakoff; we had a light fair wind, and
our little bark was gliding along at the rate of
six or seven miles an hour.   We were congratu-

lating ourselves on our great good luck, and just coming to the conclusion that all we had heard and read of the gales on this coast were so many "travellers' stories;" but we were soon compelled to come to a different conclusion. Towards dark the sky began to wear a lowering appearance in the north-east, and in less than half an hour we were in the midst of a gale of wind. Sail after sail was taken in, and at last it was deemed advisable to lie to until some change in the weather should take place. The sea also rose with great rapidity, and, except in a typhoon in China, I never recollect such a gale and such a sea. Our little bark behaved admirably, rising and falling with the sea, and shipping comparatively little water.

For two days it was necessary for us to remain in this uncomfortable position; and when the gale moderated, and we were able to get a little sail upon the vessel, the winds were foul, and carried us considerably to the southward of our course. But it cannot always blow a gale, even in Japan; so, whether the winds were tired of persecuting us, or whether it was owing to the influence of sundry old shoes which were thrown overboard, 1 cannot say, but the gale ceased, and a fair wind sprang up from the westward. On the evening of the 28th we were abreast of Cape Idsu—that Cape of Storms where it is said to blow always. Our experience, however, was rather different; for we seemed to run into a dead calm, with a heavy tumbling sea.

At daybreak on the 29th we were opposite a group of islands situated not very far from the entrance to the Bay of Yedo. One of them— Vries's Island—rises to the height of 2530 feet above the sea, and has an active volcano on its summit. The smoke, which continuously rises from this mountain, forms an excellent landmark for mariners approaching this part of the coast. As we sailed past we observed that on the sides of the mountain, and particularly down near the shore, there were numerous villages and small towns. There were apparently some fertile valleys and hill-sides at a low elevation, but near the summit all appeared barren, while huge volumes of smoke were seen following each other at short intervals.

On our left, on that same morning, was spread out to our admiring gaze the fair land of Nipon; and very beautiful it was to look upon. The land was hilly and mountainous as in China; but there appeared, some fifty or sixty miles inland, Mount Fusi, or Fusi-yama, the "Matchless," or Holy Mountain of the Japanese. Its northern slopes were covered with snow, but on its southern sides green streaks of verdure were visible. This mountain is the highest in Japan. It was formerly supposed to be only 10,000 or 12,000 feet above the level of the sea, but later observations made by Mr. Alcock's party in 1860 give it a height of 14,177 feet.

In the evening we passed Cape Sagami at the

View of Fusi-yama — From a Japanese sketch.

entrance of the Bay of Yedo, and at daybreak
next morning we were well up the bay, and only
a short distance from the Yokuhama anchorage.
On our right, in the direction of Yedo, we observed a cloud of boats under sail, composed
chiefly of fishing-boats which supply the markets
of the capital and the surrounding towns with fish.
During our voyage from Nagasaki I had observed

very few native vessels or fishing-boats, such as
may be seen crowding the waters of the Chinese
coast.   In so far as sea-going vessels are concerned, I was quite prepared to see but few, as the
Japanese are not a maritime nation, and do not
send ships to foreign countries; but I fully expected to see fleets of fishing-boats along the shore,
and their absence leads me to doubt whether the
Japanese islands are as populous as they are generally supposed to be.

We anchored abreast of the town of Yokuhama
at eight o'clock on the morning of the 30th of
October.   This is one of the ports opened by treaty
to foreigners, and it is the one nearest to the
capital.   It was here that in March, 1854, Com-
modore Perry, of the United States Navy, concluded his treaty with the Japanese.   At one of
the interviews presents were delivered from the
American Government.   These consisted of American cloths, agricultural implements, firearms, and
a beautiful locomotive, tender, and passenger car,
one-fourth of the ordinary size.   The latter was
put in motion on a circular track, and went at the
rate of twenty miles an hour.   The Japanese, we
are told, were more interested in this than in anything else; but, Chinese-like, concealed all expressions of wonder or astonishment.

The town of Kanagawa, on the opposite or
northern side of the bay, is the place named as the
port in the treaty, but it was found unsuitable
owing to the shallowness of the water all along

that part of the shore.   For a long time the
ministers and consuls of the Treaty powers endeavoured to induce their respective merchants to
abstain from renting land or building on the Yokuhama side of the bay.   Curiously enough, however,
the Japanese Government took a different view
of the matter, and encouraged the merchants to
come to Yokuhama by building for them dwelling-
houses, and commodious piers and landing-places.

Both places had their advantages and disadvan-
tages.   The argument of the consuls in favour of ad-
hering to Kanagawa was that it was on the great
highway of Japan ; and that, as Japanese from all
parts of the empire were daily passing through it,
our merchandise would, through them, be carried
to all parts of the country, and would in this
manner be quickly known and appreciated.   It
was also hinted that the Government intended to
hem foreigners in at Yokuhama by means of a
broad and deep canal; that this in fact was to be
another Desima; and that we were to be made
prisoners and treated in all respects as the Dutch
were in the olden time at Nagasaki.

The advantage of Kanagawa being on the great
highway of Japan was fully admitted by the merchants, but they believed that if they located themselves there the Government would lead the main
road round by some other way, and would take
measures to have them and their Japanese customers as much under control as at Yokuhama.
As to the latter place being made a second Desima,

they argued that the time had gone by when such things were possible. Besides, if Kanagawa was chosen, the ships would have to lie a long way from the shore, where they would oftentimes be unapproachable owing to the state of the weather, which is very uncertain on this coast. Altogether Yokuhama was the most suitable place for the transaction of their business, and it was business which had brought them to Japan.

While this discussion was going on, the Japanese Government, for reasons of its own, was affording every facility to those who wished to settle at Yokuhama; and notwithstanding the opposition of the ministers and consuls of the Treaty powers, the merchants carried their point. Unhappily all this was the cause of much wrangling and ill feeling, which it will take some time to remove.

When the American squadron first visited Yoku- hama in 1854, it was but a small fishing village, containing probably not more than 1000 inhabit- ants. Now the population amounts to 18,000 or 20,000, and a large town covers a space which was formerly occupied by rice-fields and vegetable gardens. The town is built on the flat land which extends along the shores of the bay, and is backed by a kind of semicircle of low richly-wooded hills. It is about a mile long, and a quarter to half a mile in width; but it is increasing rapidly every day, and no doubt the whole of the swamp which lies between it and the hills will soon be covered with buildings.

A large customhouse has been erected near the
centre of the town, the foreign allotments being on
the east side of it, and the native town chiefly on
the west, so that foreigners and natives are kept
each by themselves. A broad and deep canal has
been dug round the town, and is connected with
the bay at each end. It will be seen, therefore,
that with the sea in front, and this canal carried
round behind, the place can easily be completely
isolated. Guardhouses are placed at the points of
egress, and no one can go out or come in without
the knowledge of the guards, and consequently of
the Government. As I have already hinted, the
Japanese have been much abused for this arrangement; but it is possible, indeed I think it highly
probable, that it has been intended more for our
protection than for anything else.

The new houses of the foreign merchants are
generally one-storied bungalows, built almost entirely of wood and plaster. The joints of the
timbers are tied together, or fastened in a way to
allow the entire structure to rock or move to and
fro during those earthquakes which are so common
and sometimes so destructive in this part of the
world. Godowns for the storing of merchandise
are generally erected near the house of the merchant; and in many instances there is also a fire-
proof building on the premises, used for the protection of specie and the more valuable portion of
the merchant's property. This is of the first importance in a country like Japan, where the buildings

are so combustible in their nature, and where fires are almost of daily occurrence in all the large towns.

The native town is remarkable for one fine wide street which runs down its centre. Here are exposed for sale the various productions of the country in very large quantities. Bronzes, carvings in ivory, lacquer-ware, and porcelain, are all duly represented. The bronzes are mostly modern, of ugly shapes, and are chiefly remarkable for the large quantity of metal they contain, which one would think might have been applied to a more useful purpose. The small ivory carvings and metal buckles for fastening the dress are great curiosities in their way. They are usually small, and represent men, women, monkeys, and all sorts of animals and plants. They exhibit the skill of the carver in a very favourable light, and are certainly wonderful examples of patience and industry. Some collections of these articles were shown in the late International Exhibition in London, and were much admired. A writer in the 'Times' describes them in the following terms:—"The designs in some of these [the metal buckles] are irresistibly grotesque, and at once recall to mind the little black woodcuts with which Mr. Leech began his connexion with 'Punch.' Probably every object in this collection is by a different artist; yet, though in some the designs are so minute as to require a magnifying glass to see them well, all are treated with the same broad humour, so that it is almost impossible to avoid

downright laughter as you examine them. There
is one figure of a man timidly venturing to coax a
snarling dog, which is inimitable in its funny expression; and so also is the expression on another's
face who is frightened by a ghost. And all these
works, the reader must remember, are not mere
sketches, but are solid little pieces of metal-work,
the background being of bronze, and the raised
figures in relief being either gold, silver, steel, or
platinum, or, as in most cases, of all four metals
intermixed. It is evident, from the platinum
being so freely used here, that the metal must be
much more common with the Japanese than with
us; and that the secret of melting it, to which our
chemical knowledge has only just attained, has
long been known to them. . . . In the side of the
case where the metal buckles are shown we find in
a collection of ivory carvings fresh proofs of the
art, skill, and comic genius of the people. Let any
one examine the litter of puppies sprawling over
each other, the grotesque look of pain on the face
of the woman who has been startled by a fox, and
tumbled forward with her fingers under the edge
of a basin; the triumphant aspect of the com-
panion figure, who has succeeded in clapping his
basin down on the fox; yet, notwithstanding their
wonderful finish, all these figures are so small that
they might be worn as brooches."

The modern lacquer-ware is good, but not to be
compared to the fine old Miaco ware, which is
extremely beautiful. There are a number of shops

where this can be procured ; but the prices asked, and obtained, are very high.   The fine polish of the old lac is unrivalled, and the specimens are often-times covered with figures of gold.   This ware is met with in the form of writing-boxes and boxes for holding papers, trays, cabinets, screens, &c. The finest pieces are often very small, and, although not of much use, are sufficient to show the high state of the art at the time when they were made.

I saw few examples of ancient porcelain, although we know that some fine pieces have found their way to Europe from Japan.   The porcelain-shops are full of modern ware, chiefly remarkable for the fine eggshell cups; and I found one or two examples of good colouring.   Generally I did not admire it, and considered it not equal to that now made in China, and far inferior to the ancient porcelain of that country.   I observed some cups and basins, with paintings of English ladies not badly executed.   This shows how quick and imitative the Japanese are as a people, and how different they are from the slow-going Chinese.

In some of the shops I observed some large crystal-looking balls said to be of rock crystal. These were finely polished and clear—not a flaw of any kind could be detected in their structure— and were highly prized owing to their great size and beauty.

All sorts of toys were abundant, and some of them were most ingenious and pretty.   There were glass balls, with numerous little tortoises inside them, whose heads, tails, and feet were in constant motion; humming-tops, with a number of trays inside, which all came out and spun round on the table when the top was set in motion; and a number of funny things in boxes like little bits of wood shavings, which perform the most curious antics when thrown into a basin containing water. Dolls of the most fascinating kind, with large, shaved, bobbing heads, crying out most lustily when pressed upon the stomach, were also met with in cartloads. One little article, so small one could scarcely see it, when put upon hot charcoal, gradually seemed to acquire life and animation, and moved about for all the world like a brilliant caterpillar. This large trade in toys shows us how fond the Japanese are of their children.

In one of the main streets there is a shop with an extensive collection of books, maps, charts, plain and coloured, for sale. A good map of the city of Yedo may be had here; but the inquirer for such a thing is invariably taken into a back room, when he is told that if the authorities knew of such a thing being sold the vendor would get his head taken off. To those who are ignorant of the language, a peculiar motion of the hand about the region of the neck explains the shopkeeper's meaning. This is a good stroke of policy, as it enables the seller to obtain a higher price for the map, and sends the lucky purchaser off highly delighted with his bargain. In the same shop I met with some really good illustrated books, containing views of the country and people about Miaco and Yedo, the two most famous cities in Japan. The former is the residence of the *Mikado* or Spiritual Emperor, and the latter that of the Ziogoon or Tycoon. In the art of drawing or sketching, the Japanese are far inferior to ourselves, but they are greatly in advance of the Chinese. Although foreigners have been only a short time residing in Yokuhama, their appearance, customs, and manners are faithfully represented by the Japanese artists. Here are to be found pictures of men and women—rather caricatures it must be confessed—engaged in amusements peculiar to highly civilized nations. Ladies riding on horseback, or walking—duly encompassed with a wonderful amount of crinoline—are fairly represented. Scenes in the Gan-ke-ro—a place got up by the Government for the amusement of foreigners —are also portrayed in a manner not particularly flattering to our habits and customs. Boisterous mirth, indulgence in wine and strong drinks, and the effects thereof upon those who are inclined to be quarrelsome, are all carefully depicted. Altogether, some very curious and instructive works of Japanese art may be picked up in shops of this description.

Opposite to the bookshop just noticed there is a menagerie containing a variety of animals for sale. In this place I remarked some extraordinary-looking monkeys, which appear to be a source of great attraction and amusement to the natives.

Little dogs were plentiful, and particularly noisy
when a foreigner approached them. Then there
were examples of deer, the eagle of the country,
and singing birds of various kinds in cages. But
the different varieties of fowls struck me more
than anything else. The kind which I had
already seen at Nagasaki was here also, and in
addition a *pure white* bird with a fine long arched
tail and long silky feathers hanging down from
each side of the back. This is a very beautiful
bird, and well worth being introduced into Europe
if it is not already here.

The Gan-ke-ro, to which I have already alluded,
is a large building at the back of the town, erected
by the Government for the amusement of foreigners.
Here, dinners, suppers, and plays, can always be
" got up on the shortest notice." In other respects this and the buildings in the surrounding
neighbourhood are much like the tea-houses in the
town of Nagasaki. Scenes of debauchery and
drunkenness are common, and even murder is not
infrequent. Over such matters one would willingly draw a veil; but truth must be told in order
to correct the impression which some persons have
of Japan—namely, that it is a very Garden of
Eden, and its inhabitants as virtuous as Adam and
Eve before the fall.

The country in the vicinity of Yokuhama is very
beautiful in its general features. It is evidently
of volcanic origin. It consists of low hills and
small valleys : the former having their sloping

sides covered with trees and brushwood, and their summits, which form a kind of table-land, all under cultivation. The valleys are very fertile, and, having a good supply of water, are generally used for the cultivation of rice.

The geological structure of this part of Japan is well worthy of notice. In my walks in the country I came upon a little hill with perpendicular sides, thus forming a convenient object for observation. The following is its formation in layers :—

1st layer.—Vegetable soil : black, resembling peat.
2nd   „   Shells 2 to 3 feet in thickness. Oysters and other sea shells.
3rd   „   Gravel.
4th   „   Light-coloured clay, with pumice-stone and shells.
5th   „   Blueish-coloured clay, with pumice-stone and shells.

The Yokuhama cliffs are from 60 to 100 feet in height, nearly perpendicular, and their structure is as follows :—

1st layer.—Black peaty-looking soil, evidently containing much vegetable matter.
2nd   „   Red earth much mixed with gravel.
3rd   „   · Gravel.
4th   „   Hard clay. This is intersected here and there with a layer of gravel, and sometimes with a layer of shells, principally oysters. The shells are seen sticking on the surface of this layer in all directions. Charred wood and pumice-stone are also met with in the clay.

Springs of excellent water are abundant on all the hill-sides. Some of them are deliciously cool even in the hottest days of summer, and afford a refreshing draught to the weary traveller.

CHAPTER III.

Town of Kanagawa — The Imperial highway — Travellers upon it —
Princes — Pack-horses — Mendicant priests — Blind men — Beggars,
&c. — Visit to the temple of Bokengee — The umbrella pine-tree —
Sintoo temples — Scenery — Thatched roofs — Valuable elm —
The farmer and his chrysanthemums — Tomi — His one fault —
Temple of To-rin-gee — Scenery by the way — Thujopsis dolabrata
— Farm-houses — Tea-plant — Fruit-trees — Yedo vine — Veget-
ables — Trees and shrubs of the district — The male aucuba —
Geological features.

THE port of Kanagawa, named in the treaty as the
location of foreigners, is situated on the northern
side of a deep bay or inlet; Yokuhama being
placed on its southern shore. The consuls of the
different Treaty powers were living in temples on
the Kanagawa side at the time of my arrival; and
as an old friend of mine, Mr. José Loureira, the
manager for Messrs. Dent and Co., of China, who
was also consul for Portugal and France, was
residing there, he kindly offered me quarters in his
temple during my stay. Nothing could have
suited me better than this arrangement. There
was plenty of room, both in the house and in the
garden, for any collections of natural history which
I might get together; and I was on the highway
to Yedo, and in the midst of a most fertile and
interesting country.

Kanagawa is a long narrow town stretching for several miles along the shore of the bay, and having one principal street, and that the *Tokaido* or great highway of Japan. The place is mentioned in the books of the old Dutch travellers, and is said by them to contain about six hundred houses, and to be twenty-four miles from the capital. It is probably about this distance from the *Nipon Bas*, or bridge in Yedo, from which distances are measured to all parts of the empire; but it is not more than sixteen or eighteen miles from the western end of the city of Yedo. It contains a great number of inns and tea-houses; and here the Dutch generally slept on the last night of their journey overland from Nagasaki to Yedo. On the following day they entered the capital. The shops are generally poor and mean, and contain few articles except the mere necessaries of life. A little way back from the main street, at intervals all the way along the town, are Buddhist temples and cemeteries. These temples are often found in the most charming situations, and they are the finest and most substantial buildings in Kanagawa. In some instances they are surrounded with pretty gardens, containing specimens of the favourite flowers of the country. It is in some of these temples that the consuls of the Treaty powers have been located. The good priests do not object to find quarters of an inferior kind both for themselves and for their gods, providing they are well paid for their trouble in turning out.

The Tokaida, or great highway of the country, is thronged all day long with people going to or returning from the capital. Every now and then a long train of the servants and armed retainers of one of the Daimios—lords or princes of the empire—may be seen covering the road for miles. It is not unusual for a cortége of this kind to occupy two or three hours in passing by. Men run before and call upon the people to fall down upon their knees to do honour to the great man, nor do they call in vain. All the people on both sides of the way drop down instantly on their knees, and remain in this posture until the norimon or palanquin of the prince has passed by. A *Daimio's* procession is made up in the following manner :—First comes the prince himself in his norimon, followed by his horse and retainers, armed with swords, spears, and matchlocks; then follow a number of coolies, each carrying two lacquered boxes slung across his shoulder on a bamboo pole. After these again there is another norimon, with an official of some kind; then more coolies with boxes, more retainers, and so on. The number of the followers is often very large, and depends upon and is regulated by the wealth and rank of the Daimio.

Kæmpfer informs us " that it is the duty of the princes and lords of the empire, as also of the governors of imperial cities and crown lands, to go to court once a year to pay their homage and respect. They are attended, going and returning,

STREET IN KANAGAWA.—THE TOKAIDO OR IMPERIAL HIGHWAY.

by their whole court, and travel with a pomp and magnificence, becoming as well their own quality and riches as the majesty of the powerful monarch whom they are going to see. The train of some of the most eminent fills up the road for some days."

If two or more of these Daimios should chance to be travelling the same road, at the same time, they would prove a great hindrance to one another, particularly if they should happen to meet at the same post-house or village. This is avoided by giving timely notice, and by engaging the inns and post-houses a month or six weeks beforehand. The time of their intended arrival is also notified in all the cities, villages, and hamlets, by putting up small boards on high poles of bamboo, signifying in a few characters what day of the month such and such a lord will be at that place to dine and sleep there.

When the retinue of the great man has passed by, the stream of every-day life flows on along the great Tokaido as before. No carts are used on this part of the road. Everything is carried on pack-horses, and these are passing along the road in great numbers all day long. Each horse is loaded with a pile of boxes and packages—a formidable size oftentimes, surmounted by a man in a large broad-brimmed straw hat, who, from his exalted position, is guiding the movements of his horse. Generally, however, when passing through towns, the horses are led by the drivers. In addition to the huge pile of packages, it is not unusual for a little family, consisting of the mother and children, to be housed amongst them. On one occasion, as two foreigners of my acquaintance were out riding in the country, one of their horses shied, and, coming in contact with a loaded pack-horse, its burden came tumbling off, and was scattered over the road. On stopping to render the driver some assistance in reloading his horse, my friends were horrified to find a whole family scrambling about amongst the packages, amongst which they had been snugly stowed away.

Packhorse, with grass shoes.

Besides the processions, pack-horses, and palan- quins, the pedestrians on the Tokaido demand our attention. Some are crowned with queer-looking broad-brimmed straw hats; others have napkins tied round their heads, and their hats slung behind their backs, only to be, used when it rains or when the sun's rays are disagreeably powerful; while others again have the head bare and shaven in front, with the little pigtail brought forward and tied down upon the crown. Mendicant priests are met with, chanting prayers at every door, jingling some rings on the top of a tall staff, and begging for alms for the support of themselves and their temples. These are most independent-looking fellows, and seem to think themselves conferring a favour rather than receiving one. I observed that they were rarely refused alms by the people, although the same priests came round almost daily. To me the prayer seemed to be always the same— namely, *nam-nam-nam*; sometimes sung in a low key, and sometimes in a high one. When the little copper cash—the coin of the country—was thrown into the tray of the priest, he gave one more prayer, apparently for the charity he had received, jingled his rings, and then went on to the next door. Blind men are also common, who give notice of their approach by making a peculiar sound upon a reed. These men generally get their living by shampooing their more fortunate brethren who can see. Every now and then a group of sturdy beggars, each having an old straw . mat thrown across his shoulders, come into the stream which flows along this great highway.

Then there is the flower-dealer, with his basket of
pretty flowers, endeavouring to entice the ladies
to purchase them for the decoration of their hair;
or with his branches of "*skimmi*" (*Illicium anisatum*), and other evergreens, which are largely
used to ornament the tombs of the dead.

All day long, and during a great part of the
night too, this continual living stream flows to and
from the great capital of Japan along the imperial
highway. It forms a panorama of no common
kind, and is certainly one of the great sights of the
empire. The blind travellers, of whom there are
a great number, are said to prefer travelling by
night when the road is less crowded, as the light of
day makes no difference to them.

Having settled down for a time in Kanagawa, I
now made daily excursions to different parts of the
surrounding country. I was fortunate in making
the acquaintance of the Rev. S. W. Brown, a missionary connected with the Dutch Reformed Church,
United States, and of Dr. Hepburn, a medical missionary, formerly of Amoy, in China. They were
living in some temples a short distance from where
I was lodging; and as they had been some time
in Japan, they were able to give me much valuable
information.

My first question was, whether there were any
large Buddhist temples in this part of Japan, similar
to those I had been in the habit of visiting in China.
My reason for wishing to get information on this
head was the fact that, wherever Buddhist temples

UMBRELLA PINE (*Sciadopitys verticillata*).

and Buddhist priests are found, there the timber is preserved on the hill-sides; and many of the rare trees of the country are sure to be met with adorning some of the courts of their temples. Mr. Brown informed me that there was a large monastery a short distance up one of the valleys, and kindly consented to accompany me thither. Our road led us up a beautiful and fertile valley, having low wooded hills on each side, and a little stream of pure water running down towards the sea, watering and fertilizing the rice-fields on its way. It was now the beginning of November, and the crops were yellow and nearly ready for the reaping-hook of the husbandman. It was a glorious autumnal day, the sun was shining above our heads in a clear sky, the air was cool, and everything around us was most enjoyable.

A walk of two or three miles brought us to the temple of Bokengee. A broad path led up the hill-side to the main entrance of the temple. Various ornamental trees, some of great size and beauty, stood near the gateway. Just inside and in front of one of the principal temples, I was delighted to meet with a beautiful new pine, called *Sciadopitys verticillata*, the umbrella pine, or " Ko-ya maki" —that is, " the *maki* of Mount Ko-ya"—of the Japanese. A branch of this fine tree is figured and described in Dr. Siebold's ' Flora Japonica ;' but a great mistake is made as regards its size. Siebold states that it forms an evergreen tree, for the most part twelve to fifteen feet high. On the

contrary, the specimens met with in the vicinity of
Kanagawa and Yedo were in many instances fully
one hundred feet in height. However, as Siebold
says that "he saw it cultivated in gardens," he
probably had no opportunity of seeing a full-grown
specimen. It is a tree of great beauty and interest.
It has broad leaves of a deep green colour, arranged
in whorls, each somewhat like a parasol, and is
quite unlike any other genus amongst conifers. In
general outline it is of a conical form, not spreading, and the branches and leaves are so dense that
the stem is completely hidden from the view. It is
impossible to say, until we have further experience,
whether this fine tree will prove hardy in our
English climate; but if it does so, it will be a very
great acquisition to our list of ornamental pines.

The principal hall or temple of Bokengee is not
remarkable either for its size or for its idols. But
the hill-side is covered with small detached buildings, which appear to be not only residences but
also seminaries for the Buddhist priesthood. These
houses are situated in the midst of pretty gardens,
each of which contains neat specimens, well cultivated, of the ornamental flowers of the country, and
is surrounded with hedges kept neatly clipped and
trimmed. The whole place is kept in the highest
order, the broad walks are daily swept, and not a
weed or dead leaf is to be seen anywhere.

At a higher elevation there are some large
temples, which seem to be kept always closed.
They are rather rough wooden buildings; but like

all the other temples are beautifully thatched, and
the ground and walks near them clean and in perfect order.   We did not observe any priests near
these temples ; and they probably belong to the
sect of *Sintoos* or *Sinsyu*, the original national
religion of Japan, upon which Buddhism has been
engrafted in some extraordinary manner.

At the time of our visit to the monastery, the
riests seemed all to be engaged in study or in
prayer.   Now and then the dull monotonous sound
of some one of them engaged with his devotions
fell upon our ears, but it soon ceased and all was
still again.   The sun was shining, and his rays
streaming through the branches of the overhanging
trees ; a solemn stillness seemed to reign around
us, and the whole place and scene reminded one of
a sabbath in the country at home.

There are many pleasant and shaded walks in
the woods about these temples.   Taking one of the
paths which led up the hill, we wandered to the
summit and obtained some charming views.   On
one side we looked down on the roofs and gardens
of the temples, and our eyes wandered from them
over the valley to the richly-wooded hills beyond.
Turning to the westward, the mountains of Hakone
lay before us, with the beautiful Fusi-yama half-
covered with snow, and looking like the queen of
the mountain scenery.   These were glorious views,
and will long remain vividly impressed upon my
memory.

Before quitting the monastery of Bokengee,

E

we examined minutely the manner in which the temples were built, and more particularly their thatched roofs. The walls were formed of a framework of wood nicely fitted and joined, but apparently not very massive in construction. This was rather extraordinary, owing to the great thickness and weight of the framework of the roof. No doubt, however, the sides were strong enough to support the roof, heavy though it was. All the roofs of the temples were thatched with a reed common to the country, and never, in any other part of the world, have I seen such beautiful thatching. Indeed this is a subject of admiration with every foreigner who visits Japan. On carefully examining the structure of one of these buildings, one soon sees the principles on which it is put up, and the reasons for its peculiar construction. Buildings such as we erect in England would be very unsafe in a country like Japan, where earthquakes are so common and so violent. Hence the main part of a Japanese house is a sort of skeleton framework; every beam is tied or fastened to its neighbour; so that, when the earth is convulsed by these fearful commotions, the whole building may rock and sway together without tumbling down. In order to render these buildings more secure, it seems necessary to have the roof of great strength and weight, and this accounts for their heavy and massive structure.

In the woods of this part of Japan there is a very fine elm-tree, called by the Japanese *Keaki*

(*Ulmus keaki* of Siebold). This is often used in the formation of the strong beams which support the roofs of these temples. The wood of this tree is extremely handsome ; and as all the framework is fully exposed to view, this is, of course, a matter of great importance.

On our way home we visited many of the little farm-houses which are situated at short intervals on the lower sides of the hills ; each had its little garden attached to it. In one of these gardens we found a very fine collection of chrysanthemums. I was most anxious to secure some of them for my collections, but, thinking the farmer only cultivated them for his pleasure, I did not like to offer him money, nor did I care to beg. My scruples were soon set at rest by the owner hinting that I might have any of them I pleased by paying for them at a certain rate. I need scarcely say we soon came to terms, and in a very short space of time the little farmer, with his flowers on his back, was trudging behind us on our way to Kanagawa. This was my first purchase in Japan, and I lost no time in making the following note, namely, that the Japanese were very much like their Chinese friends over the water, and that no difficulty was so great that it could not be overcome by a little liberality.

My next object was to procure a native of this part of the country to assist me with my collections, and more particularly to act as a guide. A man named Tomi was recommended to me as a

person likely to suit my purpose. Tomi had been
a kind of pedler, and had wandered up and down
the country for many years. Everybody knew
Tomi, and Tomi knew everybody. Latterly he
had been in the service of some foreigners at
Kanagawa, who gave him a high character for
intelligence and activity. But it was rumoured
that Tomi had, in common, 1 am sorry to say,
with many of his countrymen, one serious fault,
and that was, he was particularly fond of saki—the
wine, or rather whisky, of Japan. It was added,
however, that he rarely indulged until the evening,
and that he was generally to be depended upon
during the day. As his knowledge of the country
was of great importance in my investigations, I
thought he would perhaps suit me better than any
one else, and so I engaged him.

Tomi was now my daily guide all over the
country, and I must do him the justice to say he
performed his work to my entire satisfaction. In
the mornings he looked rather red about the eyes,
as if he had been indulging freely during the
preceding night; but he kept sober, for the most
part, during the day.

The weather was delightful; day after day the
sun was shining in a clear sky, the air was cool,
and I could walk all day long with the greatest
comfort. The seeds of the different trees and
shrubs of the country were now ripening; and my
great object was to secure a supply of all the
ornamental kinds for exportation to Europe.

More particularly I was desirous of procuring.
seeds of the *Sciadopitys*, already described, of the
Thujopsis dolabrata, and of the different pines,
yews, and arborvitæ.

One morning Tomi informed me he had found
out a temple in the country where there were
some fine trees of *Thujopsis dolabrata*. This was
good news; so we started·off together to see the
trees, and if possible to procure some seeds. Our
road led us up a valley somewhat like that by
which I had gone to Bokengee. The scenery was
of the same beautiful character—fertile valleys
and richly wooded hills, which even at this time
of the year (November) had a green and summer-
like appearance, owing to the number of evergreen trees and shrubs which are indigenous
to the country. Sometimes our road gradually
ascended, and carried us along the tops of the
hills, which here form a kind of table-land, the
whole of which is under cultivation. It is impossible for me to describe the beautiful views
that were continually presenting themselves as we
passed along. Looking seaward, the smooth
waters of the Bay of Yedo lay before us, dotted
all over with the little white sails of fishing-boats,
whose produce was to supply the market of that
populous capital. Strange ships, of another build
and rig, lay quietly at anchor abreast of Yokuhama. Their tall masts and square yards pro-
claimed them to belong to the nations of the far
West. Looking inland, the view from the hill-

tops was ever-changing but always interesting and beautiful. Rice valleys, farmhouses, and temples lay below us; beyond them were low hills, then valleys again, and so on, until the eye rested on a sea of hills on the far-off horizon.

A walk of a few miles brought us to a little temple nestled amongst some woods on a hill-side. The name of this temple was To-rin-gee. A small avenue of trees leads up from a rice valley to the temple, and ends at a flight of stone steps. On each side of the steps there is a grassy bank covered with bushes of azalea, aucuba, and other ornamental shrubs. Ascending the stone steps we found ourselves on a level with the temple, and in a pretty garden filled with flowers, and kept in the most perfect order.

The temple of To-rin-gee is a small one, and has only one priest and priestess to minister at its altars. It is cleanly kept, the floors are covered with mats, and many of the walls are ornamented with pictures. Works of art are highly appreciated by these people; and I afterwards, at their urgent request, presented them with some pictures from 'Punch' and the 'Illustrated London News,' with which they were highly pleased. The priest and priestess received us most kindly, and, as they appeared to be well acquainted with Tomi, we soon found ourselves quite at home. The screens of the little verandah were drawn, and we were invited to seat ourselves on the clean mats that covered the floor. Some delicious tea, made, in Chinese

fashion, without milk or sugar, was set before us,
and proved very agreeable.

While we sipped our tea I had time to make
some observations on the surrounding scenery.
A quiet and secluded rice valley formed the fore-
ground to the picture; hills were on each side of
us and behind us, densely covered with trees of
many different kinds.   Pines, evergreen oaks,
chesnuts, bamboos, and palms—the latter giving a
somewhat tropical character to the scenery—were
the most common species.   On a hill-side to the
right of where we sat I observed a grove of the
beautiful *Thujopsis dolabrata*, which I had come to
look for.

A stillness, almost solemn, reigned amongst
these woods and temples, broken at times only by
the call of the cock pheasant, or the rich clear note
of some songster of the woods.   What a charming
place for a hermit, or for some one tired of the
busy scenes and oppressing cares of the world!

But I had not come here to meditate only; and,
therefore, setting down my teacup, I intimated to
the good priest that I wished to pay a closer visit
to the " *Asnero*," the Japanese name for *Thujopsis
dolabrata*.   The old man kindly led the way.   On
arriving at the grove of these trees we found an old
cemetery amongst them; and they had, no doubt,
been planted there, along with a number of *Crypto-
merias*, at the time the cemetery was first made.

The " Asnero " is a beautiful tree, straight,
symmetrical, attaining a height of 80 to 100 feet,

and having leaves of a fine dark-green colour. They are imbricated, or overlap each other on the stems, and look almost as if they had been plaited. Beneath they are of a. silvery hue, which gives them a somewhat remarkable appearance when blown about by the wind. We could observe some bunches of seeds on some of the higher branches. These were not very easily reached; but both Tomi and I being good climbers, we pulled off our shoes and mounted the trees, much to the astonishment of our good friend the priest, who stood quietly looking on at our proceedings.

The afternoon was far advanced before we had completed our researches in the vicinity of To-rin-gee, and therefore, bidding adieu to the priest and priestess, we took our departure, choosing, on our homeward journey, a different road from that by which we came. As this road led us through a number of highly-cultivated valleys, I noted the state of the crops. The low rice-lands were now covered with that grain, yellow, and nearly ready for the sickle. On all the higher lands the young wheat and barley crops were now (Nov. 10th) above-ground. The seed is not sown broadcast as with us, but in rows two feet three inches apart. It is dropped in the drills by the hand, in patches, each containing from twenty-five to thirty grains of seed, and about a foot from each other in the drill. The land is particularly clean, and the whole cultivation resembles more that of a garden than of a farm.

FARM-HOUSES NEAR YEDO, WITH IRIS ON THE ROOFS.

Every now and then we came to a farm-house. These are generally situated on the dry land at the lower sides of the hills, having the wooded hills behind them and the rice valleys in front. All had thatched roofs like the temples I have already noticed, although not built in such an expensive and substantial way. In almost every instance a species of iris, "*Sho-bu*," was growing thickly on the flattened ridge of the roof, thus giving it a rural and not unpleasing appearance.

On the road-sides, and also in the little gardens of the farmers and cottagers, I frequently met with the tea-plant in cultivation. It was not cultivated largely in this part of the country, but, apparently, only in sufficient quantities to supply the wants of those around whose houses it was growing. Fruit-trees of various kinds were common also on the lower sides of these hills, and, generally, in the vicinity of the villages. Pears, plums, oranges, peaches, chesnuts, loquats, Salisburia nuts, and *Diospyros kaki*, are the most common fruit-trees of this district.

The vine in this part of the country produces fruit of great excellence. The bunches are of a medium size, the berries of a brownish colour, thin-skinned, and the flavour is all that can be desired. This grape may be valued in England, where we have so many fine kinds, and most certainly will be highly prized in the United States of America. A few years ago I was travelling from Malta to Grand Cairo, in company with Mr. Bryant the celebrated American poet, and a genuine lover of horticultural pursuits. This gentleman informed me that, owing to some cause, our European vines did not succeed very well on the other side of the Atlantic, and suggested the importance of introducing varieties from China, where the climate, as regards extremes of heat and cold, is much like that of the United States. I had never met with what I consider a really good variety of grape in China, and therefore have not been able to act on Mr. Bryant's suggestion. At last, however, we had here a subject for the experiment; and I urged its importance on Dr. Hall, of Yokuhama, who is an American citizen, and who has already introduced a number of plants into his country from China. He entered warmly into the matter, and no doubt will accomplish the object in view.

The winter vegetables met with were carrots, onions of several kinds, " lobbo " (a kind of radish), " gobbo " (*Arctium gobbo*), nelumbium roots, lily roots, turnips, ginger, *Scirpus tuberosus, Arum esculentum*, and yams.

Many of the forest-trees of this district are identical with those found about Nagasaki, which I have already noticed. The largest and most useful seem to be such as *Pinus Massoniana, P. densiflora, Abies firma, Retinospora pisifera, R. obtusa*, and *Cryptomeria japonica;* the latter attains a very great size, and seems peculiarly at home. I have already mentioned *Thujopsis dolabrata* and *Sciadopitys verticillata.* The maiden-

hair tree (*Salisburia adiantifolia*) is common about
all the temples, and attains a great size.   Here,
as in China, the natives are very fond of its
fruit, known in the Japanese shops by the name
of " *Gingko*," and in China as " *Pak-o* " or white-
fruit.   Evergreen oaks, of several species, are common in the woods over all this part of Japan.
They attain a goodly size, and are most ornamental trees.   Chesnuts, of several kinds, are also
common ; the leaves of one species (*Castania japonica*) are used to feed a kind of silkworm.   Acers
or maples are also common trees ; many of the
leaves of these are beautifully marked with various
colours, and almost all of them take on deep colours
as they ripen in the autumn, and produce a most
beautiful and striking appearance upon the landscape.   But the elm already mentioned (*Ulmus
keaki*) is perhaps the most valuable timber-tree in
Japan.   It was introduced into Europe, by Dr. Siebold, some years ago, but I have not heard whether
or not it is suitable to our English climate.

Amongst shrubs a species of *Weigela* was common, which at first I supposed to be the *W. japonica*
of Thunberg, but it now proves to be *W. grandi-
flora*.   It is covered with flowers during the summer
months, and is really very ornamental.   *Osmanthus
aquifolius*, covered with sweet-scented white flowers,
was also met with.   It belongs to *Oleaceæ* (the olive
tribe), and is a fine ornamental evergreen bush.
In the gardens there is a variety with variegated
leaves, looking somewhat like the variegated holly.

This is a charming shrub, and if it proves hardy in our climate will be a great favourite. A new species of *Aucuba*, not variegated like the one in English gardens, but having leaves of the deepest and most glossy green, was found common in the shady parts of the woods and hedges, and has now been introduced into England. As a fine evergreen bush it will be greatly prized; and, in addition to this, it produces a profusion of crimson berries nearly as large as olives, which hang on all the winter and spring, like the holly-berries of our own country.

One of my objects in visiting Japan was to procure the male variety of the common *Aucuba japonica* of our gardens. This is perhaps the most hardy and useful exotic evergreen shrub we possess. It lives uninjured through our coldest winters, and thrives better than anything else in the smoke of our large towns. Hence it is met with everywhere, and is one of the most common plants in the parks, squares, and houses of London; but no one in this country has ever seen it covered with a profusion of crimson berries, as it is met with in Japan. It belongs to a class of plants which have the male and female flowers produced on different individuals. Curiously enough, all the plants in Europe were females, and hence the absence of fruiting specimens. On my arrival in Japan I lost no time in looking out for the male of this interesting species. I found it at last in the garden of Dr. Hall at Yokuhàma, who has also a very interesting collection of the plants of Japan, and to whom I am indebted for much valuable information and assistance. This plant was sent home in a Wardian case, and I am happy to say it reached England in good health, and is now in the nursery of Mr. Standish at Bagshot. I look forward with much interest to the effects of this introduction. Let my readers picture to themselves all the aucubas which decorate our windows and gardens, covered, during the winter and spring months, with a profusion of crimson berries. Such a result, and it is not an improbable one, would of itself be worth a journey all the way from England to Japan.

The geological formation of this part of the country differs entirely from that about Nagasaki. The latter bears a striking resemblance to the hilly part of China in the same latitude; that is, the upper sides of the hills are generally barren, with rocks of clay-slate and granite protruding in all directions. About Yedo we meet with quite a different formation. (I have already described the substrata as exhibited by the sea-cliffs at Yokuhama.) The country inland consists of hill and valley; and with the exception of the celebrated mountain named Fusi-yama, and some others in its vicinity, the hills are only a few hundred feet above the level of the sea. The soil in the valleys, in which rice is the staple summer crop, is of a blackish-brown colour, almost entirely composed of vegetable matter, and resembles what we meet with in a peat-bog in

England. Like that land it springs beneath the
feet when one walks over it. The sloping sides of
the hills are covered with trees and brushwood, the
latter oftentimes being apparently of little value.
Passing upwards through the belt of trees and
brushwood, we next reach the tops of the hills.
These are all comparatively flat, and thus a kind of
table-land is the result. The soil of this table-land is
exactly similar to that found in the marshy valleys
below, that is, it is a soil closely resembling what is
found in peat-bogs. Scarcely a stone or rock of any
kind is met with, either in the valleys, on the hill-
sides, or on the table-land on the summits. A casual
observer, on examining this black and apparently
rich-looking soil, would think it very fertile, and
capable of producing large crops ; but in reality it
is not so fertile as it looks, and foreigners generally
remark·on the little flavour the vegetables have
which are grown on it.

How this peculiar formation was originally produced I am unable to explain. Whether this part
of Japan was at some early period a flat peat-moss,
and these hills formed by one of those fearful earthquakes for which the country is still famous, and
which, according to tradition, forced up Fusi-yama
in a single night to the height of more than 14,000
feet, I must leave to geologists to determine.

CHAPTER IV.

Journey from Kanagawa to Yedo — Native body-guard — The Tokaido — Civility of the people — Beggars by the wayside — Tea-houses — Kawasaky — River Loga — "Mansion of Plum-trees" — The ladies' platform — Hostess and waiting-maids — Japanese and Chinese ladies compared — Tea-gardens — Sinagawa — English Legation — Hospitality of Mr. Alcock — Large cemetery — Garden and trees — The Yakoneens.

I GLADLY availed myself of an invitation from his Excellency Mr. Alcock to visit Yedo, and made preparations to start for that city on the 13th of November. On these occasions the stranger is always accompanied by mounted *Yakoneens*, or Government officers, who are in fact the police of the country. Their rank, however, seems of a much higher grade than that of such persons in Europe, and they are treated with marked respect by all classes of the natives, who appear to stand greatly in awe of them. These officers are armed, each having two swords; and they are supposed to guard the foreigner in case of attack or insult by the way.

As we rode out of the courtyard of Mr. Loureira's house, I could not help smiling at the queer-looking individuals who came on behind me. Each of them wore a round, broad-brimmed straw hat, and as the

day was wet they had loose rain-cloaks over their
dresses. Their two swords, which were fixed in
their belts at an angle of forty-five degrees, made
their dresses stick out behind ; and as we trotted
or galloped along the road, they had a curious fly-
away sort of appearance. As a general rule, they
are but indifferent horsemen.

Our road—the Tokaido, or Imperial highway
already mentioned—led us to the eastward, along
the shores of the Bay of Yedo. Small shops, tea-
houses, sheds for the accommodation of travellers,
and gardens, lined each side of the way. Now
and then we came to an open space with trees
planted in the form of an avenue. These were
chiefly of such species as *Cryptomeria japonica,
Pinus Massoniana, Celtis Orientalis,* and *Ulmus
keaki.* The glimpses which were obtained, from
time to time, through these trees and across the
gardens behind them, were very beautiful. On
the left, at a little distance, the view was bounded
by some low hills of irregular form, crowned with
trees and brushwood ; while on the right the
smooth waters of the Bay of Yedo were spread out
before us, here and there studded with the white
sails of fishing-boats.

The people along the road were perfectly civil
and respectful. "*Anata Ohio,*" or "Good morning,
sir," was a common salutation. Kæmpfer informs
us that in his time "multitudes of beggars crowded
the roads in all parts of the empire, but particularly
on the so much frequented Tokaido." Some of the

members of Lord Elgin's embassy, if I remember
right, seem to doubt the truth of this, as they did
not meet with any on the occasion of their visit to
Kawasaky; but on this occasion beggars were probably kept out of the way by the authorities.
Truth compels me to state that at the present day,
as in the days of Kæmpfer, the beggars in Japan
are numerous and importunate. As I rode along
the road, there were many who " sat by the wayside begging." These were " the maimed, the
halt, the lame, and the blind," who, as I passed by,
prostrated themselves on the ground and asked for
alms.

Tea-houses for the refreshment and accommodation of travellers formed the most remarkable feature on the road, and were met with at every few
hundred yards. These buildings, like the shops,
are perfectly open in front, and have the floors
slightly raiséd and covered with mats, on which
customers squatted and took refreshment. The
cooking apparatus was always fully exposed to
view, with its necessary appendages, such as pots,
kettles, teacups, and basins. On approaching one
of these tea-houses some pretty young ladies met us
in the middle of the road with a tray on which
were placed sundry cups of tea of very good quality. This they begged us to partake of to refresh
us and help us on our journey. When about six
miles from Kanagawa we arrived at one of these
tea-houses which was rather larger than usual.
Here it seemed to be the duty or privilege of the

F

landlord to provide water for the horses of travellers and Government officials, and consequently
we found a man ready with a pail of water for our
horses. It is customary to leave a small present
in the coin of the country in return for these
civilities.

With the exception of a few hundred yards here
and there, the whole road from Kanagawa to Yedo
is lined on each side with houses. Now and then
the single row expands into a village or town of
considerable size, teeming with a dense population.
One of these, named Kawasaky, stands about seven
or eight miles east from Kanagawa. It seemed a
busy market-town. The road which formed the
main street was lined with shops and tea-houses,
and crowded with people passing to and fro,
buying and selling, or lolling about looking on.
Travellers too were numerous, who were either
going to the capital or returning from it on the
great highway. Now and then we met a long
train of coolies and armed men in the wake of a
norimon containing an official or person of rank.
The coolies were carrying the luggage, and the
retainers were in attendance probably as much for
show as for the protection of their master.

When we arrived at the further end of Kawasaky we were again politely stopped by mine host
of the "Hotel of Ten Thousand Centuries," a tea-
house of the first class, who insisted on our entering
his establishment for refreshment to ourselves and
our good steeds. His invitation was seconded by

three or four Japanese beauties, but we were un-
gallant enough this time to decline the hospitality,
as it was unnecessary, and as these frequent stop-
pages were rather expensive.

At this place the river Loga intersects the main
road. According to treaty, foreigners are not
allowed to pass further than this point in the direction of the capital, unless they belong to the Legations of those nations who have treaties with Japan.
Special permissions are however granted by the different ministers, with the sanction of the Japanese
Government. In all other directions from Kanagawa, except this one, foreigners are allowed to
travel to the distance of ten *ri*, or about twenty-five
miles. It will be seen, therefore, that there is a
large tract of country available either for recreation or for researches in natural history, geology,
and other sciences.

Dismounting from our horses, we crossed the
Loga in flat-bottomed boats, the horses being put
into one, and the yakoneens and myself going in
another. This river is but a small stream of one
hundred feet in width, and quite shallow. Our
boats were guided and propelled across by long
bamboo poles. When we had crossed the river we
rode onwards in the direction of the capital. For
some distance the road, the houses, and other objects, were just a repetition of what I have already
described. After riding about two miles we arrived
at a place called Omora, where there is a celebrated
tea-house named Mae-yaski, which being interpreted

means the " Mansion of Plum-trees." Here we
were met by mine host and some pretty damsels,
and invited to partake of the usual refreshment.

The " Mansion of Plum-trees " is one of the best
of the class to which it belongs. It is arranged in
the usual' style,—that is, it has a number of apartments separated from each other by sliding doors,
and raised floors covered with mats kept scrupu-
lously clean, upon which the natives sit down to
eat their meals and drink tea or saki. In front of
the door there is a matted platform, raised about
a foot from the ground and covered overhead.
Ladies travelling in norimons or kangos, when
about to stop at the tea-house, are brought alongside of this platform, the bearers give the conveyance a tilt on one side, and the fair ones are literally
emptied out upon the stage. They seem quite accustomed to this treatment, and immediately gather
themselves up in the most coquettish way possible, and assume the squatting posture common in
Japan.

Whether we really needed refreshment, or whether we could not resist the laughing-faced damsels
above mentioned, is not of much moment to the
general reader ; one thing is certain, that somehow
or other we found ourselves within the " Mansion of Plum-trees," surrounded by pretty, good-
humoured girls, and sipping a cup of fragrant tea.
One lady, not particularly young, and whom I took
for the hostess, had adorned herself by pulling out
her eyebrows and blackening her teeth, which cer-

tainly in my opinion did not improve her appearance. However, there is no accounting for taste; and certainly our own taste, in many respects, is not so pure as to warrant us in "throwing the first stone" at the Japanese. The young girls who were in attendance upon me had glittering white teeth, and their lips stained with a dark crimson dye. The Japanese innkeeper always secures the prettiest girls for his waiting-maids, reminding me in this respect of our own publicans and their barmaids.

These inns and their waiting-maids seem to have been much the same in the days of Kæmpfer, in the year 1690, as I found them in 1860. "Nor must I forget," he says, "to take notice of the numberless wenches the great and small inns, and the tea-booths and cook-shops, in villages and hamlets, are furnished withal. About noon, when they have done dressing and painting themselves, they make their appearance, standing under the doors of the house, or sitting upon the small gallery around it, whence, with a smiling countenance and good words, they invite the travelling troops that pass by to call in at their inn, preferable to others. In some places, where there are several inns standing near one another, they make, with their chattering and rattling, no inconsiderable noise, and prove not a little troublesome."

The Japanese ladies differ much from those of China in their manners and customs. It is etiquette with the latter to run away the moment they see

the face of a foreigner; but the Japanese, on the
contrary, do not show the slightest diffidence or
fear of us. In these tea-houses they come up with
smiling faces, crowd around you, examine your
clothes, and have even learnt to shake hands!
Although in manners they are much more free
than the Chinese, I am not aware they are a whit
less moral than their shy sisters on the other side
of the water.

In addition to tea, my fair waiting-maids brought
a tray containing cakes, sweetmeats of various
kinds, and a number of hard-boiled eggs, which
one of them kept cracking and peeling, and pressing
upon me. As I was seated in the midst of my
good-humoured entertainers, the scene must have ¬
been highly amusing to a looker-on, and would, I
doubt not, have made a capital photograph.

My yakoneens were in a different room, and,
apparently, had good appetites, and were making
good use of their time. Leaving them to finish
their meal, I took the opportunity of having a
stroll through the large garden in front of the
" Mansion." As its name implied, it contained a
large number of flowering plum-trees, planted in
groups and in avenues. Little lakes or ponds, of
irregular and pleasing forms, were in the centre of
the garden, in which gold fish and tortoises were
swimming about in perfect harmony. These little
lakes were spanned by rustic bridges, and surrounded with artificial rockwork, in which ferns
and dwarf shrubs were planted. Altogether the

place was pretty and enjoyable, even at this time of the year. In spring or summer, when the trees are in full bloom, or covered with leaves, the " Mansion of Plum-trees " must be a charming place.

Bidding a polite adieu to our fair entertainers, we mounted our horses and continued our journey along the great highway. For the last three or four miles of the journey, the road had taken a direction more inland, and we had lost sight of the bay. Now, however, the bay came again into view, and the road led along its banks as before. Gradually it became more crowded with people, the buildings and shops appeared of a better class, and everything indicated our near approach to the imperial city.

We now entered the suburb of Sinagawa, a place often mentioned in the writings of the Dutch travellers. On our left we observed many fine houses and temples, and some stately trees ; while on our right the upper part of the bay lay spread out to our view. Before us lay the great city, encircling the head of the bay in the form of a crescent, and stretching away almost to the distant horizon. Far out in the bay a square-rigged vessel of war was lying at anchor ; it proved to be the United States frigate 'Niagara,' which had just brought home the Japanese ambassadors from their visit to America. A crowd of small trading vessels and fishing boats lay in the shallow water near the shore ; and a chain of batteries commanded the anchorage.

While I was quietly observing all these objects, one of my yakoneens, who was riding ahead to show the way, suddenly turned in to the left and intimated that we had arrived at the residence of the English Minister. I found his Excellency at home; he received me most kindly, introduced me to the gentlemen of the Embassy, and gave me quarters in the Legation.

The British Legation is located in a large temple, or rather in buildings adjoining, such as are attached to nearly all the large temples in Japan, and which are probably intended to receive visitors, or as seminaries for the Buddhist priesthood. It stands at the head of a little valley, backed behind and on each side by low richly-wooded hills, somewhat in the form of a horse-shoe, and open in front to the Bay of Yedo. The situation is exceedingly picturesque and beautiful. A fine wide avenue, some 200 yards in length, leads up from the bay to the residence of the English Minister. Ornamental gateways stretch over the avenue and give it a pretty appearance, and here and there I observed some large examples of *Pinus Massoniana, Cryptomeria japonica, Salisburia adiantifolia, Podocarpus macrophyllus,* camellias, &c.

On the west side of the temple there is a large cemetery covered with many thousands of stone tombs, some of them apparently of great age. One of these cemeteries is attached to almost every temple about Yedo, but this is the largest that came under my observation. They seem, in almost all instances, to be placed on the west side of the temples. The Japanese, like their neighbours in China, pay great attention to the graves of their dead. They frequently visit them, and place branches of *skimmi* (*Illicium anisatum*), laurels, and other evergreens, in bamboo tubes in front of the stones. When these branches wither they remove them and replace them by others. The trade of collecting and selling these branches must be one of considerable magnitude in Japan; they are exposed, in large quantities, for sale in all the cities and villages; one is continually meeting with people carrying them in the streets; and they seem always fresh upon the graves, showing that they are frequently replaced.

A garden situated in the rear of the buildings of the Legation, although small in extent, is one of the most charming little spots I ever beheld. The circular hill already noticed rises up behind, and forms a background to the picture: this hill is richly covered with trees of great size and beauty; particularly some fine evergreen oaks, seeds of which Mr. Alcock has sent to Kew. On the lower part of the hill there is some pretty rockwork covered with maples, azaleas, camellias, and other plants, with a species of plum, whose branches hung down like a weeping willow. At the base there is a small lake of irregular and pleasing form, extending the whole width of the garden, and between this and the temple there is a little lawn which gives a quiet and pleasing finish to the whole.

To complete the picture as it appeared to me : it was a bright autumnal day; an old maple-tree, with blood-red leaves, was hanging over the lake at one end—an azalea, with leaves of a glowing crimson, was seen in groups at the other; patches of red, purple, and of almost every hue, met the eye in all directions, and produced a striking effect, backed as they were by the deep green of the camellia, evergreen oak, and pine. As the large trees in the background threw a shade over some parts of the garden, while the sun's rays streamed through other parts, or shone full upon the varied colours, the effect produced made one almost fancy oneself in some fairy land. Little walks led through amongst the bushes over the hill-side, where the different plants can be minutely examined, and where shade can be had from the fierce rays of the sun. A fine avenue has been made on the top of the eastern spur, extending down towards the bay, whence a delightful view to seaward can be obtained, and where exercise and the cool morning and evening breezes can be enjoyed, without the nuisance of being followed by the officials of the Japanese Government, an annoyance to which every one has to submit if he moves out of the grounds of the temple.

The garden I have been describing is purely Japanese, Mr. Alcock having found it much in the same state as I saw it. The French Consul-General, and his able secretary the Abbé Gerard, have each a garden, which they found attached to the temples

given up to them as their places of residence.
These gardens are all remarkable for azaleas of
extraordinary size, which have been kept carefully
clipped; and if they are covered with flowers in
the spring, as I believe they are, they must be
indeed charming objects to look upon.

The gardens and grounds of the Legation are
surrounded by a high wooden fence, and the gates
are guarded by armed yakoneens. If any of the
members of the Legation or their visitors pass out
of this enclosure, they are immediately followed by
some of these men. If the foreigner prefers a walk
they walk after him; or if he goes out on horseback they follow in the same style. For some time
this proceeding was thought to be quite unnecessary, and it was supposed that these men
acted merely as spies, to report all the doings of
the foreigners. The Japanese Government have
always maintained that the system was necessary
for our protection; and although it has no doubt
signally failed in some instances, as for example,
in the case of poor Mr. Heuskin the American
interpreter, yet I have no doubt in my own mind
that many lives have been saved by means of it.
In so far as the Government is concerned, I believe
there is every desire to prevent disturbances with
foreigners, and this is one of the means it uses to
accomplish that object.

At the time of my visit there were an unusually
large number of foreigners living in Yedo. In
addition to the members of the English, French,

and American Legations, whose countries had
already made treaties with Japan, there was a
deputation from Prussia engaged in making a
treaty for that country, and a number of American
officers who had come out in the ' Niagara ' with
the Japanese ambassadors.　Everything was going
on quietly ; and although a short time before
Mr. Alcock's servant—a Japanese—had been
murdered, and an attempt had been made upon
the life of a Frenchman in the service of the French
Consul-General, the impression was, that these
men were probably not altogether blameless, and
had brought such punishments upon themselves.
Be that as it may, no one seemed to have any
hesitation in moving about, and I thus had an
opportunity of seeing all the most remarkable parts
of the city, as well as many suburban places of
great interest.　It is true that we were always
followed by the guard of yakoneens, but one had
only to fancy himself a person of great importance
—a prince or a noble in the far East—and this
body-guard was easily endured.　I found them
always perfectly civil, and often of great use in
showing me the right road.

CHAPTER V.

ON the day after my arrival in Yedo Mr. Alcock was good enough to invite me to accompany him in a ride through some of the most interesting parts of the city. The Legation is situated in the south-west suburb, and the main portion of the great city lies to the eastward from our starting point. There was nothing to indicate to a stranger the point where the western suburb ended and the city commenced; indeed, as it has been justly observed, " the suburb of Sinagawa merges into Yedo much in the same way as Kensington straggles into London." Taking then an easterly course, a portion of our road led us through lanes fringed with fields and gardens, and through streets somewhat resembling those of a country town in England. During the first part of our route there was nothing particularly striking to attract our attention. Soon, however, we arrived at a spot of great interest. This was a little hill, one of the highest of the many hills which are dotted about all over the city. Its name was Atango-yama, which means the "Hill of the god Atango." On its summit there is a temple erected to the idol, and a number of arbours where visitors, who come either for worship or for pleasure, can be supplied with cups of tea.

Leaving our horses at the foot of the hill, we ascended it by a long flight of stone steps, which were laid from the base to the summit. When we arrived at the top of the steps, we found ourselves in front of the temple and its surrounding arbours. Here we were waited upon by blooming damsels, and invited to partake of sundry cups of hot tea. But the temple, the arbours, and even our fair waiting-maids, were for the time disregarded as we gazed upon the vast and beautiful city which lay below us spread out like a vast panorama. Until now I had formed no adequate idea of the size of the capital of Japan. Before leaving China I had heard stories of its great size, and of its population of two millions; but I confess I had great doubts as to the truth of these reports, and thought it not improbable that, both as to size and population, the accounts of Yedo might be much exaggerated. But now I looked upon the city with my own eyes, and they confirmed all that I had been previously told.

Looking back to the south-west over the wooded

suburb of Sinagawa from which we had just come, and gradually and slowly carrying our eyes to the south and on to the east, we saw the fair city of Yedo extending for many miles along the shores of the bay, in the form of a crescent or half-moon. It was a beautiful autumnal afternoon, and very pretty this queen of cities looked as she lay basking in the sun. The waters of the bay were smooth as glass, and were studded here and there with the white sails of fishing-boats and other native craft; a few island batteries formed a breastwork for the protection of the town; and far away in the distance some hills were dimly seen on the opposite shores. Turning from the east towards the north, we looked over an immense valley covered with houses, temples, and gardens, and extending far away almost to the horizon. A wide river, spanned by four or five wooden bridges, ran through this part of the town and emptied itself into the bay.

On the opposite side of a valley, some two miles wide and densely covered with houses, we saw the palace of the Tycoon and the "official quarter" of the city, encircled with massive stone walls and deep moats. Outside of this there are miles of wide straight streets and long substantial barn-looking buildings, which are the town residences of the feudal princes and their numerous retainers.

To the westward our view ranged over a vast extent of city, having in the background a chain of wooded hills, whose sloping sides were covered with houses, temples, and trees. A large and

populous portion of Yedo lies beyond these hills,
but that was now hidden from our view.

Such is the appearance which Yedo presents
when viewed from the summit of Atango-yama.
This hill now bears the modern title of "Grande
Vue," and well it deserves the name. After we
had enjoyed this magnificent view for some time,
we descended by the stone steps and resumed our
ride. Our road now skirted a hill clothed with
noble timber-trees and surrounded with walls.
This was the Imperial cemetery. A short distance
beyond this we crossed the first or outer moat, and
were then in the " official quarter," amongst the
residences of the Daimios and their retainers. Here
the streets are wide, straight, and cleanly kept, and
altogether have quite a different appearance from
those we had already passed through. Good drains
are carried down each side to take off the super-
fluous water. All we saw of the houses of the
Daimios was the outer walls, the grated windows,
and the massive-looking doors, many of them deco-
rated with the armorial bearings of their owners.
These buildings were low—generally two stories
high; their foundations and lower walls were
formed of massive stonework, and the upper part
of wood and chunam. Judging from the general
length of the outer street walls, the interior of these
places must be of great size; indeed such must
necessarily be the case, to enable them to accommo-
date the large number of retainers which these
princes always keep about them. As we rode along,

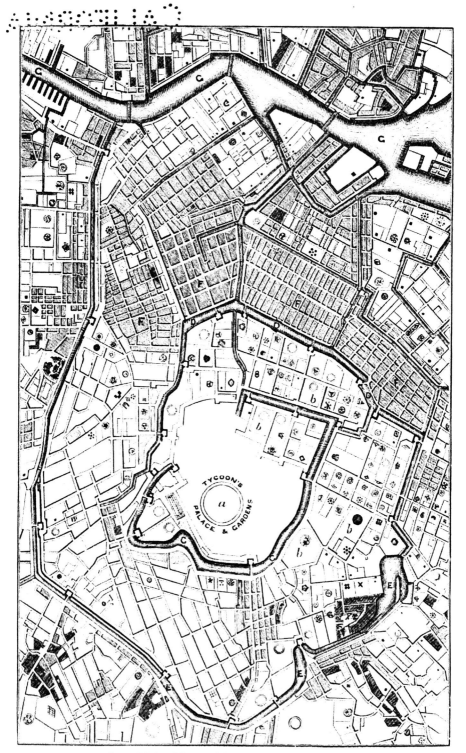

TYCOON'S
PALACE & GARDENS
a

PLAN OF CENTRAL PORTION OF THE CITY OF YEDO.

a. Tycoon's Palace and Gardens.

b. Residences of the Daimios, each circular mark representing the Symbol (Crest) of Owner

E. Outer Moat.

F Commercial Quarter

G. River Todogawa, with which Moats and Canals

many of these retainers showed themselves at the grated windows. It might be only fancy on my part, but I thought I could discern little good-will or friendly feeling towards ourselves in their countenances.

I have just stated that we crossed a bridge over a deep moat before entering the Daimios' quarter. In order to give an idea of the plan of this part of the city, I may compare the moat to a rope loosely coiled; the end of the outer coil dipping as it were into the river, and supplying the whole with water. It is not correct to say, as is sometimes said, that there are three concentric circles, each surrounded by a moat. The Tycoon's palace and the offices of his ministers are situated in the centre of the coil, while the outer and wider portion encircles the mansions of the feudal princes.

The second or inner moat and enclosure was now in view in front of us, with its houses and palaces on rising ground. On the inner side of this circling-moat there are high walls on the water's edge formed of large blocks of stone, of a polygonal form, and nicely fitted into each other without the aid of lime or cement. This is a favourite mode of building in Japan in all cases in which stone is used. The plan is probably adopted in order to render such structures more secure in a country like this which is so subject to earthquakes. In some places sloping banks of green turf rise steeply from the edge of the moat, and are crowned at the top with a massive wall. A landslip in these banks,

however, showed that the wall which apparently
crowned their summits had its foundation far below,
and that the banks themselves had been formed in
front of the wall.   On many of these green banks
there are groups of juniper and pine trees, while
inside the wall itself tall specimens of the same
trees rear their lofty heads high above the ramparts.   No embrasures or places for guns were
observed in these walls, although one would imagine
they had been erected for the purposes of defence.
Kæmpfer, however, assigns another reason; he
says, "Yedo is not enclosed with a wall, no more
than other towns in Japan, but cut through by
many broad canals, with ramparts raised on both
sides, and planted at the top with rows of trees, not
so much for defence as to prevent the fires—which
happen here too frequently—from making too great
a havoc."

   A few months previous to the time of my visit,
the *Gotiro*, or Regent of the Empire, had been
waylaid and murdered in open day, as he was
proceeding from his residence to his office in the
inner quarter.   The scene of this tragedy was
pointed out to me.   A writer in the 'Edinburgh
Review' gives the following graphic account of
this horrid murder :—

   "Within the second moated circle facing the
bay, the causeway leads over a gentle acclivity,
near the summit of which, lying a little back-
ward, is an imposing gateway, flanked on either
side with a range of buildings, which form the

outer screens of large courtyards. Over the
gates, in copper metal, is the crest of the noble
owner — the chief of the house of *Ikomono*, in
which is vested the hereditary office of Regent,
whenever a minor fills the Tycoon's throne.
From the commanding position of this residence
a view is obtained of a long sweep of the ram-
part; and midway the descent ends in a long
level line of road. Just at this point, not 500
yards distant, is one of the three bridges across
the moat, which leads into the inner enclosure,
where the castle of the Tycoon is situated. It
was about ten o'clock in the morning of the 24th
of March, while a storm of alternate sleet and
rain swept over the exposed road and open
space, offering little inducement to mere idlers
to be abroad, that a train was seen to emerge
from the Gotiro's residence. The appearance
of the *cortége* was sufficient to tell those familiar
with the habits and customs of the Japanese
that the Regent himself was in the midst, on his
way to the palace, where his daily duties called
him. Although the numbers were inconsiderable, and all the attendants were enveloped in
their rain-proof cloaks of oiled paper, with great
circular hats of basket or lacquered ware tied to
their heads, yet the two standard-bearers bore
aloft at the end of their spears the black tuft of
feathers,. distinctive of a Daimio, and always
marking his presence. A small company of
officers and personal attendants walk· in front

and round the foremost norimon, while a troop
of inferior office-bearers follow, grooms with led
horses, extra norimon-bearers, baggage-porters
—for no officer, much less a Daimio, ever leaves
his house without a train of baggage—empty or
full, they are essential to his dignity.   Then
there are umbrella-bearers—the servants of the
servants — along the line.   The cortége slowly
wound its way down the hill, for the roads were
wet and muddy even on the high ground, while
the bearers were blinded by the drifting sleet,
carefully excluded only from the noromons by
closed screens.   Thus suspended in a sort of
cage, just large enough to permit a man to sit
cross-legged, the principal personage proceeded
on his way to the palace.   Little, it would seem,
did either he or his men dream of possible
danger.   How should they, indeed, on such a
spot, and for so exalted a personage ?   No augur
or soothsayer gave warning to beware of the
' Ides of March.'   .   .   .   .   The edge of the
moat is gained.   A still larger cortége of the
Prince of Kiu-siu, one of the royal brothers, was
already on the bridge, and passing through the
gate on the opposite side, while, coming up from
the causeway, at a few paces distant, was the
retinue of the second of these brothers, the
Prince of Owari.   The Gotiro was thus between
them at the foot of the bridge, on the open
space formed by the making of a broad street,
which debouches on the bridge.   A few strag-

gling groups, enveloped in their oil-paper cloaks, alone were near, when suddenly one of these seeming idlers flung himself across the line of march, immediately in front of the Regent's norimon. The officers of his household, whose place is on each side of him, rushed forward at this unprecedented interruption — a fatal move, which had evidently been anticipated, for their place was instantly filled with armed men in coats of mail, who seemed to have sprung from the earth—a compact band of some eighteen or twenty men. With flashing swords and frightful yells, blows were struck at all around, the lightest of which severed men's hands from the poles of the norimon, and cut down those who did not fly. Deadly and brief was the struggle. The unhappy officers and attendants, thus taken by surprise, were hampered with their rain gear, and many fell before they could draw a sword to defend either themselves or their lord. A few seconds must have done the work, so more than one looker-on declared ; and before any thought of rescue seemed to have come to the attendants and escorts of the two other princes, both very near (if, indeed, they were total strangers to what was passing), one of the band was seen to dash along the causeway with a gory trophy in his hand. Many had fallen in the *mêlée* on both sides. Two of the assailants, who were badly wounded, finding escape impossible, it is said, stopped in their flight, and

deliberately performed the Harikari,* to the
edification of their pursuers; for it seems to be
the law (so sacred is the rite, or right, which-
ever may be the proper reading) that no one
may be interrupted, even for the ends of justice.
These are held to be sufficiently secured by the
self-immolation of the criminal, however heinous
the offence; and it is a privilege to be denied to
no one entitled to wear two swords. Other
accounts say that their companions, as a last act
of friendship, despatched them to prevent their
falling into the hands of the torturer. Eight
of the assailants were unaccounted for when all
was over; and the remnant of the Regent's
people, released from their deadly struggle, hur-
ried to the norimon to see how it fared with
their master in the brief interval, to find only a
headless trunk. The bleeding trophy carried
off had been the head of the Gotiro himself,
hacked off on the spot. But strangest of all
these startling incidents, it is further related
that *two* heads were found missing, and that
which was seen in the fugitive's hand was only
a lure to the pursuing party, while the true
trophy had been secreted on the person of
another, and was thus successfully carried off.
The decoy paid the penalty of his life. After
leading the chase through a first gateway down
the road, and dashing past the useless guard, he
was finally overtaken; the end for which he

---

* The act of suicide by ripping open the stomach.

had devoted himself having, however, as we have seen, been accomplished. Whether this be merely a popular version or the simple truth, it serves to prove what is believed to be a likely course of action; and how ready desperate men are to sacrifice their lives for an object. The officer in command of the guard, who allowed his post to be forced, was ordered the next day to perform the Harikari on the spot. The rest of the story is soon told. All Yedo was thrown into commotion. The wardgates were all closed; the whole machinery of the government in spies, police, and soldiers, was put in motion, and in a few days it was generally believed the whole of the eight missing were arrested, and in the hands of the torturer. What revelations were wrung from them, or whether they were enabled to resist the utmost strain that could be put upon their quivering flesh and nerve, remains shrouded in mystery."

Riding onwards, and keeping the citadel on our left, we passed two or three bridges which crossed the inner moat, and led into the palace and offices of the ministers. These personages and their servants may be seen daily going to office about nine or ten o'clock in the morning, and returning to their homes about four in the afternoon, much like what occurs at our own public offices. Some walk to office, some ride on horseback, and others go in norimons. Almost every man we met was armed with two swords.

Now and then we met or passed a Daimio, or official of rank, accompanied by his train of retainers, armed with swords, spears, and matchlocks, and with the usual amount of luggage, large umbrellas, led horses, and other signs of his rank.

No foreign visitor to Yedo is allowed to enter the sacred precincts of the inner enclosure which we were now riding round. A short time before this, a portion of the palace of the Emperor had been burned down, and it was now being rebuilt. Judging from the part of it which came under my observation in the distance, it did not seem a very imposing structure. Kæmpfer writes in glowing terms of the palace of his day: "It had a tower many stories high, adorned with roofs and other curious ornaments, which make the whole castle look, at a distance, magnificent beyond expression, amazing the beholders, as do also the many other beautiful bended roofs, with gilt dragons at the top, which cover the rest of the buildings within the castle." As this work, however, professes only to give the reader a description of what came under my own observation, I must leave to others the description of the interior of the Tycoon's castle.

We had approached the citadel on the south, passed round it to the eastward, and were now on a rising ground on the north. Here another of those splendid views over the city and bay was obtained. This point has been named "Belle

Vue" by foreigners, and deservedly so.   It would be a mere repetition of what I saw from the "Hill of Atango" to describe the scene which we now again beheld.   Suffice it to say, that a vast city, bounded on one side by a beautiful bay, and on the other by the far off horizon, lay spread out beneath us.   The land appeared studded all over with gardens ; undulating ground and little hills were dotted about in every direction, crowned with evergreen trees, such as oaks and pines, and, although it was now far on in November, there was nothing to indicate the winter time in Yedo.

The population of this fine city has been estimated at about two millions of souls.   The extent of ground covered by Yedo, and the main parts of its suburbs, has been stated by Kæmpfer, on Japanese authority, to be about sixteen English miles long, twelve broad, and fifty in circumference.   Judging from a native map of the city now before me, and from having ridden through it in all directions, I think the following is about its true size: From the southern suburb of Sinagawa to the north-eastern suburb the distance is about twelve miles, and from east to west it is about eight miles. Of course miles of extensive suburbs lie beyond these points, but these must be looked upon as being in the country and not in the town.

We could have lingered long on Mount " Belle Vue," and gazed upon the beautiful panorama which lay before us ; but the last rays of an autumnal sun reminded us that it was time to return home. Having completed the circle of the Tycoon's castle, we took a southerly course; and winding our way through streets which sometimes led us over little hills, sometimes through lanes and gardens, we in due time reached the gates of the British Legation.

A Yedo Gentleman, with Servant carrying Sword, and Custom-house Officer with Fan.

CHAPTER VI.

.

The country round Yedo — Hill and valley — Trees — Autumnal foliage — Views of Fusi-yama — Cottages and farm-houses — Flowers
and vegetables — Signs of high civilization — Public baths — Beautiful lanes and hedges — Avenues and groves — Civility of the
people — Dogs and their prejudices — Street dogs — Lapdogs —
Fire at the British Legation — Mode of giving alarm — Organization
of Fire-brigade — Wretched engines — Presents from foreign governments — More suitable ones pointed out.

DURING my stay in Yedo I made many excursions
into the surrounding country — sometimes on
horseback, and at other times on foot — but
invariably accompanied with a guard of yakoneens. If the reader will accompany me on one
of these excursions, I shall endeavour to show
him something of the country, as I have already
done of the town. Our road leads us to the
westward, and we are soon clear of the straggling
suburb of Sinagawa. The land is undulating in
its general features, and consists of a succession
of hills and valleys. The valleys are low and flat,
and capable of being irrigated by the streams
which flow down from the surrounding hills.
Rice is the staple crop of these low lands, and it
was now of a yellow hue and ready for the reaping-hook of the farmer. The hills which encircle

the valleys are covered with brushwood and lofty trees. Here the gigantic *Cryptomeria japonica*, the noble pine, and the evergreen oak are peculiarly at home. Clumps of bamboos and the palm of the country (*Chamærops excelsa*) give a sort of tropical character to the scenery. The vivid hues of the autumnal foliage are most striking, and produce a wonderful and beautiful effect upon the landscape. The sumach and various species of maples have now put on their varied shades of colour—yellow, red, and purple; the leaves of the azalea are changing into a deep, glowing crimson; and these masses of "all hues" contrast well with the green foliage of the oaks and pines. As the eye wanders over these valleys and hills, it rests at last on a conical mountain in the background, some 14,000 feet in height, and nearly covered with snow: this is Fusi-yama, the holy mountain of Japan. It would certainly be difficult in all the world to find a scene of greater natural beauty than this.

As we rode onwards we passed many snug little suburban residences, farm-houses, and cottages, having little gardens in front containing a few of the favourite flowering-plants of the country. A remarkable feature in the Japanese character is, that, even to the lowest classes, all have an inherent love for flowers, and find in the cultivation of a few pet plants an endless source of recreation and unalloyed pleasure. If this be one of the tests of a high state of civilization amongst a people, the lower orders amongst the Japanese come out in a most favourable light when contrasted with the same classes amongst ourselves. Vegetables, too, were observed in abundance. All foreigners who visit Japan remark on the little flavour possessed by the vegetables of the country. This is probably owing to the peaty nature of the soil. Although dark in colour and apparently rich in vegetable matter, yet it has not the strength or substance of the soil which is found (for example) in the rich alluvial plain of the Yang-tze-kiang in China.

In one of the villages through which we passed we observed what appeared to be a family bathing-room. The baths at the time were full of persons of both sexes, old and young, apparently of three or four generations, and all were perfectly naked. This was a curious exhibition to a foreigner, but the reader must remember we are now in Japan. Bathing-houses or rooms, both public and private, are found in all parts of the Japanese empire—in the midst of crowded cities, or, as we here see, in country villages. The bath is one of the institutions of the country; it is as indispensable to a Japanese as tea is to a Chinaman. In the afternoon, in the evening, and up to a late hour at night, the bath is in full operation. Those who can afford it have baths in their own houses for the use of themselves and their families; the poorer classes,

for a very small sum, can enjoy themselves at
the public baths.   After coming in from a long
journey, or when tired with the labours of the day,
the Japanese consider a bath to be particularly
refreshing and enjoyable ; and it is probably on
this account, as well as for cleanliness, that it is so
universally employed.   The stern moralist of
Western countries will no doubt condemn the
system of promiscuous bathing, as it is contrary
to all his ideas of decency; on the other hand,
there are those who tell us that the custom only
shows simplicity and innocence such as that which
existed in the Garden of Eden before the fall
of man.   All I can say is, that it is the custom
of the country to bathe in this way, and that, if
appealed to on the subject, the Japanese would
probably tell us that many of the customs amongst
ourselves—such, for example, as our mode of
dressing and dancing—are much more likely
to lead to immorality than bathing, and are not
so useful nor so healthy ; at any rate, the practice
cannot be attributed to habits of primitive innocence in this case, as no people in the world
are more licentious in their behaviour than the
Japanese.

Never in my wanderings in any other country did I meet with such charming lanes as we
passed through on this occasion.   Sometimes
they reminded me of what I had met with in
some of the country districts of England ; but I
was compelled, notwithstanding early prejudices,

to admit that nothing in England even could be compared to them. Large avenues and groves of pines, particularly of *Cryptomeria*, were frequently met with, fringing the roads, and affording most delicious shade from the rays of the sun. Now and then magnificent hedges were observed, composed sometimes of evergreen oaks of various species, sometimes of *Cryptomeria japonica* and other evergreens. These were kept carefully clipped, and in some instances they were trained to a great height, reminding one of those high hedges of holly or yew which may frequently be met with in the parks or gardens of our English nobility. Everywhere the cottages and farm-houses had a neat and clean appearance, such as I had never observed in any other part of the East. Frequently we came upon tea-houses for the refreshment of travellers; and these had little gardens and fish-ponds in their rear, of which glimpses were obtained as we rode slowly by. The scene was always changing and always beautiful—hill and valley, broad roads and shaded lanes, houses and gardens, with a people industrious, but unoppressed with toil, and apparently happy and contented.

Such is the appearance of the sylvan scenery in the vicinity of Yedo. I could scarcely fancy myself on the borders of one of the largest and most populous cities in the East, with a population of two millions of human beings, and covering nearly a hundred square miles of land. As we rode through this charming scenery, the stillness was broken only by the rustling of the leaves of the trees and the tread of our horses' feet. The people in the villages through which we passed were quiet and civil, and did not annoy us in any way. Little urchins sometimes shouted out To-jin, To-jin, as we passed by—a term which means *Chinaman*, but which probably is also used to designate a foreigner, or one who is not a native of Japan. I am not aware that the term is meant as an offensive one, and it certainly does not appear quite so bad as Fan-kwei, or Pih-kwei — that is, foreign devil, or white devil — terms applied to us in China rather too frequently. The dogs were the only animals which showed their enmity to us, and this they did in a manner not to be mistaken. They rushed out of the houses, and barked at us in the most furious manner; but they are cowardly withal, and generally keep at a prudent distance.

These dogs appear to be of the same breed as the common Chinese dog, and both have probably sprung originally from the same stock. It is curious that they should have the same antipathy to foreigners as their masters. For, however civil and even kind the natives of Japan and China appear to be, yet there is no doubt that nine-tenths of them hate and despise us. Apparently such feelings are born with them, and they really cannot help themselves.

That we are allowed to live and travel and trade in these countries is only because one class makes money out of us, and another and a larger one is afraid of our power. I fear we must come to the conclusion, however unwillingly, that these are the motives which keep Orientals on their good behaviour, and force them to tolerate us amongst them. The poor dogs have the same feelings implanted in their nature, but they have not the same hypocrisy, and therefore their hate is visible. As watch-dogs they are admirable, and that is almost the only use to which they are applied. Old Dutch writers inform us that these street dogs belong to no particular individual, but that they are denizens of particular streets— public property, as it were—and that they are regarded with a kind of superstitious feeling by the natives. They are " the only idlers in the country." I think these statements may be received as doubtful, or only partially true. Although some of these dogs may have neither home nor master, yet by far the greater portion have both; and if the inhabitants look upon them as sacred animals, and have any superstitious feelings regarding them, they certainly show these feelings of reverence in a peculiarly irreverent manner. On a warm summer afternoon these animals may be seen lying at full length in the public highway, apparently sound asleep; and it was not unusual for our attendants to kick and whip them out of our road in a most unceremoni-

ous way. On many of them the marks of the sharp
swords of the yakoneens were plainly visible;
and everything tended to show, that, if the dogs
are regarded as sacred by some, the feeling fails
to secure them from being cruelly ill-treated by
the common people. It was not unusual to meet
with wretched specimens in a half-starved condition, and covered with a loathsome disease. The
fact that such animals were tolerated in the
public streets almost leads one to believe that they
must be regarded with superstitious feelings.

The lapdogs of the country are highly prized
both by natives and by foreigners. They are
small—some of them not more than nine or ten
inches in length. They are remarkable for snub-
noses and sunken eyes, and are certainly more
curious than beautiful. They are carefully bred;
they command high prices even amongst the
Japanese; and are dwarfed, it is said, by the use
of saki—a spirit to which their owners are particularly partial. Like those of the larger breed
already noticed, they are remarkable for the intense
hatred they bear to foreigners.

After a most pleasant excursion we found ourselves at the gates of the British Legation, just as
it was getting dark. The evenings were now cold,
and some new stoves had been put up in the
dining-room. The first gong had sounded, and
we were getting ready for dinner—a meal for
which the excursion into the country had fully
prepared us. But the day was not to end so

agreeably as we had supposed. A pipe leading
from the stove set fire to the roof of the dining-
room, ånd for some time it was feared the whole of
the Legation would be destroyed. The watchmen
who surrounded the premises gave the first alarm
to those outside by beating in a peculiar way
upon the hollow stem of the bamboo. This emits
a peculiar sound, which is heard a very long way
off. Then the large fire-bell sounded its alarm-
peal—a sound which was taken up by other bells,
and repeated all over Yedo. These fire-bells are
established in all Japanese towns, and the custody
of them is regularly organized. The manner in
which they are tolled informs the people whether
the fire be near or afar off—whether they ought
to come to render assistance at once, or hold themselves in readiness to come on a second warning.
On the present occasion all the arrangements
seemed to work most admirably. The gates round
the Legation were instantly closed and guarded by
armed yakoneens. The members of the fire-
brigade and those who had duties to perform were
allowed to enter, but all others were strictly excluded. In a few minutes the place was full of
armed men. Several hundreds were running
about in all directions — in the garden, in the
rooms, in the passages, and on the roofs of the different buildings; but watchful eyes were upon
them everywhere, and not an article of any kind
was stolen. The Minister's table was covered
with plate; his drawing-room contained numerous

articles of interest and value, both native and
foreign ; yet, however tempting these things might
have been, not a single article was missing. Altogether I had never seen such a perfect system
of organization. In China it would have been a
most difficult matter to have restrained the mob,
who would have seized the opportunity to plunder ;
here, however, it seemed perfectly easy, and every
one was under the most complete control. Scenes
like this must be constantly happening in Yedo.
Fires are almost of daily occurrence in some part or
other of the city ; and, owing to the houses being
principally built of wood, the fires spread with great
rapidity. The officers of the Government and the
members of the different fire-brigades have constant
practice; and this, no doubt, accounts for their
perfect system of organization, which was the
admiration of every one on the present occasion.
Here, however, our eulogium must end.

The engines which were brought to put out the
fire were the most wretched machines I ever saw.
A little pond in the garden, in which there was a
good supply of water, was not twenty yards from
the house; yet the engine had to be filled with
buckets by hand, there being no hose to connect it
with the pond. The stream of water it threw out
was little larger than that thrown by a hand-
syringe, and much less than could be discharged
from a good garden engine. A number of men
carried water in buckets up ladders to the roof of
the building, and emptied it upon the flames; but

here, strange to say, there was no system—no
passing the buckets from hand to hand; every
man was doing what was right in his own eyes;
all were giving orders, and each one was making
all the noise he could.   Luckily the fire had been
discovered early, and was easily extinguished, as
the night was calm.   Had it only got a little
ahead before the discovery, or had a smart breeze
been blowing at the time, the British Legation in
Yedo, with the surrounding temples, would, in all
probability, have been burned to the ground.

The fire was at last extinguished, but, ere this
was accomplished, a considerable amount of damage
had been done to the buildings.   The rooms,
papered in Japanese style, and divided from each
other by moving panels, were strewed with charred
wood, broken tiles, and deluged with water ; the
pretty garden was covered with rubbish, and
several valuable plants hopelessly ruined.   But in
the midst of this we were all thankful that the
flames had been subdued, and that we had still
ample room in other quarters of the Legation.
And now the last scene of all took place, and a
very sensible one it was.   The high officers who
had been superintending the fire brigade formed a
kind of procession, and, with lanterns, marched up
the ladders and over the roof, to judge for themselves and make sure that the flames were really
extinguished.   When everything was found in a
satisfactory condition, orders were given for the
people to leave, and in a few minutes the crowd

of coolies, firemen, and two-sworded yakoneens, had disappeared as quickly as they came.

A short time before I visited Japan the English Government had made the Tycoon a present of a pretty little steam yacht, which I am afraid will be of little use to His Majesty; and during my visit to Yedo the Government of the United States of America had presented to the Japanese all the newest and most destructive implements of war, and also had sent an officer over to instruct them how to use them. Should other nations in the West feel desirous of making presents, I would strongly recommend them to send out some good fire-engines, which would be of far more value to the Japanese than implements of destruction, which may one day be turned against the givers.

CHAPTER VII.

A journey in search of new plants — Japanese College — Residence of Prince Kanga — Dang-o-zaka — Its tea-gardens, fish-ponds, and floral ladies — Nursery-gardens — Country people — Another excursion — Soldiers — Arrive at Su-mae-yah — Country covered with gardens — New plants — Mode of dwarfing — Variegated plants — Ogee, the Richmond of Yedo — Its tea-house — The Tycoon's hunting-ground — Fine views — Agricultural productions — A drunken man — Intemperance of the people generally.

THE capital of Japan is remarkable for the large number of gardens in its suburbs where plants are cultivated for sale. The good people of Yedo, like all highly civilized nations, are fond of flowers, and hence the demand for them is very great. The finest and most extensive of these gardens are situated in the north-eastern suburbs, at places called Dang-o-zaka, Ogee, and Su-mae-yah. As one of my chief objects in coming to Yedo was to examine such places as these, I lost no time in paying them a visit.

As the British Legation was situated in the south-west suburb, I had to cross the entire city before I could reach these gardens. From the time occupied in going this distance I estimated the width of the city, in this direction, at about nine or ten miles. Passing in from the western suburb, I went through the "Official Quarter," with its

wide straight streets and town residences of the
Daimios or lords and princes of the Empire,
which have been already noticed. On a rising
ground on my left I observed the palace of the
Tycoon. Proceeding onward in an easterly direction, I recrossed the moat, and was again amongst
the streets and shops of the common people.
Here, on a hill-side, in the midst of some tall pines
and evergreen oaks, I observed a large building,
which, I was informed, was a college for students
of Chinese classics. A little further on I passed
the palace of the Prince of Kanga, reputed to be
the wealthiest and most powerful noble in the
empire, and to have no less than 40,000 retainers
located in his palaces in the capital, ready to do his
bidding, whether that be to dethrone the Tycoon
or to take the life of a foreigner. He was reported
to be at the head of the conservative party in the
empire, and to be unfavourable to foreigners.

After passing the residence of Prince Kanga I
found myself in the eastern suburb. One long
street, with houses on each side of the way, and
detached towns here and there, extended two or
three miles beyond this. Turning out of this
street to the right hand, I passed through some
pretty shaded lanes, and in a few minutes more
reached the romantic town of Dang-o-zaka. This
pretty place is situated in a valley, having wooded
hills on either side, with gardens, fish-ponds, and
tea-houses in the glen and on the sides of the hills.
In the principal tea-gardens the fish-ponds are

stocked with different kinds of fish; and I observed a number of anglers amusing themselves fishing, in the usual way, with hooks baited with worms.

The most curious objects in this garden were imitation ladies made up out of the flowers of the chrysanthemum. Thousands of flowers were used for this purpose; and as these artificial beauties smiled upon the visitors out of the little alcoves and summer houses, the effect was oftentimes rather startling. The favourite flowering plum-trees were planted in groups and avenues in all parts of the garden, while little lakes and islands of rockwork added to the general effect.

Having patronised this establishment by taking sundry cups of tea, I intimated to my attendant yakoneens my intention to look out for some gardens of a different kind, in which I could purchase some new plants. But pleasure was the order of the day with them, and they coolly informed me there were no other places worth seeing here, and that we had better go on to the tea-gardens of Ogee. From information I had previously received, I knew they were deceiving me, and therefore proceeded to take a general survey on my own account. When they saw I was determined to look out for myself, they pretended to have received some information about other places, and said they were willing to guide me to them. Telling them I was greatly obliged, I desired them to lead the way. A short walk to the top of the hill brought us to a long, straight,

country-looking road, lined with neatly clipped
hedges.   Here I found a large number of nursery
gardens, richly stocked with the ornamental plants
of the country.   Crowds of people followed us, and,
although they were rather noisy, and anxious to
see such a strange sight as a foreigner in these out-
of-the-way places, they were, upon the whole, particularly civil and easily managed and controlled.
As I entered a nursery the gates were quietly
closed upon the people, who waited patiently
until I came out, and then they followed me on to
the next.   The yakoneens seemed to be greatly
respected, or feared it may be, but, at all events, a
look, a word, or a movement of the fan, was quite
sufficient to preserve the most perfect order.

I visited garden after garden in succession.
Each was crowded with plants, some cultivated in
pots and others in the open ground, many of which
were entirely new to Europe, and of great interest
and value.   Every now and then my yakoneens
informed me that the garden I happened to be in
at the time was the last one in the lane, but I told
them goodhumouredly I would go on a little
further and satisfy myself.   This they could not
object to, and, as more gardens were found, they
only smiled and said they had been misinformed.
My old experience in China was of good service to
me here.   There is nothing like patience, politeness, and good humour, with these Orientals,
whether they present themselves as noisy crowds
or crafty officials.

At first the proprietors were not quite sure whether they ought to sell me the plants which I selected. A reference was invariably made to the yakoneens, both upon this point and also as to what sum they should ask. I am afraid I must confess to the impression that these gentry made me pay considerably more than the fair value or " market price." As I concluded each purchase, the plants purchased, the price, and the name of the vendor, were carefully written down by one of the officials, and this report of my proceedings was taken home to their superiors.

The day was far spent before I had finished the inspection of these interesting gardens, but I was greatly pleased with the results. A great number of new shrubs and trees, many of them probably well suited for our English climate, had been purchased. Orders were now given to the different nurserymen to bring the plants to the English Legation on the following day, and we parted mutually pleased with our bargains. It was now too late to go to Ogee or Su-mae-yah, so that journey was put off until another day.

Mounting our horses, we left the pleasant and romantic lanes of Dang-o-zaka and rode homewards. In coming out we had passed to the south of the Tycoon's palace, but in going home a different route was taken—a route which led us along the north side of these buildings. In all my excursions about Yedo with a guard of yakoneens, I have invariably observed that they

have brought me home by a different road from
that by which I went. At first I gave them credit
for a .desire to show me as much of the city as
possible, but I am now inclined to believe that
they had orders of this kind from their superiors;
and that the object was to prevent the chance of
an attack from any one who had seen us going out,
and who might lie in wait for us on our return.
Be that as it may, the fact is as I have stated.

On the following morning the whole of the
nurserymen from whom I had purchased plants
presented themselves at the British Legation, to
deliver the plants and to receive their money—
and possibly to pay a small tax to the officials.
But if the latter transaction took place, it was done
quietly and without a murmur.

A day or two after this, with a flask of wine
slung over my shoulder, and a small loaf and jar
of potted meat in my pocket, I started early in the
morning in order to explore the country and
gardens about Su-mae-yah and Ogee. The same
guard of yakoneens accompanied me, and our road,
for a good part of the way, was the same as that
by which I went to Dang-o-zaka. The places we
now proposed to visit, although in the same direction, are considerably farther off. Passing, therefore, the scene of my former visit, I rode onwards
farther out into the suburbs. The houses gradually began to get more scattered, sometimes fields
and trees lined one side of the road, and everything showed me that I had fairly left the great

city behind me. In one of these country parks I heard some soldiers going through their exercise; and the music was not unlike that of our own military bands. It was very likely an imitation of something of the kind. The high close paling and dense brushwood prevented me from seeing much, but sometimes I caught a glimpse of the flags and spears of the soldiers. The Daimios are constantly training their soldiers in all the arts of Japanese warfare. On this occasion, when passing near a Daimio's residence in the city, I heard the clattering of arms, as of men engaged in fencing; and many times, during my stay in Yedo, I have heard the same sounds. If ever any European nation has the misfortune to go to war with Japan, it will find the Japanese, as soldiers, very much superior to the Chinese. At the same time, as we do not fight with swords only, there is little doubt about the issue of such a contest. Let us hope, however, that such a thing as a war with Japan may be far distant, and that, in this one instance at least, we may have the satisfaction of opening up a country without deluging it with the blood of its people.

Park-like scenery, trees and gardens, neatly-clipped hedges, succeeded each other; and my attendant yakoneens at length announced that we had arrived at the village of Su-mae-yah. The whole country here is covered with nursery-gardens. One straight, road, more than a mile in length, is lined with them. I have never seen, in any part of the

world, such a large number of plants cultivated for
sale.   Each nursery covers three or four acres of
land, is nicely kept, and contains thousands of
plants, both in pots and in the open ground.   As
these nurseries are generally much alike in their
features, a description of one will give a good idea
of them all.

On entering the gateway there is a pretty little
winding path leading up to the proprietor's house,
which is usually situated near the centre of the
garden.   On each side of this walk are planted
specimens of the hardy ornamental trees and shrubs
of the country, many of which are dwarfed or
clipped into round table forms.   The beautiful little
yew (*Taxus cuspidata*) which I formerly introduced
into Europe from China, occupies a prominent place
amongst dwarf shrubs.   Then there are the different species of Pines, Thujas, Retinosporas, and
the beautiful *Sciadopitys verticillata*, all duly represented.

Plants cultivated in pots are usually kept near
the house of the nurseryman, or enclosed with a
fence of bamboo-work.   These are cultivated and
arranged much in the same way as we do such
things at home.   The Japanese gardener has not
yet brought glass-houses to his aid for the protection and cultivation of tender plants.   Instead of
this he uses sheds and rooms fitted with shelves,
into which all the tender things are huddled together for shelter during the cold months of winter.
Here I observed some South American plants, such

as cacti, aloes, &c., which have found their way
here, although as yet unknown in China—a fact
which shows the enterprise of the Japanese in a
favourable light. A pretty species of fuchsia was
also observed amongst the other foreigners. In one
garden I saw a large number of a species of acorus
with deep green leaves. These were cultivated in
fine square porcelain pots, and in each pot was a
little rock of agate, crystal, or other rare stone,
many of these representing the famous Fusi-yama,
or " Matchless Mountain" of Japan. All this little
arrangement was shaded from bright sunshine and
protected from storms by means of a matting which
was stretched overhead. There was nothing else
in this garden but the acorus above mentioned, but
of this there must have been several hundred specimens. The pretty Nanking square porcelain pots,
the masses of deep green foliage, and the quaint
form and colouring of the little rocks, produced a
novel and striking effect, which one does not meet
with every day.

In Japan, as in China, dwarf plants are greatly
esteemed; and the art of dwarfing has been brought
to a high state of perfection. President Meylan, in
the year 1826, saw a box which he describes as
only one inch square by three inches high, in which
were actually growing and thriving a bamboo, a
fir, and a plum-tree, the latter being in full blossom.
The price of this portable grove was 1200 Dutch
gulden, or about 100l. In the gardens of Su-mae-
yah dwarf plants were fairly represented, although

I did not meet with anything so very small and very expensive as that above mentioned. Pines, junipers, thujas, bamboos, cherry and plum trees, are generally the plants chosen for the purpose of dwarfing.

The art of dwarfing trees, as commonly practised both in China and Japan, is in reality very simple and easily understood. It is based upon one of the commonest principles of vegetable physiology. Anything which has a tendency to check or retard the flow of the sap in trees, also prevents, to a certain extent, the formation of wood and leaves. This may be done by grafting, by confining the roots in a small space, by withholding water, by bending the branches, and in a hundred other ways, which all proceed upon the same principle. This principle is perfectly understood by the Japanese, and they take advantage of it to make nature subservient to this particular whim of theirs. They are said to select the smallest seeds from the smallest plants, which I think is not at all unlikely. I have frequently seen Chinese gardeners selecting suckers for this purpose from the plants of their gardens. Stunted varieties were generally chosen, particularly if they had the side branches opposite or regular, for much depends upon this; a one-sided dwarf-tree is of no value in the eyes of the Chinese or Japanese. The main stem was then, in most cases, twisted in a zigzag form, which process checked the flow of the sap, and at the same time encouraged the production of side-branches at those parts of the stem where they were most desired. The pots in which they were planted were narrow and shallow, so that they held but a small quantity of soil compared with the wants of the plants, and no more water was given than was actually necessary to keep them alive. When new branches were in the act of formation they were tied down and twisted in various ways; the points of the leaders and strong-growing ones were generally nipped out, and every means were taken to discourage the production of young shoots possessing any degree of vigour. Nature generally struggles against this treatment for a while, until her powers seem to be in a great measure exhausted, when she quietly yields to the power of Art. The artist, however, must be ever on the watch; for should the roots of his plants get through the pots into the ground, or happen to receive a liberal supply of moisture, or should the young shoots be allowed to grow in their natural position for a time, the vigour of the plant, which has so long been lost, will be restored, and the fairest specimens of Oriental dwarfing destroyed. It is a curious fact that when plants, from any cause, become stunted or unhealthy, they almost invariably produce flowers and fruit, and thus endeavour to propagate and perpetuate their kind. This principle is of great value in dwarfing trees. Flowering trees—such, for example, as peaches and plums—produce their blossoms most profusely under the treatment I have described; and as they expend their energies in this way, they have little inclination to make vigorous growth.

The most remarkable feature in the nurseries of Su-mae-yah and Dang-o-zaka is the large number of plants with variegated leaves. It is only a very few years since our taste in Europe led us to take an interest in and to admire those curious freaks of nature called variegated plants. For anything I know to the contrary, the Japanese have been cultivating this taste for a thousand years. The result is that they have in cultivation, in a variegated state, almost all the ornamental plants of the country, and many of these are strikingly handsome. Here is a list of a few to give some idea of the extent and number of these extraordinary productions :—Pines, Junipers, Retinosporas, Podocarpus, Illiciums, *Andromeda japonica*, Euryas, Eleagnus, *Pittosporum Tobira*, Euonymus (yellow), Aralia, Laurus, *Salisburia adiantifolia*. I have already said we must look upon the *Aucuba japonica* of our gardens as only a variegated variety of that species. Then there is a variegated orchid! a variegated palm! a variegated camellia! and even the tea-plant is duly represented in this "happy family!" The beautiful *Sciadopitys verticillata*, which is no doubt "one of the finest conifers in Asia," has produced a variety which has golden-striped leaves.

It may readily be imagined that I was able to select a great number of new ornamental shrubs and trees which will one day, it is hoped, produce a

striking and novel effect upon our English parks
and pleasure-grounds. Having settled the prices
of the different plants selected, all the particulars
were carefully written down by my attendant
yakoneens, as on a former occasion, and the vendors
were requested to bring my purchases to the
British Legation on the following morning. We
then took our departure for Ogee.

Ogee is the Richmond of Japan, and its celebrated tea-house is a sort of "Star and Garter
Hotel." Here the good citizens of Yedo come out
for a day's pleasure and recreation, and certainly it
would be difficult to find a spot more lovely or more
enjoyable. Our road led us down a little hill, and
was lined on each side with pretty suburban residences, gardens, and hedgerows. On approaching
the village crowds of people came out to look at the
foreigner, although a species of that genus had not
been particularly rare of late. Giving some of the
boys our horses to hold, we were conducted to the
interior of the tea-house, and attended by pretty,
good-humoured damsels. A small garden, with
a running stream overhung with the branches
of trees, green banks, and lovely flowers, was in
the rear of the tea-house; and, taken as a whole,
the place was extremely pretty and well worthy of
being patronized by the pleasure-seekers of Yedo.
Having partaken of the cakes, tea, hard-boiled
eggs, and other delicacies which were set before
me, I went out for a stroll in the surrounding
country. As my yakoneens were busy with their

dinner, I tried to induce them to remain and finish it, telling them I was only going for a short walk, and that I would soon return. This they would not listen to, so I let them have their own way, and we all set out together. My chief object was to get upon the top of a hill in the vicinity, in order to have a good view of the country. A few minutes brought me to the top, which formed a kind of table-land, uncultivated, but having here and there a few groups of lofty trees. This forms the hunting-grounds of his Imperial Majesty the Tycoon. It is here that on certain occasions he watches the flight of the falcon in pursuit of the heron of Japan—a bird held sacred by the Japanese, and rigidly preserved by the authorities. There is also on this hill an archery-ground for the Imperial soldiers, and a refectory for preparing a repast for his Majesty's retinue.

The view from the top of this eminence was exceedingly fine. To the northward, a highly cultivated agricultural country lay spread out. It was the period of the rice-harvest, and the fields were now yellow with the ripening grain. The young crops of wheat and barley, already several inches above ground, were of the liveliest green, and contrasted well with the yellow rice-fields. The country was well-wooded, and a little river was seen winding through the valley on its way to the head of the Yedo bay. Taking the place as a whole, his Majesty the Tycoon could scarcely have found a more pleasant hunting-ground.

The day was now far advanced; indeed, my yakoneens had been hinting some time before this that it was time to return to Yedo. First, they looked to the heavens, and gravely informed me they thought it was going to rain; and when they saw this did not produce the desired effect, they told me evening was approaching, and that it was dangerous for me to be out after dark. This was no doubt quite true, and during my residence in Yedo I invariably made it a rule to get back to the Legation as soon after nightfall as possible. On the present occasion I intimated to them that I was now quite ready to return to the city, and we were soon on our way.

On our way back, and just when we were opposite to the residence of the Prince of Kanga—the Daimio whom I have already mentioned as unfavourable to foreigners—a drunken man was monopolizing the road, who, I was afraid, might give us some trouble. He had a long wooden pole in his hands, and was endeavouring to strike all who came in his path. One of my betos, or grooms, was struck by him; but as the poor wretch could scarcely stand, it was very easy to get out of his way. He had no idea that a foreigner was behind him; and I shall never forget the peculiar wild and drunken stare he gave me when he observed me. Under the circumstances I judged it prudent to leave him in his trance of astonishment, and trotted onwards.

Intemperance in the use of ardent spirits is one

of the vices of the Japanese. In this respect, if we can trust Thunberg, the Swedish physician, they must have degenerated sadly during the last hundred years. Amongst a long catalogue of their virtues, Thunberg says, they have "no play or coffee-houses, 'no taverns nor alehouses, and consequently no consumption of coffee, chocolate, brandy, wine, or punch ; no privileged soil, no waste lands, and not a single meadow; no national debt, no paper currency, no course of exchange, and no bankers (!)." It may have been so in Thunberg's time, although I confess to some doubts upon the subject; but it will be seen, from what came under my own observation, that things are very different now.

In these days it is a common saying that " all Yedo gets drunk after sunset !" This is, of course, an exaggeration ; but, no doubt, drunkenness prevails to a degree happily unknown in other countries at the present day. Even before the evening closes in, the faces of those one meets in the streets are suspiciously red, showing plainly enough that *saki* has been imbibed pretty freely. Nor is it in the capital city only that such a state of things exists. We learn from Dr. Pompe, the Dutch physician at Nagasaki, that one-half of the whole adult population are more or less inebriated with saki by nine o'clock every evening ! When I state that a great proportion of these drunken people in the capital are armed with two rather sharp swords, and that in this condition they are often ill-natured and quarrelsome, it will be readily seen that the city of Yedo is not a very safe place for foreigners to be about in after nightfall.

The remainder of our ride home from Ogee was without any incident worth relating, and I arrived at the house of the English Minister, well pleased with the successful issue of the day's excursion. On various occasions during my stay in Yedo I repeated my visits to Dang-o-zaka, Su-mae-yah, and Ogee, and was thus enabled to add to my collections a very large number of the ornamental trees and shrubs of Japan.

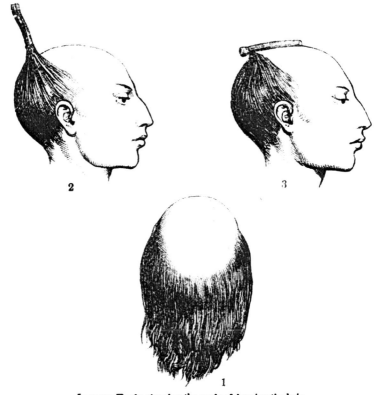

Japanese Heads, showing the mode of dressing the hair.
1. Back of head before the hair is tied up. 2. Second process. 3. Full dress

CHAPTER VIII.

On the 23rd of November I had an appointment with the Abbé Girard, who was formerly a missionary in Loochoo, and was now interpreter to M. de Bellecourt, the French Consul-General, or *Chargé d'Affaires*, in Japan. The Abbé, who was well acquainted with Yedo, was good enough to offer to take me to some places of interest which I had not yet seen. I found him residing in a little temple near the French Legation, and well guarded with yakoneens. He had in his house some rare specimens of Japanese singing-birds, particularly one known to foreigners as the Japanese nightingale. This is a curious bird, if the stories which are told about its habits are true. It is said to inhabit the recesses of dark woods, and to shun the light of day. Hence in a domestic state it is usually kept in comparative darkness, a wooden box being dropped over its cage. This box has a small paper window, in order to admit a little subdued light. In this condition it sings charmingly, and has a full, clear, ringing note, wonderfully loud for so small a bird. The Japanese name of this little songster is Ogo-yezu.

After breakfast the Abbé and I mounted our horses, and, accompanied by our two sets of yako-neens, set out to visit the temple of Ah-sax-saw, which lies on the eastern or south-eastern side of Yedo. Our route led us, not only through a portion of the "official quarter," which I had frequently visited, but also through the main streets of the trading part of the city. I confess I was rather disappointed. The streets were much wider and cleaner than those of the Chinese towns; but the contents of the shops appeared to be of little value. One must, however, bear in mind that Yedo is not a manufacturing or trading town in the usual sense in which the term is used. Hence, perhaps, I ought to have expected to see only the necessaries, or perhaps a few of the luxuries of life, exhibited in the shops here. Silk and cotton shops were numerous, and, if they did not obtain custom, it was not for want of the use of means. Men and boys were stationed in front of the doors trying all their arts to induce the passers-by to go in and spend their money. Lacquer-ware, bronzes, and porcelain were exhibited in abundance, as were also umbrellas, pipes, toys, and paper made up into every conceivable article.

I may here mention in passing that Japanese
paper is made chiefly out of the bark of the paper
mulberry (*Broussonetia papyrifera*).   It is particularly well suited for decorative purposes, such
as the papering of rooms.   It has a glossy, silky,
and comfortable appearance, and many of the
patterns are extremely chaste and pretty.   The
fan pattern, which looked as if fans had been
thrown all over the surface, used to be much
admired by the foreign residents.   For some reason
it is made in very small sheets, which would
render it rather inconvenient to our paper-hangers.
This, however, is no detriment in Japan, where
labour is cheap.   Japanese oil-paper is of a very
superior quality, and is used for a variety of
purposes.   For a very small sum one can be clothed
in a " Mackintosh " coat and trowsers capable of
keeping out any amount of rain.   As a wrapper
to protect silk goods and other valuable fabrics
from wet and damp it is invaluable, and owing to
its great strength it is often used instead of a tin
or lead casing.   Despatch-boxes, looking like
leather, and very hard and durable, are also made
of paper, and so are letter-bags, purses, cigar-cases,
umbrellas, and many other articles in daily use.
In addition to those purposes to which paper is
applied in western countries, in Japan it is used
for windows instead of glass, for the partitions of
rooms instead of lath and plaster, for fans and
fan-cases, for twine, and in a variety of other
ways.

Articles used as food were displayed in abundance in all the streets of the commercial quarter. The vegetables and fruits of the country, such as I have named elsewhere, were in profusion everywhere, and apparently cheap. The bay supplies the good people of Yedo with excellent fish, and consequèntly the fishmonger was duly represented amongst the shopkeepers, where his wares could be purchased either dead or alive, fresh or salted. Butchers' shops were also observed as we rode along, showing that the Japanese do not live on vegetables and fish only. It is true that in these shops we did not observe any beef, for the Japanese do not kill their bullocks and eat them as we do ; and, as the sheep is not found in the country, we, of course, could not see any mutton. Venison, however, was common, and monkeys were observed in several of the shops. I shall never forget the impression produced upon me when I saw the latter hanging up in front of a butcher's door. They were skinned, and had a most uncomfortable resemblance to the members of the human family. I dare say the Japanese consider the flesh of the monkey very savoury ; but there is no accounting for prejudices and tastes, and I must confess that I must have been very hungry indeed before I could have dined off these human-looking monkeys.

In our ride through the town we remarked a large number of fire-proof houses, or godowns, for the protection of money or valuable goods in case of fire. These have thick walls of mud and stone,

and are most useful in a country like this, where
fires occur so frequently.   Wooden watch-towers
were also numerous in all parts of the city.   These
are posts of observation, from which a fire can
be observed at a distance and an alarm given.
Buckets of water were seen in every street, and
frequently on the tops of the houses; and a kind
of fire-police are continually on the watch by night
and by day, ready to give instant notice and
assistance.

After riding in an easterly direction for some
time, we arrived at the celebrated *Nipon-Bas,* or
" Bridge of Japan."   This crosses a canal which is
fed by a river a little to the south of the bridge,
and which is apparently connected with the moat
which encircles the official quarter and the palace
of the Tycoon.   The bridge is a strong wooden
structure resting on piles, and riveted together
with massive clamps of iron.   To a foreign eye
there is nothing very remarkable in its appearance; but by the Japanese it is considered one of
the wonders of Yedo.   From this bridge the distances to all parts of the empire are measured in *ri*;
and hence it is usual to say, such a place is so
many *ri* distant—not from Yedo, but—from Nipon-
Bas.   A *ri* is about equal to two and a half English
miles.

A ride of about two hours brought us to Ah-sax-
saw.   Its massive temple was seen looming at the
further end of a broad avenue.   An ornamental
arch, or gateway, was thrown across the avenue,

which had a very good effect; a huge belfry stood
on one side ; and a number of large trees, such as
pines and *Salisburia adiantifolia*, surrounded the
temple.   Each side of the avenue was lined. with
shops and stalls, open in front like a bazaar, in
which all sorts of Japanese things were exposed
for sale.   Toys of all kinds, such as humming-tops,
squeaking-dolls with very large heads, puzzles, and
pictures were numerous, and apparently in great
demand.   Looking-glasses, tobacco-pipes, common
lacquer-ware, porcelain, and such like articles,
were duly represented.   Had the whole been
covered over with glass, it would have been not
unlike the Lowther Arcade in London.   Crowds of
people followed us as we entered the avenue, who
had evidently seen little of Europeans before ; but
although somewhat noisy, they treated us with the
most perfect civility and respect.

On our arrival at the head of the avenue, we
found ourselves in front of the huge temple, and
ascended its massive steps.   Its wide doors stood
open ; candles were burning on the altars, and
priests were engaged in their devotions.   It was
the old story over again — unmeaning sounds,
beating of drums, tinkling of bells, &c., which I
had so often heard when a guest in the Buddhist
temples of China.

The temple has numerous tea-houses attached
to it for the accommodation of visitors and devotees.   Adjoining them are many pretty gardens
with fish-ponds, ornamental bridges, artificial rock-

work, and avenues of plum and cherry trees, which
seem the favourite ones at all the tea-houses and
temples of Japan.

This place is most famed in the vicinity of Yedo
for the variety and beauty of its chrysanthemums.
At the time of our visit they were in full bloom,
and most certainly would have delighted the eyes
of our English florists had they found themselves
so far away from Hammersmith, the Temple, or
Stoke Newington. I procured some extraordinary
varieties, most peculiar in form and in colouring,
and quite distinct from any of the kinds at present
known in Europe. One had petals like long thick
hairs, of a red colour, but tipped with yellow,
looking like the fringe of a shawl or curtain;
another had broad white petals striped with red
like a carnation or camellia; while others were
remarkable for their great size and brilliant colouring. If I can succeed in introducing these varieties into Europe, they may create as great a change
amongst chrysanthemums as my old *protégee* the
modest " Chusan daisy " did when she became the
parent of the present race of pompones.*

In order to make sure of getting the finest
varieties, I determined to take suckers from those
in bloom at the time of my visit, and further to
take these same suckers home under my own care.
Having settled the price with some difficulty, I
then intimated to the proprietor my wish that he
should dig them up forthwith. To this he made

* Most of them have arrived safely in England.

many objections, not on his own account, but on mine. "They would be inconvenient for me to carry," he said, and "he was quite willing to dig them up next morning and bring them himself to the Legation." I do not know that the man wanted to deceive me by bringing different and inferior kinds to those I had purchased, but I had been taken in once or twice in this way in China, and had determined not to be taken in again. I therefore expressed my best thanks for his good intentions towards me, but got him to let me have the suckers, to take home under my own charge.

The Japanese gardener understands the art of chrysanthemum culture rather better than we do, and produces blooms of wonderful size. This is done by great care, good soil, and by allowing only one or two blooms to be perfected at the end of a shoot.

The tea-plant was common in these gardens, and was frequently used as an edging for the walks. In this position it was kept clipped, and had a pretty and novel appearance. In other places in this district I observed it cultivated rather extensively for the sake of its leaves. There is also in the gardens of Ah-sax-saw a collection of living birds and other animals for the amusement of visitors who may happen to be fond of this branch of natural history. I observed green pigeons, speckled crows, a fine large eagle, gold and silver pheasants, mandarin ducks, rabbits, and squirrels amongst the collection. Altogether, there are many things here calculated to amuse and instruct the good people of Yedo when they come out for a holiday; and when the plum and cherry trees are in blossom, these gardens must be very enjoyable.

Leaving Ah-sax-saw, with its temples, tea-gardens, and chrysanthemums, we returned up the avenue by which we came, and were again followed by crowds of wondering natives. Taking now a southerly direction, we came upon a broad river which flows from the eastward, and empties itself into the bay of Yedo. It is about as large as the Thames at Richmond or Kew. We crossed it by a wooden bridge, and then entered that part of the town called by the Japanese *Moo-co-gee-me*, or " island opposite to Yedo." This is, in fact, the Southwark or Borough of the capital. It is large and densely populated; the streets run mostly at right angles with each other; and it is intersected by a number of wide canals.

Riding along the banks of the river, we soon found ourselves nearly clear of houses and in the country. As we looked back over the river, the city of Yedo, with its temples, watch-towers, and undulating wooded hills, lay spread out before us, and formed a picture of striking beauty. Nearly all the land where we were was one vast garden; or to speak more correctly, it was covered with tea-gardens and nurseries. There were hedges of single camellias (*C. sasanqua*), white and red, and China roses, all in full bloom, although it was now late in November. Many evergreen trees were there, clipped into fanciful shapes; and the indispensable flowering plums and cherries were in great abundance, although now leafless and having put on their wintry garb.

We paid a visit to a number of tea-houses and gardens; and from the way in which they were arranged and planned, no doubt they are patronized by thousands during the spring and summer seasons, when picnic-loving and pleasure-seeking Yedoites go out to enjoy themselves. Everywhere we were politely received, and tea pressed upon us by the proprietors of the gardens.

We were now some ten or twelve miles from the foreign Legations, and declining day warned us to hasten our return. On our way back we followed for some distance the course of the river. There is a fine broad embankment all the way along the left bank, which we could not help contrasting with that which is now being formed at Pimlico and Chelsea. But the Yedo embankment has probably been in existence for many generations —a monument of the foresight and enterprise of this extraordinary people.

In this part of Yedo there is a celebrated Buddhist temple named *Eco-ying*, which was erected to the memory of 180,000 human beings who lost their lives in one night about 150 years ago. As

K

the story runs, on that night occurred one of those
fearful earthquakes which so heavily afflict this
beautiful country.   Houses were thrown down in
all directions, and hundreds were buried alive in
the ruins; conflagrations naturally followed, and
this city of wooden houses was almost destroyed.

Our attendant yakoneens kindly offered to take
us to this celebrated temple, which was only a very
little out of our way on our route homewards.   As
we approached it I observed in front a statue of
Buddha, and some upright stones carved with an
inscription which told the visitor of the fearful
catastrophe and where the victims were buried.
When we ascended the stone steps in front of the
temple, a noisy crowd followed and surrounded us;
we being now in a part of the town densely populated, and seldom if ever visited by foreigners.
In an instant we had the yakoneens of the district
in addition to our own by our sides, in order to protect us from insult or injury.   Although noisy
enough in all conscience, this crowd of people were
good-humoured, and, although naturally anxious
to look upon such strange beings as we were considered to be, they were perfectly civil, making way
for us in any direction we wished to go.

On entering the temple a curious scene was presented to our eyes.   Candles were burning dimly
on the altars, and incense filled the murky atmosphere with a heavy perfume.   An old reverend-
looking man occupied a kind of pulpit, and was
engaged in a sermon or address to a number of

young men, women, and children. This reverend
gentleman and his youthful congregation had a
part of the temple to themselves—a sort of chapel
in fact, which was separated from the rest of the
building by a network of string; not strong certainly, but perfectly sufficient for the purpose in
this orderly country. On our entrance, followed
by a noisy crowd, the preacher continued his discourse apparently as if he was perfectly unconscious
of our presence. It was very different, however,
with the members of his congregation: all of them
transferred their attention from the preacher to us;
turning round, they fixed their eyes upon us, and
commenced laughing and chatting in a manner
which, if complimentary to us, certainly was not so
to their reverend instructor. Not willing to annoy
the old man, we did not prolong our visit in the
temple, but left him to finish his discourse, and
his youthful audience to profit by his teaching.

Earthquakes such as that which this temple and
its monuments were designed to commemorate are
fortunately rare even in Japan. In the days when
Taiko-sama was king (about the year 1595), we
are told that an earthquake of frightful violence
took place. " The sea rose to an extraordinary
height, especially in the strait between Nipon and
Sikok, attended with terrible destruction of life
and property." In 1793 another terrible earthquake took place. " The summit of a high mountain in the province of Fisen, west of Simbara, sunk
entirely down. Boiling water rushed in torrents

from all parts of the cavity, and a vapour like a
thick smoke covered the mountain. Three weeks
after, there was an eruption from a crater about
half a league from the summit. The boiling lava
flowed down in streams, and for many days the
surrounding country was in flames. A month
after, the whole island of Kiu-siu was shaken by an
earthquake, felt principally, however, in the neighbourhood of Simbara. It reduced that part of the
province of Figo opposite to Simbara to a deplorable
condition ; and even altered the whole line of coast,
sinking many vessels which lay in the harbours."
The last visitation of any great violence occurred
in 1854. In Yedo alone it is supposed that
200,000 human beings were destroyed at this time,
partly by the falling buildings and partly by fires,
which were raging in all parts of the city, occasioned
by the earthquake. The little town of Simoda, a
few miles outside of Yedo bay, was laid in ruins at
this time, and the Russian frigate 'Diana' was
wrecked in the harbour.

During my residence in Japan, earthquakes,
although not of a violent character, were of frequent occurrence, and generally took place during
the night. The sound of creaking timbers used to
remind me of my experience in the cabin of a small
steamer labouring in a heavy sea during or after a
gale of wind. Then my bed used to move about
in a most uneasy manner, as if some strong power
was endeavouring to carry it bodily away, but,
changing its mind, had set it down again. Bishop

Smith, in his 'Ten Weeks in Japan,' gives an amusing account of his first experience in this way. He says, " At 4 a.m. on the morning following my first night of sleeping in the Legation, I was suddenly awoke by a loud rattling noise at my door, and a forcible lifting up of my bed, and its heavy descent with a violent jerk to the ground. I shouted again and again to no purpose, warning the supposed intruder from my room, and making it perceptible that I was on the alert. A continued shaking of the bed, and a rumbling noise throughout the building, at first suggested the suspicion that our native guards were right, and that I had to prepare myself for the irruption of some invader. The foe, however, came from a quarter which I little suspected. An English voice in a distant apartment exclaimed, ' An earthquake! ' The sign of panic amongst the native population was soon audible. The priests rushed to the temples and. commenced reciting their Buddhist chants. The monks began their ringing of bells, and beating of drums and gongs at the neighbouring shrines. The Japanese domestics fled into the open air, and for the moment all was confusion and dismay."

The natives of the country seem to dread these earthquakes even more than the foreigners who are now located amongst them. An intelligent Japanese, who spoke English well, expressed his fears that his country would one day disappear from the surface of the globe, and sink down under the waves of the ocean. He had been told that an island out at sea, once fair and verdant, covered with people and houses and trees, was now nowhere visible, and that ships sailed over the spot where it once was.

Earthquakes are so common in Japan that meteorologists have a division in their tables in order to mark their occurrence. Dr. Hepburn, to whom I am indebted for a table showing the temperature of Kanagawa, and which I shall have occasion to mention hereafter, has one of these columns in his table. By a reference to it, it will be found that from the 1st of November, 1859, to the 31st of October, 1860, no less than twenty-eight shocks had been felt. In November, 1861, four are marked, and in February, 1861, there are the same number. This will give some idea of the frequency of the shocks, and of the volcanic nature of .the country. When we consider how often these earthquakes happen, and how awfully violent they sometimes are, it is scarcely to be wondered at if the natives of the country view them with feelings of awe and dread, and express their fears that some day their fair and beautiful land may disappear in the waters of the sea.

As the Temple of Eco-ying is situated in a part of the town rarely visited by foreigners, crowds of people came to see us take our departure. The police of the district escorted us beyond their boundary, and we were soon out of the crowd and trotting onwards through the principal streets of

the town.   On the way home I observed that our
road was strewed with straw shoes which had been
worn by men and horses.   All the horses wear
shoes of straw, which, when worn out, are replaced
by others, the old ones being left on the road where
they are cast off.

CHAPTER IX.

WHILE engaged in making observations on the
city of Yedo and the country around it, I had been
daily adding to my collections of new trees and
shrubs. Now and then a bit of ancient lacquer-
ware, or a good bronze, took my fancy, and was
carefully put by. The gardens I have already
described were visited frequently, and each time
something new was discovered and brought away.
Mr. J. G. Veitch, the son of one of our London
nurserymen, had also been in Yedo, endeavouring
to procure new plants for his father, and consequently our wants in this way were generally
known amongst the people. Almost every morning, during my stay at the Legation, collections of
plants were brought for sale, and it was seldom
that I did not find something amongst them of an

ornamental or useful character that was new to our English gardens. This, however, could not last for ever; and the time came when I had apparently exhausted the novelties in the capital of Japan. Baskets were now procured, in which the plants were carefully packed and sent down by boat to Yokuhama, where Ward's cases were being made, in which they were to be planted and sent home to England.

On the 28th of November I left the hospitable quarters of the English minister, on my return to Kanagawa. I returned by the way I came—along the Tokaido, or great highway of Japan. Again we passed through the scenes I have already described: beggars on the wayside, mendicant priests, *Bikuni* or begging nuns, travelling musicians, coolies carrying manure as in China, lumbering carts * and pack-horses, and travellers of all ranks, were met and passed on the road.

Here are some Bikuni, or mendicant nuns, sketched on the spot by my friend Dr. Dickson. Kæmpfer gives us the following description of this religious order:—"They live under the protection of the nunneries at Kamakura † and Miaco, to which they pay a certain sum every year, of what they get by begging, as an acknowledgment of their authority. They are, in my opinion, much the handsomest girls we saw in Japan. The

---

* Carts are used extensively all over the city and suburbs of Yedo, but are not met with on country roads.

† Kamakura. See Chap. XIV.

Bikuni or Mendicant Nuns.

daughters of poor parents, if they be handsome and
agreeable, apply for and easily obtain this privilege of begging in the habit of nuns, knowing that
beauty is one of the most persuasive inducements
to generosity. The *Jamabo*, or begging mountain
priests, frequently incorporate their own daughters
with this religious order, and take their wives from
among these Bikuni. Some of them have been bred
up as courtezans, and, having served their time,
buy the privilege of entering into this religious
order, therein to spend the remainder of their youth
and beauty. They live two or three together, and
make an excursion every day a few miles from their

dwelling-house. They particularly watch people of fashion, who travel in norimons, or in kangos, or on horseback. As soon as they perceive somebody coming they draw near and address themselves, not all together, but singly, every one accosting a gentleman by herself, and singing a rural song; and if he proves very liberal and charitable, she will keep him company and divert him for hours. . . . They wear a large hat to cover their faces, which are often painted, and to shelter themselves from the heat of the sun."

A number of shops, established for the sale of sea-shells, were observed on the road-side, but they did not contain many species of interest. Dried fruits for sale were numerous and plentiful, such as oranges, pears, gingko-nuts (*Salisburia adianti-folia*), capsicums, chesnuts, and acorns. The fruit of *Gardenia radicans* is used here as a yellow dye, in the same way as in China. Amongst vegetables I noticed carrots, onions, turnips, lily-roots, ginger, gobbo (*Arctium gobbo*), nelumbium-roots, *Scirpus tuberosus*, arums, and yams. Fish of excellent quality was exposed for sale in large quantities.

A little way out of Sinagawa my yakoneens pointed out the place where criminals are executed. It is an uninviting-looking piece of ground close by the highway. I find that Kæmpfer notices the same spot as observed by the Dutch embassy upwards of two hundred years ago. Near to Sinagawa they passed " a place of public execution,

offering a show of human heads and bodies, some
half putrefied and others half devoured—dogs,
ravens, crows, and other ravenous beasts and birds,
uniting to satisfy their appetites on these miserable
remains." On the present occasion I did not notice
any of these revolting sights, and it is to be hoped
that the Japanese have, like ourselves, become less
addicted to judicial bloodshedding than they were
at the time of Kæmpfer's visit. It will be remembered that such exhibitions were not uncommon .
amongst Western nations at a later period even
than that alluded to.

When we had crossed the river Loga we put up
our horses at the inn of " Ten Thousand Centuries,"
and proceeded on foot to visit a famous Buddhist
temple situated about a mile and a half from the
ferry. Our road led us through fields and gardens,
all in a high state of cultivation. Rice appeared
to be the staple summer crop of the low land of
this district. Many gardens of pear-trees were also
seen on the road-side. The branches of these trees
were trained horizontally when about five or six
feet from the ground, sometimes singly in the
shape of a round table, or in groups in the form of
an arbour. The branches are supported by a rude
trelliswork of wood. The pear of the district is a
pretty round brown kind, good to look upon, but
only fit for kitchen use. There are no fine melting
pears in Japan ; at least none came under my
notice during my stay in the country. On the
roadside there were many little shops in which tea

and dried fruits were exposed to tempt the weary pilgrim on his way to worship at the temple. Begging priests were also passed, ready to bestow prayers and blessings on the heads of those who gave them alms.

As we approached the sacred building, one of my yakoneens ran before to announce our arrival. On entering the main gateway there was a tank of holy water on our right hand. Every devotee, on entering, visits the holy well, and sprinkles himself with water before he enters the temple. For this privilege he pays a small sum, the amount expected · being in accordance with the means of the giver. In most cases the poor give only a few cash of the country, about the value of a farthing of our money. My attendant yakoneens did not fail to perform the ceremony like good Buddhists, after which we ascended the broad flight of steps which led up to the main hall of the temple. Many native visitors came in while we were there, and each one, as he reached the door of the edifice, was observed to bow low before its altars, and to mutter some prayers. Inside there were a number of priests of the Buddhist faith, who had evidently an eye to the good things of this world, and who were busily engaged in selling books and pictures connected with the temple to the ignorant and superstitious who came to worship at its altars. The temple itself appeared to be a strong and massive structure. Huge paper lanterns were hanging from the roof, and a few Buddhist deities were observed on the altars.   Otherwise it was not remarkable, and was far inferior to the chief temples commonly met with in China.

When we got back to the inn of " Ten Thousand Centuries " a number of the waiting-maids of the place came running out to welcome us with the usual " Ohio," or " Good morning ; how do you do ? " of the Japanese.   I know that the main object of all this excessive civility is to bring custom to the establishment, and sundry *itzeebus** out of the pockets of the traveller ; but after all, there is much gratification in a kind reception, and it is not worth while to look too closely into the motives of those who give it.   In the present instance we had had a long walk over a dry hard road, the sun had been hot, and we were glad to accept the invitation given to us by the pretty damsels to enter the inn and refresh ourselves after our journey.   The same scene was now exhibited as I have already described at the " Mansion of Plum-trees."   A low square table was placed before me, covered with different kinds of sweet cakes, dried fruits, and cups of tea. The young girls of the tea-house, kneeling in front and on each side of me, poured out my tea, and begged me to eat of the cakes and fruits, while one of them busied herself in taking the shells off some hard-boiled eggs, dipping them in salt, and putting them to my mouth.   Surely all this was enough to satisfy and refresh the most weary traveller, and to send him on his way rejoicing.

* A silver coin of Japan, worth about eighteenpence.

But the best of friends must part at last, so I was obliged to bid adieu to mine host and his fair waiting-maids of the "Ten Thousand Centuries," and pursue my way to Kanagawa.   Nothing particularly worthy of notice presented itself during the remainder of my journey.   The same motley groups and queer-looking travellers were met and passed on the highway; dogs barked, and children ran out of the houses to look at the foreigner, and to cry out, as loudly as their little lungs would

Nursery Maids.

permit, "Anato, Ohio."   The number of little girls, each having a child tied on her back, was one of the most amusing sights during our progress.   As these ran hobbling along, and the little heads of the children bobbed about, in danger apparently of being shaken off, one could not help laughing. On reaching the temple in Kanagawa, in which my quarters were, my yakoneen guard informed me that their presence was no longer necessary, and I was free again to roam about by myself in any direction I pleased. I must confess that, however highly honoured I had felt during my visit to Yedo, by having a mounted armed guard attending me wherever I went, yet the departure of the yako-neens was a decided relief, and greatly did I enjoy a return to my former lowly estate.

Mr. M'Donald, of Her Majesty's Legation in Yedo, from whom I had received much kindness and assistance, had been good enough to forward my collection of plants in boats to Kanagawa, and these arrived in safety. My guide Tomi had been employed during my absence in making collections of seeds and plants; but I am bound to confess that, according to the accounts I received of his pro-ceedings during my absence, it appeared his fa-vourite saki had had more attractions for him than natural history. As I had now secured living specimens and seeds of all the ornamental trees and shrubs of this part of Japan which I was likely to meet with at this season of the year, the whole were removed across the bay to Yokuhama, and placed for safety in Dr. Hall's garden, until Ward's cases were ready for their reception.

The collection which had been got together at this time was a most remarkable one. Never at any one time had I met with so many really fine plants, and they acquired additional value from the fact that a great portion of them were likely to prove suitable to our English climate. Amongst conifers there was the beautiful parasol fir (*Sciadopitys verticellata*), *Thujopsis dolabrata*, *Retinospora obtusa* and *R. pisifera*, *Nageia ovata*, several new pines and cypresses, and varieties of almost all these species having variegated leaves.

Amongst other shrubs there was a charming species of Eurya, having broad camellia-looking leaves, beautifully marked with white, orange, and rose colours; a pretty variegated Daphne; several species of privets, yews, hollies, box, and ferns. In addition to these there were two or three new species of *Skimmia*—shrubs which bear sweet-scented flowers, and become covered with red berries, like the holly, during winter and spring; a palm with variegated leaves, a noble species of oak, some new Weigelas, and a number of curious chrysanthemums.

This list of beautiful trees and shrubs, all new to English gardens, may appear a long one, yet I must add to it several representatives of other two genera which are particularly worthy of notice. The first is a shrub or small tree called *Osmanthus aquifolius*. This genus is closely allied to the olive; it produces sweet-scented white flowers, and has dark-green prickly leaves like the holly. Curiously enough, the leaves on the upper branches and shoots of the Osmanthus are produced without

L

spines, exactly as we see on old holly-trees. All
the species of Osmanthus have variegated varieties
in Japan, many of which are very beautiful objects
for garden decoration.

The other genus to which I would call attention
is the well-known Aucuba. In Europe we know
only the variegated variety of *Aucuba japonica*,
which is one of the most useful of our evergreens,
inasmuch as it is perfectly hardy in our climate,
and flourishes even in the smoke of large towns
where our indigenous shrubs refuse to live. But
in the shaded woods near the capital of Japan I
met with the true species of *Aucuba japonica*, of
which the variegated one of our gardens is, no
doubt, only a variety. This species has beautiful
shining leaves of the brightest green, and becomes
covered, during the winter and spring months,
with bunches of red berries, which give it a pretty
appearance. In fact, the Aucuba of the woods near
Yedo is the " Holly of Japan." I frequently met
with hedges formed of this plant, which were very
ornamental indeed. In the woods there are
numerous varieties of both sexes, some of which
show the faintest traces of variegation, while others
are nearly as much marked as the Aucubas found
in our English gardens. In addition to the
Aucubas found in a wild state, I had, in this collection, several garden varieties, with distinct and
beautiful variegation, and the *male* plant of our
common garden species, to which I have alluded
in an earlier chapter, the introduction of which is

likely to add much to the beauty and interest of
that useful shrub, inasmuch as we may now expect
to have it covered, during winter and spring, with
a profusion of crimson berries.

Many other species of interest might be named
in the collection which I had now got together,
but the above will suffice to show how fruitful the
field for selection had been in and near the capital
of Japan. From the list which I have given, no
one will be surprised when he hears others tell of
the lovely sylvan scenery of the Japanese islands.
I have already endeavoured to give a faint idea of
such scenery; and it was now my intention to
transfer to Europe and America examples of those
trees and shrubs which produce such charming
effects in the Japanese landscapes.

But the latter part of the business was no easy
matter. To go from England to Japan was easy
enough; to wander amongst those romantic valleys
and undulating hills was pleasure unalloyed; to
ransack the capital itself, although attended by an
armed guard, was far from disagreeable; and to
get together such a noble collection as I have just
been describing was the most agreeable of all.
The difficulty—the great difficulty—was to trans-
port living plants from Yedo to the Thames, over
stormy seas, for a distance of some 16,000 miles.
But, thanks to my old friend Mr. Ward, even this
difficulty can now be overcome by means of the
well-known glass cases which bear his name.
Ward's cases have been the means of enriching

our parks and gardens with many beautiful
exotics, which, but for this admirable invention,
would never have been seen beyond those countries
to which they are indigenous.

In a foreign country, however, even Ward's
cases cannot be made without some difficulty.
The carpenter who contracted to make the framework of the cases would have nothing to do with
the glazing, because he did not understand it. A
Dutch carpenter, residing in Yokuhama, under-
took to do the glazing, but unfortunately broke his
diamond and could not procure another to cut the
glass! Luckily, however, these difficulties were
got over at last, and a sufficient number of cases
were got ready to enable me to carry the collection
on to China. The steam-ship 'England,' Captain
Dundas, being about to return to Shanghae, I
availed myself of the opportunity to go over to
that port with my collections, in order to ship them
for England, there being as yet no means of send-
ing them direct from Japan. Mr. Veitch had
also put his plants on board the same vessel, so
that the whole of the poop was lined with glass
cases crammed full of the natural productions of
Japan. Never before had such an interesting and
valuable collection of plants occupied the deck of
any vessel, and most devoutly did we hope that
our beloved plants might be favoured with fair
winds and smooth seas, and with as little salt
water as possible—a mixture to which they are
not at all partial, and which sadly disagrees with
their constitutions

ON the 17th of December, 1860, the good steam-ship 'England,' in which I was passenger, weighed anchor and proceeded to sea. The wind, which had been blowing a gale the day before, was now light and fair, so that we were able to crowd on all sail and made rapid progress. The headlands which had lately been christened as " Mandarin Bluff " and " Treaty Point," were soon passed, and the pretty little towns of Yokuhama and Kanagawa were lost to our view in the distance. In the afternoon we passed Cape Sagami and the volcanic islands at the entrance of the Bay of Yedo, and were once more in the great Pacific Ocean. Cape Idsu—that stormy

cape, the dread of mariners, but which, I am bound
to say, has as yet treated me kindly—was also
passed, and then darkness set in, and the fair land
of Nipon was hidden from our eyes.

On the following morning I was up and on
deck before sunrise, and was well rewarded by
the beauty of the scene. Landward, Fusiyama,
or the " Holy Mountain," was seen towering high
above all the other land, covered with snow of the
purest white, and its summit already basking in the
rays of the morning sun, although that luminary had
not yet shown himself to the denizens of our lower
world. Sailors and passengers alike looked often
and long upon that lovely mountain, and it was
with regret we watched it gradually disappear
from our view and sink in the horizon.

In the afternoon of this day we were abreast of
Cape Oo-sima, and soon afterwards entered the
Kino Channel, which lies between the islands of
Sikok and Nipon, and leads into the Inland Sea.
A reference to the map of Japan will give a better
idea of the position of this sea than any description.
No foreign vessel, except ships of war or transports,
had been allowed to navigate its waters, and, as it
had not been surveyed, it was necessary, in all cases,
to obtain pilots from the Japanese Government
before attempting the passage. The ' England '
was not a ship of war nor in any way connected
with the Government, and, in ordinary cases, would
not have been permitted to pass through the
sacred waters of the Inland Sea. But as Captain

Dundas and his passengers were all anxious to view the beautiful scenery of which they had often heard, a request was sent to the authorities for permission and pilots, backed by the following powerful reasons. Her Majesty the Queen of Great Britain had presented a handsome steam-yacht to the Tycoon of Japan, and the latter had made a selection of lacquer-ware, paper screens, swords, and a variety of other articles, to send to Her Majesty in return. Now, although the good ship 'England' was not a "man of war," and had no great warrior amongst her crew and passengers, yet she had on board the presents for the Queen, and on that account was surely entitled to all the honours of a ship of war. Besides, she might be wrecked if exposed to the stormy waters of the North Pacific Ocean, the presents might be damaged or lost, and that was an additional reason why she ought to be allowed to take the smooth-water passage. The propriety and prudence of the course suggested was perceived at once by the authorities, and pilots were granted forthwith.

As the night was calm and clear, we steamed onwards slowly, and found ourselves in the morning on the eastern side of the island of Awadji, or Smoto as it is called in some English charts. There is a passage on the south-east side of this island, but in its centre is a dangerous whirlpool, which all mariners carefully avoid. We therefore took the northern passage. As daylight was breaking the ship got ashore on a bank of soft mud. Our Japanese pilots appeared to be steering right on to the island, thinking, no doubt, that the wonderful English vessel, that went along without sails or paddles, could pass over land and villages as easily as she could plough the waters of the deep sea. Without much difficulty we got the ship afloat again, and proceeded on our voyage, but our confidence in the knowledge of our pilots was considerably lessened. Going onward in a north-westerly direction, we approached the entrance to the bay of Hiogo and Osaca.

This beautiful Inland Sea was greenish in colour and smooth as a mill-pond. In the direction of the towns just mentioned it was studded with the white sails of small junks, showing that this portion of the Japanese islands must be densely populated. Fishing-boats were seen in all directions busily employed in securing food for the teeming population; and pleasant-looking villages and Daimios' castles were observed scattered along the shores of the bay.

The town of Hiogo, which is the seaport of the imperial city of Osaca, is one of the ports which, according to the treaty, should be opened to foreign trade in 1863; and from all accounts it is likely to prove the most important place in Japan. Kæmpfer, who passed through Osaca about 170 years ago, tells us that he found it "extremely populous, and, if we can believe what the boasting Japanese tell us, can raise an army of eighty thousand men among its inhabitants. It is the best trading town in Japan, being extraordinarily well situated for carrying on commerce, both by land and water. This is the reason why it is so well inhabited by rich merchants, artificers, and manufacturers. . . . Whatever tends to promote luxury, or to gratify sensual pleasures, may be had at as easy a rate here as anywhere, and for this reason the Japanese call Osaca the universal theatre of pleasures and diversions. Plays are to be seen daily, both in public and private houses; mountebanks, jugglers who can show artful tricks, and all the raree-show people who have either some uncommon or monstrous animal to exhibit, or animals taught to play tricks, resort thither from all parts of the empire, being sure to get a better penny here than anywhere else." In proof of this demand for luxuries in Osaca, Kæmpfer tells us that the Dutch East India Company "sent over from Batavia, as a present to the Emperor, a casuar, a large East India bird who would swallow stones and hot coals. This bird having had the ill luck not to please our rigid censors the governors of Nagasaki, and we having thereupon been ordered to send him back to Batavia, a rich Japanese assured us that, if he could have obtained leave to buy him, he would have willingly given a thousand taels for him, as being sure, within a year's time, to get double that money by showing him at Osaca."

Hiogo and Osaca were visited by Mr. Alcock in the summer of 1861, and his despatch to Earl

Russell fully confirms Kæmpfer's account. "The
approach to Hiogo is good and easy, the anchorage secure; the navigation to Osaca for cargo-
boats short and easy also, not more than four or
five miles from the bay, though some fifteen from
Hiogo, which is to Osaca what Kanagawa is to
Yedo. Only this last is a capital filled chiefly with
Daimios and their retainers—dominant classes,
which consume much and produce nothing, and
are decidedly hostile to foreign commerce, as
diminishing their own share and endangering its
easy and secure appropriation; while Osaca is a
great mercantile centre, situated on a plain intersected by twenty branches of a river, and spanned
by innumerable bridges, some of them 300 paces
across; with this great advantage (above all others)
over Yedo, that, although an imperial city, it, is
comparatively free from the two-sworded generation of locusts and obstructives. There are a large
number of Daimios' residences, occupying more
than a league of the river's banks, but I fancy
these are seldom occupied, or only temporarily, by
their owners. Immense activity reigns everywhere; and although it was difficult to make much
way in finding out the true prices, with yakoneens
whose business it was to mislead us and fill their
own pockets, I saw enough to satisfy myself that,
if anything like free interchange could once be
established, this would supply a market more than
equal in importance to all the other ports com-
bined."

It would appear, therefore, that the towns of
Hiogo and Osaca are likely to be places of considerable importance in a mercantile point of view.
In situation these towns possess great advantages.
They are in the central and most populous part of
the empire, are easily approached from the sea,
and there is good anchorage for ships in Hiogo
Bay, or the Gulf of Osaca. Moreover, Osaca is
only a day's journey from Miaco, the residence of
the spiritual Emperor, and the sacred capital of
Japan. Thunberg left Osaca by torchlight in the
morning, and reached Miaco the same evening.
He says, "Except in Holland, I never made so
pleasant a journey as this with regard to the
beauty and delightful appearance of the country.
Its population, too, and cultivation, exceed all
expression. The whole country on both sides of
us, as far as we could see, was nothing but a fertile field ; and the whole of our long day's journey
extended through villages, of which one began
where the other ended." These ports are not only
placed in a most favourable position for commerce,
but they also swarm with merchants; and they
have few of those idle, two-sworded gentry, who
are the curse of Yedo, and who will render that
capital unsafe as a residence for foreigners certainly during the lives of the present generation.
The great tea-producing districts of Japan are also
situated in this part of the country, a circumstance.
which will render these ports of considerable value
to the foreign merchant. In fact, if we can rely

upon the statements of Kæmpfer, Thunberg, and other travellers—and their statements would seem to be confirmed in Mr. Alcock's despatch which I have just quoted—Osaca appears to be to Japan what Soo-chow was to China in the days before the rebellion, and what it may one day become again —namely, the great emporium of trade and luxury.

As we were not at this time bound for Hiogo or Osaca, we did not proceed further up the bay, but, bearing southward through a narrow strait between the islands of Awadji and Nipon, we soon reached a wider part of the sea. As we steamed along, the scenery was very lovely and enjoyable. A calm and glassy sea was skirted on each side by hills of various heights from 800 to 2000 feet, sometimes apparently rugged and barren, and sometimes covered with trees and brushwood. Thick clouds of morning mist rested here and there for a while amongst the hills and sometimes on the water, and then became dispersed, allowing us to view the charming scenery, which for a time had been obscured. Fishing-boats were swarming in all directions, and their pretty white sails added not a little to the beauty of the scenery. The excitement experienced by the passengers, and even by the sailors, was something most unusual; sketch-books, pencils, and journals were all in great request, and impressions were produced upon us all which will not easily be forgotten.

We were now in what is called the Harama-nada Sea. It gradually widens until the distance be-

tween the two shores—that is, between the islands
of Nipon and Sikok—is about thirty miles.   Our
course lay nearer the eastern than the western side
of the passage.   In the afternoon we came to a
group of islands, through which we sailed until the
evening. ' Some of these are remarkable for their
peculiar forms.   One named Ya-sima had a rocky
summit, giving it the appearance of a huge camel
kneeling to receive its load.   Viewed from a different point, it looked like the ruins of an
ancient castle.   Another, called the Che-se-Fusi,
or Little Fusiyama, was a remarkable representation, although in miniature, of its snow-capped
namesake.   Both these islands will no doubt prove
valuable landmarks to mariners in this sea, as
they have probably been for ages past to the
Japanese.

The scenery in this part of the sea was quite
a panorama—ever shifting as we sailed onwards.
Now we opened up a beautiful bay, with a fishing
village on its shores, and terraced cultivation
extending a short way up the side of the hills.
Losing sight of this, other islands, bays, and
coves came constantly into view to charm and delight the eye.   In one flat valley on our left we
had a good view of a town of considerable size, in
which a Daimio of great power resided and reigned
supreme.   His castle appeared to be strongly forti-
fied, and had numerous watch-towers on its walls.
These castles are apparently numerous in all parts
of the empire, for many of them were seen on the

shores of the "Inland Sea" during our passage through it.

Although the scenery through which we had passed had been most picturesque and beautiful, yet the land did not appear to be rich or fertile. With the exception of little patches of terraced-work near the sea-shore, the ground seemed in a state of nature where the hand of the agriculturist had never ventured to turn over the soil. Rocks, apparently of granite and clay-slate, with red barren earth, were seen everywhere in patches amongst the scanty vegetation of stunted fir-trees. Perhaps in spring, or during the rainy season, when the hills are green, these islands may not present such a barren appearance; and no doubt, as in China, the interior may be rich and fertile, although the land is barren near the sea-shore. But though not rich in an agricultural point of view, the strange and romantic hills and valleys, the rugged rocks, and those sights of nature " stern and wild," contrasted with towns and villages nestled in snug coves, and basking on the shores of this beautiful " Inland Sea," made more than one of our little party express a wish to be set on shore, and to become a " hermit of the glade " for the remainder of his days amongst such scenery.

I was rather disappointed in the number of trading-junks and fishing-boats seen during the day. The weather was fine, and there was nothing to keep them in their anchorages near the shore had they really existed. A place like this in China would have swarmed with them; and, as I have already stated, they were numerous in the vicinity of the ports of Hiogo and Osaca—towns which we know to be large and populous. This fact, together with the sterile character of the land, would lead to the conclusion that the southern part of Nipon, and the western part of Sikok, do not possess a large population or an extensive trade. Time will show whether these surmises are correct, or whether this absence of marine traffic be due to some other cause.

There are numerous well-sheltered anchorages in many parts of this sea; but, as in China, there seem to be some special ones which alone the natives are accustomed to use, to the total neglect of the others, and no doubt for native craft these are the best ones. We passed one of these favoured places about three o'clock in the afternoon, and our pilot wanted the captain to go in there and anchor for the night. This proceeding, however, did not suit the ideas of Englishmen, who are always in a hurry, and it was intimated to our good pilot that it was too early in the day to anchor, and that we must go on until the evening. Before dark another place was pointed out as a safe anchorage for the night. A fishing-junk was at anchor a short distance ahead of us; and our pilot thought, naturally enough, that there must be good anchorage in her vicinity. But when we got up with the junk, a cast of the lead showed us that she was at anchor in a place where there were twenty-three fathoms of water! She had, no doubt, only a light kedge out, and had taken up that position for fishing operations. We therefore steamed onwards until our soundings gave twenty fathoms, when Captain Dundas, fearing to approach nearer the shore, dropped anchor for the night. A few minutes before we anchored the sun went down behind the islands of the west, and, in bidding the " Inland Sea " adieu for the day, lighted up the clouds in the most gorgeous manner, and gave them the appearance of mountains of fire and gold. And thus ended my first day in the Harama-nada Sea.

Next morning (Dec. 20), at daylight, we weighed anchor with considerable difficulty, owing to the length of chain we had out in our deep anchorage. We discovered, too, that, at a short distance from where we had spent the night, there was an excellent anchorage, with only eight fathoms of water over it. During the forenoon we came up with a pretty-looking village of considerable size, named Ino-sima. Here the land appeared much more fertile than we had seen since entering the sea. The houses were scattered over the sides of the hills amongst fields and gardens of terraced land, and surrounded with healthy fruit-trees, apparently pears. The young crops of wheat and barley were above ground, forming broad patches of the liveliest green, most pleasing to look upon. Half-way up the hills cultivation

INO-SIMA, "OUR PILOT'S HOME."

ceased, and beyond all was barren or in a state of
nature.   One of our pilots informed us that he
was a native of this place, and it was sketched
immediately and romantically called "The Pilot's
Home."

Our passage during the morning of this day had
been straight and broad, and of easy navigation,
even for a sailing vessel; but about 1 P.M. we
entered a pass between some islands which was
certainly not more than half a mile in width.
Here the scenery was very remarkable, and perhaps
the finest we had yet seen.   Pretty villages,
temples, and farm-houses were observed on every
side of us.   Now and then we passed a fertile
valley, in a high state of cultivation, stretching
far back amongst the hills.   The houses, too,
seemed to be nicely thatched and tiled, and had an
air of comfort and cleanliness about them rarely
seen in oriental countries.   We appeared to be
sailing down some smooth river, which every now
and then widened or narrowed according to the
formation of the land.   Around us there were hills
and mountains, of various heights and of every
conceivable form.   The lowest rose but a few feet
above the water, while the highest seemed fully
two thousand feet high.   Here and there, in our
progress, I observed a column of stone erected
upon the top of a sunken rock to warn the
mariner of the hidden danger.   On one of the
banks of this river-like sea a broad road was observed skirting the beach under an avenue of

M

trees.   Our pilots informed us that this was a portion of the *Tokaido*, or imperial highway, which
leads all the way from Yedo to Nagasaki.   Sometimes the sea appeared completely land-locked, and
resembled a lake with its bays and inlets; at
other times it had the river-like appearance I have
already noticed.   Some of us compared it to Loch
Lomond, Loch Katrine, or the Kiles of Bute; but,
although probably it had a partial resemblance to
all these places in the Scottish Highlands, yet it
had a character peculiarly its own.

In the afternoon we had a good view of the
castle and fortress of Meara-sama, situated at the
head of a deep bay.   This castle is said to be
remarkable in Japan for its great strength.   It is
supposed to be one of the strongest in the empire,
and perfectly impregnable.   A massive sea-wall
was built along the sea-shore; while behind this
wall were seen castles, turrets, and watchtowers,
inhabited by this feudal chief and his numerous
retainers.   Leaving this bay and its stronghold on
our right and to the westward, our course led us in
a more southerly direction, the channel still narrow
and winding.   This part continued as populous as
that which I have already noticed when we entered
the " narrows," and large villages, composed of
comfortable-looking houses—not densely packed
together, but divided by fields and gardens—were
everywhere seen along the shores.

In the evening we passed out into a wider part
of the sea, and anchored for the night at a place

called Metari. Boats in large numbers, filled with
wondering natives, had been sculling round us to
get a sight of the ship that went ahead without
wind or sails, and of the strange beings from some
far-off foreign land who crowded her deck. While
we were sitting at dinner, and speaking of the
strange and beautiful scenery through which we
had passed during the day, a messenger came on
board to inform us that the high officers of the
place were coming off to pay us a visit. In a few
minutes three quiet, modest-looking individuals
were ushered into the cabin, and led up to the
head of the table, where Captain Dundas was
seated. They wanted to know whence we came,
what we wanted, and whither we were bound—all
of which questions, with many others, were an-
swered to their entire satisfaction. They were
then politely offered wine, biscuits, and sundry
other things which were upon the table. Each of
them tasted what was set before him, and then,
pulling out a piece of paper, wrapped up in it the
remainder of the solids, and thrust the parcel into
his wide sleeve. Such is the custom of the country, and such is termed politeness in Japan. A
numerous retinue of servants attended these high
officials, all of whom were delighted with what was
given to them, and begged for more! As these
gentry took their departure, they intimated to us
that an officer of a yet higher rank than theirs was
coming on board. This personage presented himself soon afterwards, and, giving his swords to an

M 2

attendant, walked up to the head of the table as
the others had done. The ceremony of questioning,
drinking, eating, and pocketing was gone through
a second time, and then, with many low bows and
expressions of thanks, the great man and his attendants took their departure for the shore.

Dec. 21st.—We weighed anchor this morning as
usual at daylight. We were now in what is called
the Suwo-nada Sea. It is wide, has few islands,
and is connected with the Pacific Ocean by a wide
passage known as the Bun-go Channel. We were
too far from the land to note anything worthy of
interest on its shores. This sea is chiefly remarkable for gales of wind of great violence, owing,
probably, to the Bun-go Channel forming a sort of
funnel between this Inland Sea and the Pacific
Ocean. We were destined to experience one of
these gales on the present occasion. It commenced in the morning, and by the afternoon had
increased to a hurricane. The wind was not
steady, but came down in fearful gusts, strong
enough, almost, to blow any one overboard who
ventured on the poop of the vessel. A trysail,
which had been set, was riven from the sheets, and
its block shaken with fearful violence and thrown
into the sea. The scene reminded me of a powerful bulldog tearing and shaking a cat, and then
casting it away in anger when he had deprived it
of life. In this state of things the 'England'
made but little headway, and it was determined
that we should look out for a safe anchorage for

ENTRANCE TO KAMINO-SAKI HARBOUR.

Page 165.

the night. We therefore bore up for the mainland of Nipon, to the westward, and made for a
place called, in Japanese charts, Kamino-saki.
This is a most extraordinary anchorage, and well
worth the attention of those who navigate this sea.
As we approached the land there seemed to be
no shelter except an open bay, protected indeed by
the land on the west, but fully exposed to the
eastward. On nearing the shore, however, we
observed an opening on our left, not more than
sixty yards wide, which looked at first sight almost
artificial, but was merely natural nevertheless, and
which led into a beautiful land-locked harbour.
We steamed through this narrow passage, and
anchored in thirteen fathoms water.

The place in which we now were had all the
appearance of an inland lake, and was protected
from the wind in all directions. On each side of
us two small towns were observed, pleasantly situated on the banks of the lake, and forming little
crescents along its shores. The houses had white-
washed walls, and appeared to be clean and comfortable looking buildings. Little temples also
appeared on the hill-sides, surrounded by pine-
trees; and Buddhist priests were seen about the
doors. Hills filled the background, well-wooded in
some parts, and terraced in others all the way up
to their summits, showing that here the soil was
fertile and productive. *Pinus Massoniana* seemed
to be the most common timber-tree in this quarter.
On our approach the whole of the inhabitants of

these quiet and secluded villages came out of their
houses to look at the strange *He-funy*, or fire-ship;
but the water being rather rough, the wind tem-
pestuous, and night closing in, none of them
ventured off from the shore. This evening we
were therefore allowed to dine in peace, and were
not honoured with the presence of yakoneens and
other " high officers" at our table.

Next day our progress was slow, as the gale was
still blowing, and we anchored about eight o'clock
in the evening. At daylight on the following
morning the Southern Strait, which leads out of
the Inland Sea into the Corea Strait and China Sea,
was visible ahead of us, and distant some ten or
twelve miles. A large fleet of junks and boats
was seen coming out from the strait, having, no
doubt, taken shelter during the gale of the previous days. The entrance to this strait is about
half a mile in width; it is bounded on the north
by the southern end of Nipon, and on the south by
Kiu-siu. Two small towns, one on each side, were
visible on its shores. As we passed along, the
strait widened considerably; and a large town,
named Simone-saki, was observed on our right
hand. A little further on, to the left, the residence
of a Daimio named Korkura was pointed out, and
we met that worthy himself in a painted barge,
going in the direction of Simone-saki.

The scenery in the vicinity of the strait is hilly,
the hills being often conical in form, and covered
with trees and brushwood. Generally the country

has that barren and uncultivated character which I
have already often alluded to in describing our
voyage down this sea. It presents a striking contrast to the volcanic regions near Yedo, where
every inch of land is capable of being profitably
cultivated, although, for some reason, thousands of
acres are lying waste, or covered with brushwood
of little value. But although the shores of the
Inland Sea,—beautiful though they are,—present
a barren aspect to the voyager, yet there must be
many rich valleys amongst these hills capable of
producing abundant crops to supply " the wants of
man and beast." Glimpses of these were caught
as we sailed along the shores, and there must have
been many more which were hidden from our
view. These the streams which flow down from
the mountains irrigate and fertilise, while the
climate of Japan is probably one of the finest in
the world.

Before we got clear of the strait some alarm
was felt owing to the shallowness of the water, and
it must be confessed we had no great confidence in
the knowledge of our pilots. After having had
for some time only three and three-and-a-half
fathoms of water, we suddenly felt an unusual
motion, which old sailors like myself knew to be
an intimation from the ship that she was "hard
and fast ashore." And so it was ; we had touched
a bank having only two fathoms of water on it,
which our good ship refused to go over, and from
which she could not recede. Our Japanese pilots

took the matter very coolly, and told us we should
have to remain in our present position until the
tide rose, when we should have water enough. This
was all very well, and it turned out quite true;
but what if one of those sudden gales for which
this coast is famous had come on in the mean time!
We had no fear for our lives, as we might easily
have reached the shore in boats, but my beautiful
collection of plants, which was on board, I certainly
looked upon as being in the greatest danger.
While matters looked rather gloomy, a good-
natured gentleman came up to me, and "hoped my
collections were insured!"

Although the circumstances in which we were
placed at this time were far from being pleasant,
we could not resist having a good joke with two of
our fellow-passengers. Dr. —— and Mr. ——
had both been unfortunate at sea, and had related,
during our voyage, the stories of their various
shipwrecks. On more than one occasion they had
been told that we held them responsible for any
ill-luck that might befall us during the present
voyage; that both of them were evidently Jonahs;
and that, if we chanced to get into danger, they
must be prepared to go overboard in order to
ensure the safety of the ship. When, therefore, all
our efforts to get into deeper water appeared
fruitless, and when the 'England' began to bump
uncomfortably on the ground, an intimation was
conveyed to these gentlemen that their time had
come, and that they had better prepare for the

fatal plunge. The sacrifice, however, was not required, as the tide rose before we could carry out our benevolent intentions, and the vessel floated safely into deeper water.

As we had now passed out of the Inland Sea, Captain Dundas determined not to trust the native pilots any longer, and kept well out from all the dangers of the coast. It was now bitterly cold, and the tops of all the hills were covered with snow. We encountered another gale of wind when off the Gotto Islands, and reached the quiet little harbour of Nagasaki without any further adventures, all of us highly pleased with our voyage through the Inland Sea. As the 'England' remained three days at Nagasaki, I employed the time in visiting a number of places in the vicinity, and added several novelties to my collections. The face of the country had undergone a great change since my former visit. It was now winter; deciduous trees were leafless, the rice-lands were lying fallow, and the hill-sides were green with the young crops of wheat and barley. The dress of the people had changed with the season; and the children, instead of being carried on the backs of children as before, were now borne about on their bosoms.

As my Ward's cases were all quite full, it was necessary to pack the Nagasaki plants in baskets, and these were put away in the long-boat on the starboard side of the ship. On the 29th of December we bade adieu, for the present, to the pleasant shores of Japan, and sailed for China. A short time after we had put to sea I felt some regret at not having put my plants in the boat on the port side, which, being to leeward, was less exposed to spray from the sea. It was lucky, as it turned out, that no alteration was made, for on the following day we encountered a heavy gale of wind; the ship rolled dreadfully; and a quantity of planks piled on the house in midships gave way, and carried the long-boat, that hung on the port side, headlong into the sea! On the 2nd of January we arrived at Shanghae, where I was kindly received by Mr. Webb, the worthy successor of my old friend the late Mr. Beale.

My time was now fully occupied in repacking and preparing the plants for the long voyage which was yet before them. The most important portion was confided to the care of Captain Taylor, of the ship 'Tung-yu,' who, a short time before this, had had the honour to introduce into Europe the living salamander now in the gardens of the Zoological Society of London. Captain Taylor delivered these plants in the most excellent condition. Some of them were exhibited before the Horticultural Society, at South Kensington, three days after their arrival in England; and it was remarked that they looked as if they had been luxuriating all their lives in the pure air of Bagshot, instead of having just been landed from a sea voyage of sixteen thousand miles.

CHAPTER XI.

IN the spring of 1861 I returned to Japan, my object being to inspect the natural productions of the country during the spring and summer months, as I had already done in the autumn and winter. The steam-ship 'Scotland,' Captain Bell, in which I had taken my passage, was bound for Kanagawa, but called at Nagasaki on her way. The day of our arrival at Nagasaki was a holiday with the natives, and all were dressed up in their gayest clothing. One of the chief sources of amusement appeared to be kite-flying. In the air above the town, and all over the country, there was a swarm of paper kites, which I at first sight mistook for a flock of seagulls. The kites were generally of a diamond shape, and were painted in gay colours of red, white, and blue. In every street, on the house-tops, on the hill-sides, and in the fields, there were numbers of both sexes and of all ages thus amusing themselves, and all seemed gay, contented, and happy.

There is a famous temple, named Dyto-cutch, situated on the hill-side above the town, which is well worth a notice. The view from this place, at the time of my visit, was extremely beautiful and full of interest. The whole town, the lake-like harbour, and the panorama of hills near and far off lay spread out before me. Many of the plum and cherry trees were now in full bloom. Most remarkable amongst them was a double-blossomed cherry, a variety producing bunches of flowers nearly as large as noisette roses. This is an ornamental tree of the first class. Being spring-time (April 13th), many other trees were bursting into flower; the leaves of all were freshly green; and, as the sun was shining brightly in a clear sky, the place was most enjoyable.

As the 'Scotland' remained in the harbour for two days, I had an opportunity of taking an excursion into the country to note the condition of its agricultural productions. The barley and wheat crops were now in ear, and would be fit for the sickle at the end of the month or the beginning of May. The cabbage-oil plant (*Brassica sinensis*) was now in full bloom, and filled the air with the fragrance of its yellow blossoms. These winter crops, when ripe, would be removed, and their places occupied by beans, sweet potatoes, melons, &c., the summer productions of this part of Japan. Most of the low rice-lands had been lying fallow during the winter, but would soon be irrigated and prepared for this crop, which is the staple production in all parts of the East.

On the hill-sides and in gardens numerous varieties of the azalea were in full bloom, but the largest garden-plants belong to the *Azalea variegata* tribe,and these were not yet in flower. *Kerria japonica, Prunus sinensis* (single and double), camellias, and many other plants identical with those of China, were also covered with their pretty blossoms.

Many pleasant and agreeable days might have been spent at this time in Nagasaki, but it was necessary that the good ship 'Scotland' should "move on." As we passed out of the harbour, I could well have wished to steer north for the entrance to the Inland Sea, in order to feast my eyes once more on its wild and romantic scenery. But the 'Scotland' had no "Queen's presents" on board, and as the outer passage, if not the most agreeable, was the safest in the present state of our knowledge, and the quickest, we steered in a southerly direction along the coast of Kiu-siu, for Van Dieman's Strait. This strait, with its peaked mountains and active volcanoes, has been noticed in a former chapter. It seems to be remarkable for the fearful storms which sweep through it from the Pacific Ocean. The first time I passed through we had a very heavy gale, and now, about the same place, we were doomed to encoun-

ter another equally severe. In order to get a little
shelter we made for the high land near Cape
Chichakoff. This time I had the advantage of
being in a steamer. As the coast is not well
known, we did not make any attempt to find an
anchorage, but steamed under the high land and
then stopped the engines. A current carried us
slowly to the eastward towards the Pacific, and
the gale told us, in language not to be mistaken,
whenever the ship had drifted beyond the shelter
of the land. Whenever this was felt, steam was
got up, and we moved back again under the
shelter of the Cape. For two days we were
detained by this gale, now drifting outwards with
the current, and now steaming back for the shelter
afforded by the land.

On the evening of the second day the gale
moderated a little, and it was determined to steam
out into the waters of the North Pacific Ocean,
where we spent anything but a pleasant night.
During the next two days we were sailing up
along the land, and passed the Bungo and Kino
channels, which lead into the Inland Sea. On the
morning of the 19th we were abreast of Cape
Idsu, inside of which is the Bay of Simoda and
the town of that name, so long the residence of
Mr. Townsend Harris, the United States Minister.
The weather was now fine, the sea was smooth,
and a considerable number of junks were passed
sailing in the direction of Yedo bay. Still, there
was nothing on this coast like the busy, bustling

scenes which are daily observed in fine weather on the coast of China.   We must have more knowledge of the interior of the Japanese islands before we can say whether this be owing to the less populous condition of the country or to the habits of the people.   The fact is as I have stated; the reason of such a difference will, no doubt, be explained in due time.   In the afternoon we were opposite the islands near the entrance to Yedo bay, and the same night dropped our anchor abreast of the town of Yokuhama.   I left the ship on the following morning, and took up my residence on shore.

Besides timber trees and other ornamental plants suitable to our climate, and likely to prove valuable in England, I had determined to make a collection of various other objects of natural history, particularly insects and land-shells.   With this view I had secured the services of Tunga, my old Chinese servant, and had brought him over with me from China to Japan.   We were now out all day long, ransacking every valley and every hill for the objects we had in view.   Tunga soon picked up a few words of the language of the country; and, as he was civil and inoffensive in all his ways, and carried a few *cash* in his pocket to reward those who assisted him, he grew very popular amongst the country people.   When making collections of insects and shells in China, we always found it a matter of the first importance to enlist in our service the children about

the cottages and farm-houses amongst the hills.
In this way we were able to secure many specimens of great interest which never came under
our own observation during the day. I therefore
determined to pursue the same course with the
Japanese. Some of my friends, to whom I mentioned my plans, informed me that such a system
would not succeed in Japan, for that it had been
already tried and had failed. Liberal rewards in
money had been offered again and again, but the
country people apparently did not want money,
or, at all events, would not take the trouble to
earn it. An experience of eighteen or nineteen
years amongst Orientals led me to doubt the truth
of the conclusion at which my friends had arrived.
Human nature, I argued, must be much the same
all over the East, if not all over the world; and
what a little management with kindness and liberality could effect in China, might surely be
accomplished in Japan.

With these principles to guide us, Tunga and
myself went to work in this new field and upon
this virgin soil. We began by collecting for ourselves, and this excited no little wonder in the
minds of the natives. Then we sat down in their
houses, or in the verandahs at their doors, and
exhibited to them the treasures in our boxes;
and so, having got into their good graces, we encouraged them to enter into our service by small
presents of the copper cash of the country to show
them that we were really in earnest, and that they

would be paid for their exertions. I had several sketches of the rare *Damaster blaptoides*, which had been given me by Mr. Stevens of Bloomsbury Street, London. These I distributed amongst them, and offered a liberal reward for each specimen of that remarkable insect. In this way we soon had hundreds of people of all ages enlisted in our service. The country round Yokuhama was divided into districts; each district was visited at stated times, and, as we were seen approaching in the distance, the fact was telegraphed from village to village, and from hill to hill, by the clear, ringing voices of the children. The difficulty, if it ever existed, had been got over, and the Japanese proved to be as willing assistants in my researches as the Chinese had been.

While writing upon the subject of Japanese insects I take the liberty of quoting a letter published in the ' Zoologist' for June, 1860, from my friend Dr. Adams, of Her Majesty's surveying ship ' Actæon ' on the capture of *Damaster blaptoides* in Japan.

" As I am in a good humour, having just fished up a new genus of mollusca from a pretty good depth, I will tell you at the risk of being tiresome all about it, as I am sure Adam White, at least, will be interested in the narrative.

" I was walking solitarily—for all hands had gone on board to dinner—along the shell-strewn strand of *Taleu-Sima*, a jolly little island, not far from the shores of Niphon —walking along in a brown

study, smoking a little clay cutty-pipe, and thinking chiefly of the contempt in which I·should be
held if some of my ' very particular' friends saw
me in this very disreputable ' rig,' for my neck
was bare, and my coat was an old blue serge, and
as for my hat, it was brown felt, and, I must say,
a ' shocking bad one.'   However, the sun was
bright, the clear blue rippling sea was calm, the
little island was clear and verdurous, and I smoked
serenely.   On a sudden my abstract downward
gaze encountered a grotesque *Coleopteron* in a suit
of black, stalking slowly and deliberately among
the driftwood at my feet—stepping cautiously
over the spillacan twigs, like a Catholic priest in
a crowded thoroughfare.   At once I knew my
coleopterous friend to be *Damaster blaptoides*; for
although my eyes are small, yet I have been
assured by a young lady friend of mine—sometimes irreverently called ' Polly'—that they are
penetrating; and my friend Adam White, when
he warned me not to forget my ' Carabs,' had
sent me a rough outline of the ' corpus' of Damaster.   So I carefully lifted my unresisting sable
friend from his native soil, and, after giving him
a good long stare, I deposited him in a bottle.
From his name and appearances, I judge him to
be cousin to Blaps, and I turned over the rockweed
for his brothers and other relations; but though
Helops was there, Damaster was not.   Puzzled, but
not baffled, I conceived his taste might be more
particular, so I ascended the steep green sides of

the island, and cast about for rotten trees; nor was
I long in discovering a very promising stump,
nicely decayed, and full of holes enough to capti-
vate the heart of any beetle.   Being, however,
fatigued with my scansorial efforts, I sat down
before the citadel of Damaster, and assisted my
deliberations by smoking a solemn pipe.   Having
propitiated Nicotiana and matured my plan of operations, I commenced the work of destruction, when,
lo! among the vegetable débris I descried a long
dusky leg, anon two more, and then, buried among

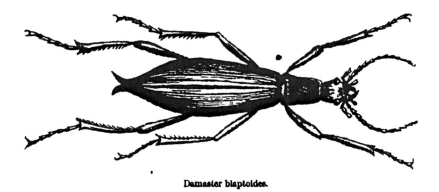

Damaster blaptoides.

the ruins, the struggling Damaster.   In this
manner was the rarest beetle known captured by
a wandering disciple of Æsculapius, and an eccen-
tric Fellow of the Linnæan Society."

I had an opportunity of seeing a portion of
Dr. Adams's treasures on board of the 'Actæon' in
China.   In addition to insects, he had a fine collection of sea-shells, which will prove of great interest
to conchologists in Europe.   His cabin was full
of specimens illustrating the natural history of

the different Oriental countries which he had visited
in the 'Actæon.'

After this digression I will proceed with my
narrative.   During the last days of April the
sea-shore was lined with natives of both sexes,
who were busily engaged in catching a curious
species of fish, which, it seems, visits these parts
for a few days at this season of the year.   The
mode of catching the fish was novel and interesting.   Each fisherman had a pair of decoys—that
is, living fish of the same kind as the intended
prey.   A long line was attached to each fish,
being fastened to the skin on the top of its head.
The slack of this line was wound up on a piece of
wood, and unrolled at the pleasure of the fisherman.   Then a net was fastened to, and slung between, two bamboo poles, these forming the two
sides of a triangle.   The third side of the triangle
was open, with the mouth of the net hanging beneath it, and in this state it was pushed forward
into the sea.   The line was now unrolled, and the
decoys were sent forth into deeper waters, to make
friends with other members of the tribe who were
still free.   A sufficient time being allowed for
these gay deceivers to get a congregation around
them and to expatiate on the luxuries of the land,
the fisherman hauls the line gently home until the
decoys and their near friends, who have followed
them, get in the water above his net.   The net
is then lifted rapidly upwards out of the water,
and decoys and decoyed are entangled in its

meshes. The latter are taken out and placed in a basket on shore, while the former are sent to sea again in search of new friends.

This mode of fishing lasted for a few days only; the species in question appeared to come suddenly on the coast, and as suddenly to take its departure, first, however, leaving a good supply of its number to assist in feeding the inhabitants of Yokuhama and Yedo. It was a curious-looking animal, short, flabby, and blown up, looking as if it consisted chiefly of wind and blubber. Some of the natives said it was poisonous; but, if so, this could be only in certain conditions, for it was a great favourite with the Japanese, who cut it up, dried it in the sun, and preserved it for future use.

One morning towards the end of April I crossed the bay from Yokuhama to Kanagawa, accompanied by Mr. Clarke, of the house of Messrs. Dent and Co., established here. Our object was to visit some of the Buddhist temples in that part of the country, and to examine the vegetable productions and other objects of interest by the way. Landing at Kanagawa, we crossed the long, narrow town, and soon found ourselves in the open country behind it. The first object which attracted my attention was the change which had taken place in the appearance of the fields and the crops since I was last here. The low rice-lands, which had been lying fallow since the crop was gathered in November, were now being dug up, flooded with water, and manured. In China, bullocks and buffaloes are employed to plough the land; but in Japan it is prepared by manual labour alone: a pronged fork is employed to dig and break up the soil. Vegetable matter is used *in a fresh state* for manure, as in China. Women, old men, and children were employed on the edges of the fields, and on every hill-side, in cutting grass and weeds for this purpose. These, being scattered over the land and mixed with mud and water, rot in a very short space of time and afford nourishment to the rice-crops. A week or two after this fresh manure is thrown upon the land every trace of it disappears from the surface. It probably goes on decaying for some time underground, thus feeding in a peculiar manner the roots of the paddy with those gases given off during the process of decomposition.

In the corners of many fields little patches of land had been carefully dug and manured as seed-beds for rearing the young paddy. Each of these patches was banked round with earth and connected with a mountain-stream, so that it could be irrigated at pleasure. Some of these seed-beds had been already sown, and we observed the natives engaged in sowing others as we passed along.

On the dry hill-lands the crops of wheat and barley were coming into ear, beans and peas were in full bloom, the cabbage oil-plant (*Brassica sinensis*) here, as at Nagasaki, was seen in patches over the hill-sides, and the air was perfumed with its fragrant blossoms.

All countries are beautiful in spring, but Japan is pre-eminently so. The trees were now clothed with leaves of the freshest green, and many of the early flowering kinds were in full blossom. On every hill-side and in every cottage-garden there was some object of attraction. The double-blossomed cherry-trees and flowering peaches were most beautiful objects, loaded as they now were with flowers as large as little roses. Camellias, forming goodly-sized trees, were common in the woods, and early azaleas adorned the hill-sides with flowers of many hues. Here the *Azalea obtusa*, with flowers of the most dazzling red, was peculiarly at home. I found this species some years ago in the gardens of China, but no doubt its native habitat is Japan, and it requires the bright sunlight of the East to bring out in perfection its brilliant colour. *Cydonia japonica* was seen in a wild state, creeping amongst the grass, and covered with red blossoms; violets, often scentless, covered every bank; and several varieties of primrose (*Primula cortusoides*) were met with under trees in the shady woods.

The Buddhist temples, always situated in the most charming positions, and having fine examples of the trees and shrubs of the country, full grown and carefully protected, are objects of attraction at all seasons, but more particularly in spring. We visited many of these on our route; all of them were interesting, and none more so than Bokengee, a place I had visited when here in the autumn.

The Bokengee Valley is a beautiful one; it leads up
between two pretty green hills covered with brushwood, evergreen oaks, and pines. The same
solemn stillness seemed to reign amongst the
temples as I had observed on a former occasion,
broken only at intervals by some priest loudly re-
hearsing his prayers. At the principal entrance of
this temple there are some large examples of the
double-blossomed cherry-tree. One of these was
one mass of bloom, and very handsome it appeared.
The broad cleanly-swept walk below it was covered
with thousands of its petals, which were falling
like thin flakes of snow.

On the 7th of May I left Yokuhama, and crossed
the bay to Kanagawa, where I took up my quarters
in a large temple which had been rented and fitted
up by Messrs. Dent and Co.; but as they had removed their establishment to Yokuhama, it was
now unoccupied. Had I searched all Japan I could ·
not have found a place better fitted for my pursuits. I had large rooms and verandahs in which
I could prepare and store my collections of dried
plants, seeds, insects, and shells, while the garden
afforded ample space for the living plants which
I was daily adding to my stores, and hoped
one day to introduce into Europe. A Japanese ·
porter, a gardener, Tunga, and myself, were the
only occupants of this temple; and I must have
had more confidence in the natives than perhaps
was prudent, for my doors were never locked,
neither by night nor by day. Itinerant florists

and nurserymen were amongst my daily visitors, and rarely arrived without bringing me something which I gladly bought and transferred to my temple garden.

About the middle of May the now well-known *Paulownia imperialis* was in full bloom in the grounds of a temple adjoining that in which I was located. Here it forms a tree about thirty feet in height; the stem is generally bare, but branches out at the top, and each branch terminates in a spike of large, lilac, foxglove-like flowers. The varieties of pinks are numerous and beautiful in this part of Japan, and they also were in bloom about this time. They are remarkable for their large blossoms of various hues, some being of the most brilliant red and scarlet, while others are coloured much like our own. The finest poppies I ever saw were met with in gardens adjoining the Imperial highway. The Japanese do not smoke opium like their friends in China, but I believe the seeds of the poppy are largely used by them for medicinal purposes. The double-flowering kinds have blossoms of great size, of many different colours, and are highly orna-mental.

But the plant remarkable above all others which were met with at this time, for its great beauty, was a new primrose.* I shall never forget the morning on which a basketful of this charming plant was first brought to my door. Its flowers,

* *Primula japonica.*

of a rich magenta colour, were arranged in tiers,
one above another, on a spike nearly two feet
in height. It was beyond all question the most
beautiful species of the genus to which it belongs,
and will, I doubt not, henceforth take its place as
the "Queen of the Primroses."

CHAPTER XII.

HAVING ransacked the country in the vicinity of Yokuhama and Kanagawa, I was very desirous of paying another visit to the capital. The nursery-gardens of Sumae-yah and Dang-o-zaka, in which I had found so many new plants during the previous winter, had no doubt many others of interest which could only be judged of in spring or early summer; but Yedo was a sealed city to all who were not officials, unless they were specially invited as guests by their minister at the Court of the Tycoon. Unfortunately his Excellency Mr. Alcock, to whom I had been indebted for much kindness and hospitality on a former occasion, was now absent in China, and it was generally reported that no Englishman would be allowed to visit the city until he returned. Under these circumstances I

was unwilling to make an application to the gentleman who had been left in charge of the Legation,
as he might not have the power to grant me my
request, and at the same time it would be disagreeable, I thought, for him to refuse. What was then
to be done? Mr. Alcock was not expected back
until the end of June, and if I could not visit Yedo
until that time all the spring-flowers would be past,
and the opportunity of adding some plants of interest and value to my collection would be lost.
Most anxious to accomplish the object I had in
view, I wrote to Mr. Townsend Harris, the United
States Minister, and asked him to receive me for a
few days at the American Legation. Mr. Harris
sent me a very kind reply, inviting me to his
house in Yedo, and begging me to remain there as
long as I pleased. Thus far everything went well,
and I was delighted with the opportunity which I
was likely to have of adding to the number of those
useful and beautiful trees and other plants which I
had discovered in Yedo the winter before; but the
sequel will show that things were not destined to
go on quite so smoothly as I had anticipated.

On the 20th of May Mr. Portman and a guard
of yakoneens were sent down to meet me at the
river Loga. I had frequently heard of a beautiful
inland road from Kanagawa to Yedo; and as I had
seen quite enough of the Imperial highway, it was
determined that we should take the new route.
Before striking into the country we paid a visit to
the celebrated tea-house at Omora, which I have

formerly noticed. The large garden attached to this "Mansion of Plum-trees" was now in great beauty. The trees were in full leaf, forming shady walks and avenues where travellers or visitors could shelter themselves from the sun's rays, which were now becoming more powerful every day. The pretty waiting-maids brought us sundry cups of tea with different kinds of cake. Pleasant, very pleasant, was that " Mansion of Plum-trees," but it was necessary to " move on."

Leaving the Tokaido behind us, we took a bridle-path which led us more inland, and soon afterwards we struck a broad country road, by which we journeyed onwards in the direction of the capital. On our way we called at a place called Nanka-nobu to see a large specimen of *Glycine sinensis*, which was one of the lions in this part of the country. It was evidently a tree of great age. It measured, at three feet from the ground, seven feet in circumference, and covered a space of trellis-work sixty feet by one hundred and two feet. The trellis was about eight feet in height, and many thousands of the long racemes of the glycine hung down nearly half-way to the ground. One of them, which I measured, was three feet six inches in length. The thousands of long, drooping, lilac racemes had a most extraordinary and beautiful appearance. People came from far and near to see the tree during the time it remained in bloom; and as it was in the garden of a public tea-house, it brought an extensive custom to the proprietor.

Tables and benches were arranged under its shade, which at the time of our visit were well occupied with travellers and visitors, all sipping and apparently enjoying the grateful and invigorating beverage. As the day was cloudless, and the sun's rays powerful, we were not slow to imitate the example they set before us, so we sipped our tea, smoked a cigar, and admired this beautiful specimen of the vegetable kingdom.

Our road during the remainder of our journey was a very pleasant one, and led us through lanes fringed on each side with pretty hedges and tall trees, the latter affording a pleasing shade. Many little villages and comfortable-looking inns or tea-houses were passed by the way. Most of these tea-houses had gardens filled with pretty flowering plants for the enjoyment of their patrons, and in more than one of them we noticed a trellis covered with the *Glycine sinensis* in full bloom. This trailing tree is evidently a great favourite with the Japanese, and it well deserves to be so. Everywhere the people seemed most inoffensive and even friendly, showing a natural curiosity to see the Tojins (Chinamen or foreigners), as they called us, and now and then saluting us with the friendly "Anata, Ohio." Japan would be a pleasant place to live or travel in were it freed from those bands of two-sworded idlers which infest the capital, and render a residence there sometimes far from agreeable.

As we entered the suburbs of Yedo we met the

young gentlemen of the English Legation going
out for a ride in the country, followed by a large
number of yakoneens.   This was rather an un-
lucky meeting, as it afterwards turned out, although
I had no idea at the time that I had done anything
wrong.   A few words were exchanged with those
of them whom I knew, and we parted apparently
good friends.   Some one told me afterwards that
the only gentleman in the party unknown to me,
and who it seems had been left in charge of Her
Majesty's Legation, looked very indignant; but as
I did not observe his countenance, I was left in
blissful ignorance of the wrath which he was
" nursing to keep warm" until some hours after-
ward.

We arrived at the American Legation between
five and six o'clock in the afternoon, where I was
most kindly received by his Excellency.   Like all
the other foreign ministers in Yedo, Mr. Harris
occupies a large and roomy temple.   An avenue
leads up from one of the streets of the town to the
temple.   Two noble trees of *Salisburia adiantifolia*
guard the entrance, and one of them is the largest
specimen of the kind I have yet met with.   Its
circumference, about six feet from the ground, is
twenty-eight feet, and it is fully a hundred feet in
height.   On one of the sides of this temple there
is the usual cemetery, and behind it is a hill
covered with lofty trees.   Then there are the usual
guardhouses filled with armed yakoneens, and a
small, quiet-looking place, which is said to be the

residence of the spy or spies by whom the sayings and doings of every one in the Legation are duly chronicled.

While we were sitting at dinner this evening I received the following letter from Her Majesty's Legation :—

"As no British subject can visit Yeddo without an invitation from, or the sanction of, Her Britannic Majesty's Minister, or, in his absence, the officer in charge of Her Majesty's Legation, from neither of whom you have received such invitation or sanction, I have to request you will take your departure from Yeddo without delay.

"I have, &c.,
"F. G. MYBURGH,
"In charge of H.B.M. Legation."

Early on the following morning I sent a reply to this letter as follows :—

"I had the honour to receive your letter of yesterday's date, upon which I beg to make the following observations. I returned to Japan a short time ago for the purpose of examining the natural productions of the country during the spring months, hoping to make some discoveries which might prove useful at home. For this purpose it was of great importance that I should be able to visit the gardens about Yedo. Unfortunately on my arrival at Kanagawa I found Her Majesty's Minister absent from Yedo, and I was given to understand that I could not obtain permission from the officer in charge of the Legation to visit the city.   His Excellency Mr. Alcock has always shown every disposition to forward my views, and had he been here I have no doubt he would willingly have granted the permission I required. Under the circumstances I wrote to his Excellency the American Minister, and asked him to grant me that permission which I am sure I would have received from Her Majesty's representative had he been in Yedo.   Mr. Harris, in the kindest manner, invited me to his house as his guest, in order to enable me to accomplish the objects I had in view.

" With this explanation, I trust you will not insist on my leaving Yedo for a few days, as it might be a matter of public regret should I be prevented from adding to our home collection some new trees or other plants of much interest."

Having despatched this letter, and trusting to receive a favourable reply, I was furnished with the usual guard of yakoneens, and we rode out to visit the nursery-gardens of Sumae-yah and Dang-o-zaka.   We took the same route through the city which I have fully described in an earlier chapter, and witnessed the same scenes.   The Sumae-yah gardens, however, presented quite a different appearance from what they had done in the autumn before.   They had put on their summer dress; the trees were covered with leaves, and many flower-

ing shrubs and herbaceous plants were in full
bloom.   Amongst those which interested me most,
because they were new to me, were a beautiful new
oak with large and handsome leaves, several new
maples with leaves beautifully marked with rich
colours, new species of Weigela, clematis, lychnis,
and a variety of Solomon's seal having its leaves
beautifully striped with broad white lines.

The Dang-o-zaka gardens, which were next
visited, were ransacked in the same way.   Every
corner was examined, and several new and important plants were added to my collections which
had not been seen by me during my former visits.
I have already stated that the town of Dang-o-
zaka is in a valley, and very pretty it seemed, with
its clean houses sheltered and adorned by richly-
wooded hills.   It is a pretty place at all seasons,
for there are so many pines and other trees that
retain their leaves all the winter, that the woods
may be said to be evergreen.   Now, however, the
leaves and flowers of deciduous trees were mixed
up with those of the evergreen oaks and pines, and
formed a pleasing contrast.

As on former occasions, an account of all the
plants I purchased and the sums to be paid for them
was carefully written down by one of my attendant
yakoneens, and no doubt a full and particular
report of my doings was forwarded to the proper
quarter.   This system has, however, one great
advantage, and it is this—the most perfect reli-
ance may be placed on the men with whom you

have made your bargains; they will certainly
bring the articles at the time appointed, and will
not attempt to demand more than the sum which
they have agreed to.

As these gardens were very numerous, the whole
day was spent in examining them; and my attendants, long before I had finished, had been giving
me sundry broad hints that it was time to set out
on our return to Yedo. When I had finished my
investigations we mounted our horses and rode
homewards, arriving at the American Legation
before nightfall. Here I found a letter waiting
for me, of which the following is a " true copy : "—

" I beg to acknowledge the receipt of your
letter of to-day, and regret that you have placed
me under the necessity of again writing to you.
I care not to be informed now for what object you
have come to Japan, or that Her Majesty's Minister would have granted you permission to visit
Yedo had he been here—I only know that you
are a private individual in a private capacity in
this country, and that you have not asked for nor
received the requisite sanction from the British
authority here to come up to Yedo.

" It is of no consequence to me now what you
were given to understand at Kanagawa; but you
must have been well aware that the American
Minister has not the power to grant you, or any
other British subject, permission to visit Yedo. It
was your duty to have communicated with me on

the subject, but this you had not the common courtesy to do; and you actually came up to Yedo without even my knowledge. I think I have said enough to show you that you have acted in an improper manner. Whether it would be a matter of public regret or not your being unable to accomplish your private ends, is not a question for me to consider. I am only performing my public duty when I call upon you a second time to quit Yedo at once. To allow you to remain would be to establish a dangerous precedent.

" I have, &c.,
" F. G. Myburgh."

This communication did not take away my breath or my appetite for dinner, as, perhaps, it ought to have done. On the following morning (for I prefer to sleep upon anything disagreeable) I sent the following reply to the insulting letter I had received—a reply which I trust will show that, although only a " private individual," I was incapable of doing anything rude or uncourteous :—

" As I am unwilling to do anything that may have the slightest appearance of disrespect to Her Majesty's Legation in Yedo, I shall leave the city at once—probably this evening, or, at latest, to-morrow morning. I may have been wrong in accepting the invitation of His Excellency the American Minister without first obtaining permission from yourself (although, I believe, such a proceeding is not without a precedent), but I had no intention of, and could have no motive for, treating you with disrespect, as my letter of yesterday might have shown you. I have therefore to complain of the very uncourteous style of your last letter, which you have thought it your public duty to address to me as a British subject, and with this remark I beg to close my correspondence."

It is stipulated in the treaties which the Japanese have made with foreign powers, that no foreigner, unless he be an official, can proceed nearer to Yedo than that point where the river Loga intersects the Imperial highway. But all the ministers who reside there had been in the habit of inviting their friends to Yedo, apparently with the knowledge and sanction of the Japanese Government. Even English ladies had been there on several occasions, and had returned highly delighted with their view of the great city. I had, therefore, no idea that I was committing a heinous offence in accepting the hospitality of the representative of a friendly Power, particularly as it was well known I had no dangerous political objects in view. But I was unfortunately a British subject, and I had come to Yedo (unwittingly, I must confess) without first bowing the knee to him who was dressed in a little brief authority. I have been travelling in Eastern countries for nearly eighteen years, and I can truly state, that, during that long period, I have on every other occasion .received the greatest and most disinterested kindness from every officer in Her Majesty's service with whom I have come in contact. I sincerely regret that I have had to mention one exception, which is perhaps not worth the prominence I have given to it in these pages. Let me turn, then, to a more agreeable subject.

On the morning after my visit to Sumae-yah and Dang-o-zaka the different nurserymen presented themselves at the American Legation, with the plants I had purchased. Notwithstanding the shortness of the time I had been allowed to stay, the collection thus brought together was one of great interest, and mostly new to science. Orders were now given to prepare baskets to pack them in for conveyance to Kanagawa; and while these were being got ready, Mr. Harris invited me to accompany him in a ride into the country.

On our way we paid a visit to the grave of poor Mr. Heuskin, formerly interpreter to the American Legation, who had been waylaid and murdered by some Japanese a few months before. The tomb is placed in a quiet and beautiful spot on the hill-side amongst some lofty trees. A neat and substantial monument, with a simple inscription, has been placed on the grave by Mr. Harris, and a hedge of evergreen oak and camellias has been planted around it by his orders.

Leaving poor Heuskin's grave, we rode on in a westerly direction for about two hours, taking many a winding path in order to see the more remarkable portions of this beautiful suburban scenery, with which Mr. Harris was well acquainted, and of which he was one of the most enthusiastic admirers. Our destination was a place called Joo-ne-shoo, or the Temple of the Twelve Altars. This temple is situated in a wood, and has a waterfall on one side, and a lake on the other. Numerous tea-houses do a thriving trade here, as the place is much resorted to by the good citizens of Yedo. Saki, which is rather stronger than tea, is also consumed in considerable quantities. Report says that many of the visitors are particularly fond of composing and reciting poetry in one of the avenues near the temple, and that sundry draughts of the favourite beverage are taken to brighten the intellect and to excite the imagination. At the upper end of this avenue there are sundry jets of water, each having a fall of about six feet, which are used in a curious way that is worth mentioning. It seems that, when the poet or philosopher, or whoever he may be, has imbibed so much saki as to render him incapable of further enjoyment—in fact, when he is what is vulgarly termed drunk—he gravely proceeds and places his head under one of these jets of cold water. This has the effect of making him a more sober, if not a wiser, man, and it enables him to return once more to the enjoyment of his saki. How often this system can be repeated in an afternoon with the same results, I am not informed. It is to be hoped, however, that it is more beneficial to the literature of the country than it can be to the constitutions of those who thus enjoy themselves at the " Temple of the Twelve Altars."

After visiting the waterfall, Poets' Avenue, and other places of interest, we sat down in one of the little sheds on the banks of the lake, and refreshed ourselves with sundry cups of hot tea. We returned home by a different road, but the same kinds of beautiful lanes, valleys, country houses, and gardens were passed as on our way out. A ride of some six miles brought us again to the great city, and we were soon threading our way amongst crowds of human beings, packhorses, and dust—a striking contrast to that sylvan scenery which we had just been enjoying.

Mr. Harris related an amusing circumstance connected with the shoeing of horses in Japan, which illustrates the ready way in which the people of the country adopt foreign customs when seen to be improvements on their own. I have already had occasion to mention the marked difference which exists between the Chinese and the Japanese in this respect. " Oula custom "— old custom—is the barrier to every foreign introduction in China, while the Japanese adopt with promptness every improvement which is set before them. When Mr. Harris first went to reside in Yedo, his horse was shod with iron shoes in the usual way. Up to this time the horses of the

Japanese either wore straw shoes, or were not
shod at all. One day an officer came to Mr. Harris
and asked him to lend him his horse, and to be
good enough to ask no questions as to the purpose
for which the animal was required. This strange
request was good-humouredly complied with, and
the horse, after being away for a short time, was
duly brought back. The officer to whom it had
been lent came to the American Legation a few
days afterwards, and told Mr. Harris, as a great
secret, that the Prime Minister had sent for the
horse to examine his shoes; and now, he said, the
Minister's horse had been shod in the same way,
and all the horses of the other officers were like-
wise being shod!

As I did not wish to embroil myself in any way
with the authorities of Her Majesty's Legation, I
left Yedo on the following morning, and took the
road to Kanagawa.

In this and in former chapters I have endeavoured to give a description of the Japanese
capital and suburbs, and I shall now end my account with a few general observations. Although
Yedo is a large city, and remarkable in many
ways, it cannot be compared with London, Paris,
or any of the chief towns in Europe, either in the
architecture of its buildings, the magnificence of
its shops, or in the value of its merchandize. It
has no Woolwich or Greenwich—no St. Paul's or
Westminster Abbey—no Champs Elysées or Ver-
sailles; it has nothing to show like the Boulevards .

in Paris or like Regent Street in London. Indeed the habits and wants of the people are so different from those of European nations, that we have little in common for a comparison. But, nevertheless, Yedo is a wonderful place, and will always possess attractions peculiarly its own in the eyes of a foreign visitor. It is of great size for an Oriental city; its palace surrounded by deep moats and grassy banks, the official quarter, the residences of the native princes, its wide streets, and beautiful bay will always be looked upon with a certain degree of interest. Then, the views which are obtained from the hills in its neighbourhood are such as may well challenge comparison with those of any other town in Europe or elsewhere. Its suburbs, too, as I have already shown, are remarkable in many ways. Those beautiful valleys, wooded hills, and quiet lanes fringed with noble trees and evergreen hedges, would be difficult to match in any other part of the world.

CHAPTER XIII.

IN due time I arrived at my old quarters in Kanagawa, and the plants which I had purchased in
Yedo were delivered·in good condition, and added
to my other collections. Tunga and myself, with
some Japanese whom I had taken into my service,
were now daily ransacking the country in all
directions in search of new plants and other
objects of natural history. One day, as I was
returning from my rambles, the last part of my
road was along the Tokaido, which forms the main
street of Kanagawa. In a tea-house, on the road-
side, a most curious operation was being performed, which attracted my attention. A woman
was sitting with her back quite naked, while
another of her sex was engaged in burning little

puffs of a pithy-like combustible substance in four holes which had been made in the skin between the shoulders. To an European the operation would have been a most painful one; but the woman who was undergoing the treatment in the present instance was laughing and joking as if she enjoyed it rather than otherwise. This was the *moxa*-burning operation, frequently noticed in the works of Kæmpfer and other writers on Japan. *Moxa* is said, in some books, to be made from the balls of a fungus, and in others to be furnished by the young leaves of wormwood (*Artemesia*). When used, it is in the form of little cones, which are placed in the holes above mentioned, and set on fire on the top. It burns slowly down, and leaves a blister on the skin, which afterwards breaks and discharges. The operation is considered very efficacious in preventing or curing the fevers of the country, as also in cases of rheumatism, gout, and even toothache. The Chinese irritate the skin for the same disorders by dipping the knuckles in hot tea, and pinching the neck, back, and other parts of the body until the skin becomes painfully tender.

Acupuncture is another famous remedy with the Japanese, although, perhaps, not so common or such an apparent luxury as the moxa-burning. It is used in cases of bowel-complaint or colic, endemic to the country. This disease is supposed by them to be caused by wind, and, in order to let it out, several holes are made with needles in the muscles of the stomach or abdomen, and in other fleshy parts of the body. These needles are exceedingly fine, nearly as thin as hairs, and are generally made of gold or silver, although sometimes of steel by persons who profess to peculiar skill in tempering them. While the needles are passed through the skin and muscle, the nerves and blood-vessels are carefully avoided : a fact which shows that the Japanese practitioners must have some knowledge of anatomy.

It is not unlikely that these two remedies for the common diseases of the country may, in many instances, prove useful; but I have no doubt the time is at hand when the Japanese will be taught to accomplish the objects they have in view in a way much more simple, and probably more efficiently. The medical men of Japan have always been remarkable for two things, when compared with the same class in China—they have always appreciated the higher character of the medical and surgical science of the Western nations, and have been attentive and eager students whenever they have had an opportunity of acquiring knowledge. Kæmpfer, Thunberg, and Siebold all bear witness to this fact, and we have seen it further confirmed by the medical members of the Embassy who lately visited England, and who appear, by their visits to our hospitals and colleges, to have been most eager to acquire this kind of information. The only drawback to their obtaining a knowledge of surgery is, their superstitious ideas;

believing, as they do, that they become polluted
by contact with dead bodies,—a circumstance which
renders dissection impossible. Could this be got
over, as it no doubt will be, their progress in the
knowledge of surgery will be remarkable.

There are little roadside altars in many of the
fields near Kanagawa, on which the natives burn
incense, and offer salt, cash, and other things to a
little deity rudely carved in stone. On one occasion I came up with three women, rather respect-
ably dressed, and looking as if they belonged to
the higher classes of Japan. They were accompanied by a man-servant, who carried in his hands a
bundle of joss-sticks and paper as an offering to
the god. They looked pleased to see a foreigner,
were very polite, and asked me where I was going
to, whence I came, and to what nation I belonged.
On my returning the compliment by asking them
the same questions, they informed me they had
come from Kanagawa, and were about to offer
incense at a little altar situated in a field some
hundred yards ahead of us. Being anxious to
witness the ceremony, I walked with them to the
altar. When we reached the little stone god, one
of the ladies, apparently the highest in rank, took
the incense out of the hand of the servant, lighted
it, and placed it in a stone basin in front of the
image. She then bent low before the altar, all the
time rubbing a string of beads which she held in
her hands and muttering some prayers.   The
second in rank stood behind her in a devout atti-

tude, while behind the second stood the third, who
made short work with her devotions, and laughed
and talked to me while the others were engaged
with their prayers.   At the conclusion of the
ceremony, which lasted only about two minutes,
the three ladies pulled short tobacco-pipes out of
their pockets, filled them with tobacco from their
pouches, and begged me to give them a light from
my cigar.   I willingly complied with the request,
and, after having a comfortable little smoke together, we parted the best of friends.

It was now the end of May, and a considerable
change had taken place in the appearance of the
country.   In the fields the barley is yellow, and
will be ready for the sickle of the husbandman in
a few days; the rape-seed is ripe already, and its
harvest has commenced.   The natives are busily
employed in sowing and planting the summer
crops between the rows of the standing corn.
These consist of soy and other beans, egg-plants,
sweet potatoes, cotton, melons and cucumbers,
turnips, hill-rice, and oily grain (*Sesamum
orientale*).

The spring flowers have now all disappeared.
The gorgeous peach and plum trees, whose falling
petals " strewed our path with flowers," are now
covered only with leaves ; azaleas, camellias,
violets, and primroses, and even the glorious
glycine itself, have all passed by, and will not be
seen again until the opening of another year.   But
although the spring beauties have gone by,

another race, equally beautiful in its way, has
come to take their places, to paint the woods and
hedgerows and gardens with masses of gay colours,
and to perfume the air with the fragrance of its
blossoms. Wild roses are now in full flower. The
hedges, banks, and uncultivated land are covered
with their white blooms. A new species of *Weigela*
is growing wild everywhere, and is also in flower.
In the end of May and in June *Deutzia scabra* and
Styrax japonica are very beautiful. They abound
on every hill-side, in the hedges, and on the banks
of streams. Later in the year the Styrax produces galls, from which a reddish dye is prepared.
Honeysuckles, too (*Caprifolium japonicum*), are
abundant, and their flowers, with those of the wild
rose, fill the air with delicious perfume.

In gardens, herbaceous peonies are out; several
beautiful kinds of pinks, quite different from the
spring sorts, are also in bloom, and there is a race
of summer chrysanthemums which come in at this
time, and which render the gardens extremely
gay. In addition to these, I noted two fine new
Weigelas, some clematises, irises, *Spiræa Reeves-
iana,* and the white Banksian rose. It is a common
remark amongst foreigners that flowers are mostly
scentless in Japan, and some have gone so far as
to attribute this to the nature of the soil of the
country. That this is not so will be apparent from
the notices of the different fragrant plants above-
mentioned. Honeysuckles, roses (particularly the
white Banksian), gardenias, peonies, tuberoses, and

a hundred other flowers, are just as fragrant in
Japan as they are elsewhere. Violets are scentless,
but this appears to be the fault of the species, and
not of the soil.

Before I left Yedo a change seemed to be about
to take place in the weather. Heavy clouds came
up and hung over the city, and every one acquainted with the climate of Japan predicted the
near approach of the rainy season. The rains commenced on the night of the 26th of May, and continued to come down heavily during the whole of
the following day. At 6 P.M. the clouds broke into
masses, and the clear blue sky appeared above them.
This evening there appeared the most beautiful and
perfect rainbow which I had ever seen, and about
the same time the clouds which rested on Mount
Fusi gradually rose, and showed us the holy mountain basking in the evening sun, and still nearly
covered with snow. One can scarcely imagine the
beauty of the scene which was now spread out
before me, and it was rendered more lovely and
enjoyable by the fresh green foliage of the shrubs
and trees, from whose leaves hung many thousands
of pearly rain-drops glistening in the sun's rays.
Heavy rains were now of frequent occurrence, and
continued at intervals up to the 15th of June. The
rainy season seems much more decided in its character here than in China; indeed it reminded me
somewhat of the same season in India, although it
did not last so long.

On the 1st of June I was awoke about three

o'clock in the morning by an earthquake of a very violent character. Some rings suspended from a canopy in the temple first indicated the motion and began to tingle, then the whole building creaked and groaned, and lastly the bed on which I lay moved under me. It occurred at about three o'clock in the morning, and lasted for a few seconds only. Several other shocks were experienced afterwards during the morning, but these were much less violent, and some of them scarcely perceptible.

June 2nd.—The natives are still busy all over the fields, sowing and planting the summer crops between the rows of the ripening corn. Blazing fires and dense clouds of smoke are now seen all over the country. The rape-harvest is finished, the seed has been trampled out, and the farmers are now engaged in burning the stalks for the sake of the ashes, which are used as manure for the summer crops.

A nursery gardener who brought me a collection of plants to-day for sale, had amongst them a genuine English strawberry covered with ripe fruit. I have already had occasion to notice, in an earlier chapter, several foreign plants which had been introduced from Western countries to Japan, as a proof of the enterprise of the people, but I was not aware until now that the real English straw-berry was also here. A species of *Fragaria* is common, in a wild state, on the banks and hill-sides, both in Japan and in China; but it has nothing to do with the species we cultivate in Europe, and is

perfectly tasteless. Here, however, was the real
" Simon Pure ;" and as many of the foreign residents had gardens round their houses, this discovery would enable them to have their strawberry-
beds, and to enjoy the old home luxury of straw-
berries and cream. I gladly purchased the plant
in question, and carried it in triumph to the house
of my friend Mr. Ross,* with whom I was to dine.
How we placed it in the centre of the table, how
we admired it, and what old scenes and old memo-
ries it brought before us, may be imagined by those
who have been long resident in such far-off lands
as Zipangu or Cathay.

During the remainder of the month of June I
discovered and added to my collections several new
plants of considerable interest, which I must now
notice. One day I was out in the country in search
of the seeds of a columbine, which were then ripe.
In the grounds of a pretty little temple I came
quite unexpectedly upon a new species of *Deutzia*,
having double rose-coloured flowers. It was in full
bloom at the time, and was very beautiful. The
good priestess of the temple kindly allowed me to
gather a few specimens of the flowers for my
herbarium, and for a few tempos † I induced her
to part with some of the plants. This shrub will
be hardy in England, and its double rose or pink
coloured blossoms will render it very ornamental in

* J. B. Ross, Esq., a resident in Yokuhama, to whom I was indebted for much kindness and hospitality.

† An oval copper coin, worth about one penny of our money.

our gardens. Curiously enough I found at this time the pretty *Spiræa callosa*, a shrub which I had first seen on the Bohea Mountains in China, and which I had imported thence into Europe. It grows wild on the hill-sides in Japan, and is also cultivated in gardens and much esteemed by the Japanese. Another *Spiræa*—a herbaceous kind, resembling our own " Queen of the Meadow," but with deep-red flowers—was also met with at this time. *Lychnis senno*, a plant which I had known from a figure in Siebold's ' Flora Japonica,' was also found in bloom, and added to my collections. It is cultivated in every cottage-garden, and is very showy and handsome when in bloom. Its leaves have a kind of violet hue somewhat resembling a Tradescantia, while its flowers are of a bright fiery red colour. There are three varieties of this—a red, a white, and one with striped flowers. They are all very ornamental, particularly the striped one. Hydrangias were also met with, and a beautiful new honeysuckle, since named *Lonicera areo-reticulata*. Summer chrysanthemums were now hawked about the streets in great variety, many of them with large flowers, and some belonging to the class called Pompones. Irises too are carried about in the same way ; the natives are very fond of these, and have a number of fine kinds.

In the markets of Kanagawa and Yokuhama there were now some good cucumbers and brinjals ; two or three kinds of peas were in season, also French beans of first-rate quality. The summer fruits of Japan are few in number and inferior in kind. At this time we had wild raspberries and loquats (*Eriobotria japonica*). A little later two kinds of plums come in, some poor peaches, apricots, and melons. As a general rule all the summer fruits of Japan are very inferior to those in cultivation in England; but as, by the late treaty, we are now enabled to give the Japanese a sample of our manufactures, the time will, no doubt, come when we shall also improve their fruits and vegetables.

From the beginning to the end of June was the most successful time for our entomological collections. The moist air and warm sun brought out insects innumerable, and some of the common kinds of beetles might be shaken off the flowers or leaves of the trees by the thousand. Tunga and myself, assisted by troops of natives, were daily adding to our stores, and many cases were now crammed full of rare species, destined to instruct and, I hope, to give pleasure to many a western entomologist. I am indebted to Mr. Stevens, of Bloomsbury Street, London, for the names of a few of the more interesting species, in the following letter.

" The best insects you have brought from Japan comprise *Damaster* (new species), described by Mr. Adams as *D. Fortunei*, three species of *true Carabi* apparently undescribed, a new genus of the carabideous group allied to *Sphodrus* or *Nebria*, two new species of *Lucani* or stag-beetles, several new

and beautiful *Longicorns*, a *Spondylus* allied to a
species found in France and Germany, and interesting on that account; also several other
coleoptera much resembling species found in
England, and two or three species identical with
English ones. Besides there is a most beautiful
and apparently new butterfly, a species of *Apatura*
or an allied genus, of which the beautiful *A. Iris*
(Purple Emperor) is found in England; some other
butterflies almost identical with our own; and
others resembling those found in the north and
south of China. Many of the insects have a great
resemblance to those found in China, and some are
identical, including *Dynastes dichotoma*."

One afternoon about this time I came upon a
group of countrymen, sitting under the shade of
some trees, busily engaged in taking a kind of
silk or gut from a large species of caterpillar.
The animal was fully four inches long, its upper
side was of a lively green colour, while the under
was white and covered with long white hairs. It
feeds upon the leaves of a species of chesnut
(*Castanea japonica*) very common on all the hill-
sides in this part of Japan. In the baskets containing the worms were a quantity of these
leaves, which, judging from the rapid manner
in which they were being eaten up, must be
very palatable. But the curious part of the
business remains to be told. These worms are
not allowed to come to maturity, and then spin
cocoons like the common silkworm, but each

individual is disembowelled alive, and two short
thread-like substances are taken out of its body.
These threads are at first about three inches in
length, and are covered thickly with a glutinous
fatty substance. When dipped in a solution of
some kind—apparently vinegar—this fatty matter
comes readily off, and the threads are drawn out to
their full length. Those which I measured on
the spot were fully five feet long. I believe they
are largely used in the manufacture of fishing-
lines, for which there is a considerable demand in
Japan. The countrymen engaged in collecting
them informed me they were also woven into
articles of clothing, but if such be the case, which
I think doubtful, such cloth must be very expensive.

   The land-shells of Japan are of some interest
to the conchologist, but the species are few in
number, and not remarkable for their beauty.
Mr. Cuming informs me that a *Helix*, with a re-
versed mouth, which I have brought home, is
H. quæsito (Deshayes), another is *Helix japonica*
(Pfeiffer), and a third, of which there are three
varieties, is a new species, and undescribed. It is
rather remarkable that a country like Japan,
which abounds in woods, gardens, and waste lands,
should have so few land-shells; such, however, is
the case, as, had they been more plentiful, I think
Tunga and myself must have met with them in our
rambles.

   During the last days of June and the first of

July a small temple, adjoining that in which I was located was daily crowded with natives who came to worship at its shrines. The wheat and barley had been gathered in, the rice was planted, and I suppose the object of the festival was to praise Buddha for an abundant harvest, and to petition for a continuance of fine weather for the young paddy. Be this as it may, the people assembled in considerable numbers, for several days in succession, to take part in the worship. Here, as in other countries, the female portion of the community seemed to be the most numerous and the most devout, for certainly nine-tenths of this congregation were women. Many had their teeth blackened and their eyebrows pulled out, showing they were married, while others were still rejoicing in white teeth and single blessedness. Jolly-looking farmers' wives with their ruddy-cheeked daughters were there, mingling with the courtesans of the tea-houses in gay dresses and painted faces. In China the priests perform the public services in the Buddhist temples, and, if any of the people should chance to be present, they are there as spectators only. Here, however, the case was entirely different. Each worshipper was furnished with a cushion or hassock on which to kneel during his or, I should rather say, her devotions. A bit of round sounding brass was laid upon the cushion, and was struck by the devotee at certain times as the service went on. The priests led off, and then the whole congregation joined, striking their brass

cymbals, and singing "Nam, nam, nam," and some
such unmeaning sounds, with their voices—unmeaning to me at least, for I did not understand them.
The service lasted, each day, for about an hour, including an interval when the worshippers refreshed
themselves with sundry copious draughts of saki.

On the 2nd of July, having heard the tinkling
and "nam, nam, nam" going on for some time, I
walked into the court in front of the little temple,
in order to see something of the ceremonies.
After remaining a few minutes I returned to my
own quarters, and was soon followed by the whole
congregation, who came, I suppose, to return my
visit. Some amongst them were old men who
could scarcely walk, but the greater part were
women and children. I received them politely,
and allowed them to examine my clothes, books,
and specimens of natural history. One lady took
hold of my wristband, another handled the neck
of my shirt, and a third examined the texture of
my trousers. But the butterflies, beetles, and
shells were to them most astonishing and incom-
prehensible. "Where could I have found such a
number of these things?"—many of which they
had never seen before. "What was I going to
do with them? Was I going to eat them?"
Those who were wiser than the rest informed the
others that I was collecting these things to make
medicine! And then some stated that I had been
over all the country gathering these objects; that
I had been paying money for them—a statement

which made some of them shake their wise heads, and evidently conclude that something was wrong with my "upper story." As all this was going on, the usual questions were put concerning my country, my age, and whether I was single or married. Many a goodhumoured joke was, no doubt, passed round amongst them at my expense; but as my knowledge of the language was very limited, it amused them without doing me any harm. Then the good ladies wanted my opinion regarding themselves, and one after another was laughingly brought forward—married and single without distinction—and proposed as a helpmate. I took all this in good part, and eventually my visitors were reminded it was time to go back to their devotions. Then came a long series of " Hé hés " and polite bowings, with many expressions of thanks, and I was left alone in my temple.

Girls meeting—an example of Japanese manners.

After leaving me, the congregation returned to the little temple in which they had been worshipping; and the singing, with the tinkling of bells and cymbals, went on as before. All at once the sounds ceased, and I concluded that the services of the day were over. In this, however, I was mistaken; for shortly afterwards I heard sounds of merriment, very different from those devotional ones which had preceded them. I was therefore induced to visit the congregation a second time, in order to satisfy my curiosity. When I reached the court in front of the temple a curious scene presented itself to my eyes. There was the same congregation in the same room in which they had been so devout a short time before, now engaged drinking saki, and already—judging from the loud laugh which was going round, and the boisterous merriment—somewhat under its influence. When I was perceived in front of the door the intelligence was quickly passed round the room, and I was received by the assembly with a scream of delight. The hospitality of these people, in so far as saki was concerned, was boundless; and many invitations were given me to join the various groups, and to pledge them in cups of the favourite national stimulant. As saki, however, is not a favourite of mine, I respectfully refused their offers, with many thanks, and considered that the most prudent course for me to pursue, under the circumstances, would be to beat a retreat. But if I had any fears that this little carousal would end unpleasantly, these fears were perfectly groundless. At an appointed time the priests appeared in their robes of office, the saki which remained unconsumed was put away, the countenances of the congregation changed from gay to grave—some of them, it is true, were a little more ruddy than before—and the religious services again commenced. The officiating priest led off, and was followed by his little congregation; and the " Nam-nam-nam-ing," and tinkling of bells and cymbals, were kept up for about another hour. At the end of this time the people left the temple, and returned quietly to their homes.

CHAPTER XIV.

A FEW miles south from Yokuhama there is a pretty
town named Kanasawa, and a little farther on is
Kamakura, said to be the ancient capital of Japan.
I had frequently heard of the beauty of these
places, and more particularly of the scenery by
which they were surrounded; and I therefore determined to visit them, and set out for this purpose
on the 4th of July. On this occasion I was accompanied by Dr. Dickson from China, and Messrs.
Ross and Hope, merchants in Yokuhama. The
first part of our road led us up through a beautiful
valley, with richly-wooded hills dipping into it on
either side, and giving it a pleasing and irregular
outline. On the edges of this valley there were
many cottages and farm-houses, and now and then
we passed pretty glens which led up amongst the

background of hills. Our road gradually ascended
to a higher elevation; and when the highest point
on the top of the hills was gained, we obtained a
glorious view of scenery which reminded me of
some of the prettiest spots in the Himalayas. We
then continued our way along the ridge of the
mountains, and looked down to the right and left
upon valleys, glens, and round hills, all covered
with the most luxuriant vegetation. A very
beautiful new lily (*Lilium auratum*) was met with
on the hill-sides in full bloom, and its roots were
dug up and added to my collections. Far away to
the eastward the sea lay spread out before us,
studded with islands, and dotted here and there
with the white sails of junks and fishing-boats.
After we had travelled along the mountain-ridge
for some distance, the road began gradually to lead
down hill, and about six o'clock in the evening we
reached the village of Kanasawa, which lies close
upon the sea-shore.

Having engaged rooms at one of the principal
inns of the .place, we strolled out to look at the
town. Kanasawa is a small place with a single
street about half a mile in length, in which there
are several inns and tea-houses. This spot is remarkable and celebrated amongst the Japanese for
its fine scenery. The sea comes in towards it
between some small islands, and presents the
appearance of a landlocked lake. Little hills,
crowned with temples and trees, are studded
about, from which charming views of sea and land

scenery can be obtained. We ascended one of these, and were kindly received by the priests attached to the temple. Some fine fresh fruit of the loquat, and sundry cups of very good tea, were presented to us, and a visitors' book was brought in which to insert our names. This book contained the names of many distinguished Japanese who had honoured the place with a visit; and numerous sketches and scraps of poetry, composed upon the spot, recorded the beauties of the situation and the fine views which it commanded. The book was examined with much interest by the members of our little party, and Dr. Dickson proposed to buy it, offering the munificent sum of fourpence halfpenny as an inducement to the priest to part with it. The Japanese are certainly a curious people; they will sell anything for money. The priest took the *tempos*, and Dr. Dickson carried off the visitors' book with its valuable autographs, clever sketches, and immortal poetry. After visiting some other places of interest, we returned to our inn, having been everywhere received with the greatest politeness by the people.

We occupied a suite of rooms upstairs. They communicated with each other by sliding doors made of paper pasted over a wooden frame; these doors could be taken out, and the whole flat converted into one room when required. The room in which we dined looked out upon the sea, and the high road of the town was under our windows. As the weather was exceedingly warm, the windows were

out, and we were fully exposed to the sea-breeze
and to a crowd of natives of both sexes and of all
ages who crowded the road in front of the inn.
After dinner we sat on a ledge at the window, and
amused ourselves with the crowd below. Strange
questions were put to us on many subjects; and as
the Japanese, as a people, have not our ideas of
morality, many of their questions and remarks
were not such as I can repeat here. Our landlord,
who was probably better acquainted with our
manners and customs than the crowd under his
windows, several times expostulated with them in
an angry tone, but produced no effect. Once or
twice a bucket of water was added to his argu-
ments; but although this induced them to scamper
away for an instant, they soon came back again.
As the night wore on the crowd gradually dispersed, and, intending to be up early next morning,
we followed their example and retired to rest.

The floors of our bedrooms were covered with
clean matting, and a padded counterpane was laid
in the middle of each room, with a wooden pillow
for the head to rest upon. Ample mosquito cur-
tains, nearly as large as the room itself, reached
from the ceiling to the floor.

Next morning at daylight we were up, and, in
order to refresh ourselves, we had a plunge in the
bay. As we intended to proceed immediately after
breakfast across the hills to the ancient town of
Kamakura, I employed the time before our meal
was ready in visiting several places of interest in

the vicinity in search of new plants. In the grounds of a native prince here I observed some trees of *Podocarpus macrophyllus* of great size, some fine examples of *Pinus massoniana*, and a new Arborvitæ (*Thuja falcata*).

The town of Kamakura was distant from Kanasawa some five miles. We sent our horses onward by the lower route, and chose the hill-road ourselves, in order to get a better view of the surrounding country. After leaving the valley this road led us gradually upwards, and then along a ridge of hills somewhat like those we had noticed the day before on the journey from Yokuhama. When we had attained a considerable elevation, the views on all sides were exceedingly fine and extensive. On our right hand and on our left we looked down upon and over a perfect sea of hills, of all sizes and of every conceivable form, covered, from their summits to the valleys below, with trees and brushwood. Many of these forests had been planted and were now yielding valuable timber, but by far the greatest portion of them were in a state of nature, very beautiful to look upon no doubt, but covered with wild trees and dense brushwood of little value. Far away down in the valleys we observed patches of culti-vated land, which, taken in connection with our mountain-road and the forests which had been planted, were the only marks of the country being inhabited by man. We did not meet one single human being during this part of our journey.

Q

And yet the climate is one of the finest in the
world ; and the soil fertile and capable of growing
excellent timber, and of yielding abundant crops
of grain.

How can this state of things be accounted for, if
we believe the statements of Thunberg, Kæmpfer,
Siebold, and other travellers, that the country is
densely populated?   But the travellers .with the
Dutch embassies from Nagasaki to Yedo rarely left
the imperial highway on their route, and must
have received their impressions from what they
observed as they went along it, and from the
crowded state of the great towns through which
they passed.   Any one, even now, whose experience
of Japan was confined to the Tokaido, would come
to the same conclusion ; but let him leave the
great highway and penetrate into the country by
its common roads, and then some doubts would
probably come across his mind on the subject.
And if he happens to know anything about agriculture or woodlands, and sees, on every hand,
thousands of goodly acres, capable of producing
crops of corn or valuable timber, lying waste or
only covered with brushwood of little value, he
will at least affirm that there are in that country
the means of supplying all the necessaries of life
to a population far greater than that which exists
in Japan at the present day.

When we reached the highest land on our
journey, we left the road and mounted the top of
an adjoining hill, from which may be obtained one

of the finest views in .Japan. On the south was the sea, with the beautiful little island of Ino-sima, famous in Japanese history; to the west was a chain of mountains, with Fusi-yama towering high above them all; while, far away in the east, the capital itself may be seen on a clear day. Down in the valley below us we could discern the roofs of the houses and temples of Kamakura, the ancient capital of the country, to which we were bound.

Having rested for a while on this beautiful spot, and enjoyed the view which lay spread out before us, we set out again on our journey. The road now led down the mountain-side, a portion of the way in a ravine, down which a clear stream was running, shaded with lofty trees. At length we reached Kamakura, which presents, at the present day, no appearance of having once been a capital town. It is simply a country village, with a few mean shops and some good inns or tea-houses. But its temples, and the scenery in the neighbourhood, will always render it a place of great attraction to foreign visitors, as it has been for ages to the Japanese. It is situated at the head of a valley, with hills on each side and behind, and open in front to the sea. A fine avenue of pine-trees extends from the temples down to the beach. Handsome broad roads intersect each other and this avenue at right angles, and these are also fringed on each side with clumps and rows of trees. *Cryptomeria japonica, Pinus massoniana,* and.

Salisburia adiantifolia, are the trees generally used for these avenues.

As we entered the village a most extraordinary circumstance occurred, which took us entirely by surprise, until we remembered that we were in Japan. A woman rushed out of a shop and placed herself in the middle of the road, holding a tobacco-pipe in one hand, and a box containing some tobacco and sundry other articles in the other. When I first saw her my impression was, that she either meant to welcome us by the offer of her pipe, or that she wished to dispose of the wares in her box. But such was not her intention. To our alarm and surprise, she threw off the only garment she wore and assumed the attitude of a naked statue, at the same time putting her pipe into her mouth and puffing out clouds of tobacco-smoke. The people came running towards us from every part of the village, and were evidently accustomed to such exhibitions on the part of the individual before us. When we recovered from our surprise we came to the conclusion that the poor creature was insane, which we afterwards found to be the case.

As the day was cloudless, with the thermometer standing somewhere about 100° in the shade, we were glad to take up our quarters in a tea-house. We were welcomed by mine host and some pretty maidens, and conducted up stairs to a suite of rooms with open windows looking out upon the village. While we were sitting fanning ourselves and enjoying the shade, after the fierce heat to which we had been exposed for some hours, crowds of people assembled on the road in front of the inn, all anxious to get a glimpse of their foreign visitors.   All at once there seemed some commotion amongst them, and they rushed away to look at some one who was coming towards our inn by a cross road not visible from the rooms we occupied.   At first we thought this excitement was caused by a fresh arrival of foreigners from Kanagawa, who had promised to come after us and join our party.   Presently, however, our mad friend came in sight, carrying in her arms a bundle of branches and some sticks of incense, as if she contemplated paying a visit to the temples or to the tombs.   Poor thing! she seemed to be good-humoured and harmless in her insanity; and even the little children, although they ran away when she approached them, did not seem much afraid of her.   She soon returned from the temples, and then employed herself in fetching water and pulling grass and weeds for our horses, which were tied up on the roadside in front of the inn. While engaged in this operation she seemed to fancy that the horses were fit objects of adoration; and as she fed each animal with grass, or gave it water, she closed her hands in an attitude of devotion, and muttered to it some Buddhist form of prayer.

When we had rested a short time in the inn we rode out to pay a visit to a large bronze statue which is considered one of the lions of the district.

We found this situated in a pretty garden about two miles from Kamakura. When we reached the entrance to the grounds we were politely requested to dismount, as no one was allowed to ride into the sacred enclosure. We entered the garden and proceeded up a paved walk lined on each side with fine specimens of trees and shrubs, many of which were trained and clipped into curious forms. At the head of the garden stood, or rather sat, the enormous bronze image we were seeking. It was not less than thirty feet in diameter at the base, and fully forty feet in height. The proportions of the figure were admirable. At first sight we were astonished at the size of the casting, but upon a closer examination we found that the huge colossus had been cast in several parts, and then joined together or built up. On the opposite page is a native sketch, bought from the priest, which gives a good idea of the image.

An old priest who lived in a small temple adjoining told us that this figure had been placed there six hundred years ago; and no doubt, had we been better acquainted with the language of the country, we might have learned some curious particulars of its history. A door at one of the sides led into the interior. This was opened by the priest, and we were invited to enter along with him. We found the inside lighted by windows placed at the back; and there were many ornaments—such as small gilded images representing Buddhist deities, and strips of paper—hanging on

the walls.   Boxes were placed here for the offerings of the devotees who visit the shrine.   Indeed
these are found in nearly all the temples of Japan,
just as they are met with in the churches of Christian countries.   Altogether, the place, the scenery,
and the statue, well rewarded us for our visit; and
our only regret on coming away was that we could
learn so little of the origin and history of this remarkable place.

Bronze image.

This part of the country abounds in temples, and
in that respect was more fitted for the site of the

capital of a Spiritual Emperor than for that of a temporal one; and this is what it very likely was in the early days of Japanese history, when the *Mikados*, or Spiritual Emperors, were the sole rulers of the country. We visited another temple in the course of the morning, not far from the bronze statue, and were shown some large tinselly-looking images which were evidently thought wonderful things by the country people. One of the most remarkable was kept in a dark place, which had to be lighted up when it was visited— another mode of getting contributions from the devout. Lithographs of this goddess were also on sale in the temple.

In Japan, as in China, noisy crowds followed us into the sacred buildings, and were anything but reverential in their demeanour. With all their noise they were good-humoured enough, and not at all unfriendly in their manner towards us. Other temples were pointed out in various directions, which we were pressed to visit; but as the day was oppressively hot, and as we had the dread of fever before our eyes, we rode back to our inn at Kamakura, determined to keep indoors until the sun's rays were less powerful.

We had ordered luncheon before we set out, and on our return we found a most substantial meal awaiting us. It consisted of excellent fish fresh from the sea, cooked in the soy of the country, and most delicious it was; fine white rice; and an omelette, rather too sweet perhaps, but very palat-

able. This we washed down with delicious cold
water from the well of the inn, mixed with a little
brandy which we had brought with us, and which
we preferred to the saki of the country. No knives
or forks, or rude things of that kind, seen at the
tables of Western barbarians, were known at our
inn at Kamakura. Chopsticks, those useful and
civilized implements which feed more than four
hundred millions of the human race, were the only
articles used during our repast. More than one of
my companions complained of the awkwardness of
these instruments; but as I had been accustomed
to their use in China, I took kindly to them in
Japan. During the time of our meal we were
waited upon by the ladies of the inn. Truth compels me to state that they were not particularly
handsome, but nevertheless they were most kind
and obliging, and very active in anticipating all
our wants.

Fatigued with the exertions of the morning, we
laid ourselves down on the clean white mats which
covered the floors of our apartments, and were soon
in the enjoyment of a comfortable siesta. I was
the first to awake, and on looking into the room
adjoining mine a curious and amusing scene presented itself. One of my companions was lying
sound asleep, while the poor maniac whose acquaintance we had made in the morning was
kneeling by his side, fanning his head, and every
now and then pausing in this operation to clasp
her hands together and mutter some words of

prayer, either to him or for him, as she had done to the horses in the morning. The most amusing part of the performance was to see our friend lying perfectly unconscious of the honours that were being paid to him. The poor woman had also brought up four cups of tea and a handful of dry rice, which she laid upon the ground as an offering to our party. As soon as she saw us awake and noticing her movements, she rose quietly and walked out of the room without paying the slightest attention to any of us.

When the day had become a little cooler we left the shelter of our inn and went to pay a visit to the temples for which Kamakura is celebrated all over the empire of Japan. They are placed at the head of the valley before-mentioned, and are approached by an avenue terminating in a broad flight of stone steps in front of the temples. They are eight in number, and are only opened, we were told, once or twice a year. We did not observe any priests about them, nor any signs of Buddhist worship; and therefore they probably belonged to the Sintoo sect, the ancient religion of Japan. Their roofs are remarkable in form, and one of them has a tower somewhat like an Indian minaret. Although we could not enter these temples, we could look through the bars of their doors and see their contents. Many of them contained wooden images of different kinds, some of which were supposed to cure certain diseases, and were worshipped and prayed to by the afflicted. One in particular was pointed out which could cure ophthalmia; and we were gravely assured by our guide that any one afflicted with sore eyes, which are very common in Japan, as well as in China, had only to look upon this image and be healed.

Among the other wonders of the place was a sacred stone, curiously formed by nature, and apparently slightly assisted by art. This stone had the remarkable property, we were told, of rendering barren women fruitful. Ladies came from afar to worship it, and at the same time to turn their faces towards the holy mountain, which is said to be one of the conditions to ensure a successful issue. A box is duly provided for the reception of offerings, which shows that there is some one who is prepared to profit by the superstitions of his countrywomen. We are surprised and we pity the poor Japanese for their superstitious delusions, and yet, if one of them were to write an account of his travels amongst ourselves, could he not tell his countrymen that in enlightened England, in the nineteenth century, a class of persons gain a livelihood by telling the fortunes of our servant-girls, and sometimes of their mistresses, and promising them rich husbands, horses and carriages, and lots of romping children? With these things in our minds we should not be too hard on the superstitions of the good ladies who visit the sacred stone at Kamakura.

The afternoon was now getting cool, for the sun was sinking rapidly behind the western hills. We therefore returned to our inn, paid our bill, mounted our horses, and took the lower road for Kanasawa, the place where we had lodged the night before. As we were leaving Kamakura I rode up to the foot of a hill on our left to see the tomb of Yuri-tomo, a celebrated general, the founder of the race of Japanese Temporal Emperors, and a man who is remembered among the people as William Wallace or Robert Bruce is in Scotland.

The name of Yuritomo is to be found in every book which professes to give a history of Japan. Before his day the country had only one sovereign, the Mikado, or Spiritual Emperor, who was believed to be descended from the gods. A personage named Zin-mu-ten-woo is said to have been the first Mikado. Having conquered the island of Nipon, he built a *dairi* or temple-palace, and dedicated it to the Sun-goddess. Historians inform us that this event took place about the year 660 B.C., and it is not unlikely that Kamakura was the place chosen for the site of this temple. For many centuries, the *Mikados*, claiming to rule by divine right and inheritance, were indeed despotic sovereigns; and even after they had ceased to head their own armies, and had intrusted the dangerous military command to sons and kinsmen, their power long remained undisputed and uncontrolled. It was perhaps first and gradually weakened by a habit into which the *Mikados* fell, of abdicating at so early an age that they transferred the sovereignty to their sons while yet children. The consequent evils of a minority the retired sovereign frequently strove to remedy by governing for his young successor.

In the course of time a *Mikado* who had married the daughter of a powerful prince abdicated in favour of his son, then about three years of age; but in this instance the *Mikado* who had abdicated was not allowed to assume the regency during the minority of his child. The ambitious and powerful grandfather of the young *Mikado* seized the government and placed the abdicated sovereign in confinement. Then ensued a civil war, in which Yuritomo first appears as the champion of the imprisoned ex-Mikado against his usurping father-in-law. Yuritomo triumphed, released the imprisoned father, and placed the regency in his hands; but the *Fowo*, as he was called, held it only nominally, leaving the real power in the hands of Yuritomo, whom he created *Sio-i-dai-Tycoon*, or generalissimo fighting against the barbarians. The ex-Mikado died, and, as lieutenant or deputy of the sovereign, Yuritomo virtually governed the empire for twenty years. His power gradually acquired solidity and stability, and when he died he was succeeded in his title, dignity, and authority by his son.*

From the days of Yuritomo, about A.D. 1185, to the present time, the empire of Japan has had two sovereigns—a *Mikado*, or Spiritual Emperor,

---

* 'Manners and Customs of the Japanese.' London, Murray, 1852.

whose residence is Miaco, and a *Tycoon*, or Temporal Emperor, residing at Yedo. Curious stories are told about the manners and customs of the Spiritual Emperor at Miaco. It is said that he is never allowed to breathe the common air, nor are his feet allowed to touch the ground; he cannot wear the same garment twice, nor eat a second time from the same dish. The dishes used by him are broken after each meal, for should any other person attempt to dine from them he would infallibly perish by an inflammation of the throat; nor could any one wearing his cast-off garments, without his permission, escape a similar punishment. He was obliged in ancient times, we are told, to seat himself every morning on his throne, with the crown on his head, and there hold himself immovable for several hours like a statue. If he happened to move ever so little, or even to turn his eyes, war, famine, fire, or pestilence was expected soon to afflict the unhappy province towards which he had squinted; but as the country was thus kept in a state of perpetual agitation, the happy alternative was finally hit upon of placing the crown upon the throne without requiring the head of the *Mikado* in it, by which it was rendered more steady, and consequently did less mischief!

Up to the end of the sixteenth century the Tycoons seem to have been active and efficient rulers, possessing much independent power and influence, although their appointment appears to have been made and confirmed by the Mikado.

From that time to the present, though they may
have become more independent of the Spiritual
Sovereign, they have degenerated into the secluded puppets of a council of state, and are
seldom seen outside of the palace-gates.

A romantic story in Yuritomo's career has been
handed down by historians. In the course of the
civil war the rebel Prince Feki fell in battle, and
his General, named Kakekigo, was taken prisoner.
This General's renown was great in Japan, and
Yuritomo strove earnestly to gain the friendship
and confidence of his captive. He loaded him
with kindness, and finally offered him his liberty.
But all was in vain. " I can love none but my
slain master," said Kakekigo ; " I owe you a debt
of gratitude, but you have caused Prince Feki's
death, and never can I look upon you without
wishing to kill you. My best way to avoid such
ingratitude, and to reconcile my conflicting duties,
is never to see you more, and thus do I insure it."
As he spoke he tore out his eyes, and presented
them to Yuritomo on a salver. The Prince, struck
with admiration, released him ; and Kakekigo
withdrew into retirement, and founded the second
order of the blind.

Yuritomo's tomb is placed near the base of a hill
in a charming situation. Behind it and on each
side were trees and brushwood, while in front were
green rice-fields extending down to the sea-beach,
the little town of Kamakura, with its temples and
avenues, lying between. It was approached by a

flight of steps, and consisted of a small plain stone tower surrounded by a dwarf wall. The whole edifice was hoary with age, having probably been erected upwards of six hundred years ago. And this was the resting-place of a General of great renown, the first of the race of Tycoons, and a man whose memory is still cherished by the natives of Nipon.

Our lowland road back to Kanasawa was a very pleasant one, leading us at one time along the banks of a clear stream, and at another through some natural gap or deep cutting in the hills. We spent a second night in "our inn," and on the following day returned to Kanagawa.

CHAPTER XV.

ON our arrival at Kanagawa we were startled by the intelligence that H. B. M. Legation at Yedo had been attacked the night before by a band of loönins,* and that the lives of Her Majesty's Minister and his staff of assistants had been in the greatest danger. From the assassinations which had taken place on several occasions, both at Yedo and at Yokuhama, since these places had become the residences of foreigners, human life was generally regarded as being somewhat insecure. And what made matters worse was the fact that no one could give any satisfactory reason for these murders. True, it was reported that Mr. Alcock's servant, who was one of the first victims, had given offence by his arrogance and overbearing manner; the murder of two Russians was attributed to a Japanese official, who, with his family, was degraded

---

* Outlaws, or disgraced retainers.

R

at the instance of Count Mouravieff, in consequence
of some insult offered to the Russians in the
streets of Yedo; and the assassination of the
American Secretary of Legation was said to have
been committed by a Daimio's retainer, struck by
him in the street, who, on returning to his master's,
was asked how he dared to do so after receiving
a blow which was still unavenged.* Offence may
have been given in this way, and the Japanese,
who are a proud and revengeful people, would
most certainly have their revenge; but none of
the foreign residents could actually affirm that
insults of this kind were the causes of the melan-
choly events that followed.

But, taking for granted that those who had
fallen victims to revenge had done something to
merit their punishment, it does not follow that the
innocent in Japan may always consider themselves
perfectly safe. The Japanese assassin is not particular as to his victim. If he can secure the real
offender, good and well; if not, a substitute must
be had; if an Englishman give offence and cannot
be found, one of his countrymen must suffer in
his stead. This being the state of affairs, it is
plain that the innocent may, at any time, suffer
for the imprudence or follies of his countrymen, or,
indeed, of any foreigner, without respect to na-
tionality; for the avenger is not particular even
on that point.

* Sir James Hope's Report to the Lords Commissioners of the
Admiralty.

Revenge is a powerful feeling in the breasts of the natives of Japan, more particularly amongst the higher classes and their numerous bands of two-sworded retainers. These gentry are always ready to resent an insult or injury, real or supposed; and as each man carries about his person two swords whose edges are extremely sharp, he has always the means of giving instant effect to his passion. Nor does this desire for revenge end with the life of the injured person. On the contrary, if he has not been able to accomplish it during his lifetime, he will leave it as an inheritance and obligation to his relations. In the autumn of 1860 an English merchant, who was returning from a shooting excursion, was seized on his way by the native police, and charged with having broken the laws of the country, no one being allowed to shoot within a certain distance of Yedo. In attempting to disarm him, a loaded gun went off, and lodged its contents in the arm of one of the officials. The wound was a dangerous one, and the foreign doctors of the place were of opinion that, unless amputation was resorted to, the man would, in all probability, lose his life. This advice, for some reason, was not listened to; but, luckily, owing to a good constitution, or perhaps to diet, the dreaded mortification did not take place, and the man recovered. It was stated to us at the time of this occurrence that the wounded man had taken an oath that, should he recover, he would not rest until he had the merchant's life, and that, should he die, his brothers would take care that he was avenged. The gentleman in question was tried at the British Consulate and sentenced to deportation; and to this sentence he probably owed his life, which, after what had happened, was not safe for an hour in Japan. During my residence in Japan there were several other instances in which foreigners were obliged to take a hasty leave of the country in order to save their lives.

But although we knew the Japanese to be proud and revengeful, and not very particular as to the identity of their foes provided they were foreigners, and although the community had to deplore the murder of several of its members, apparently innocent and unoffending men, yet nothing had taken place recently to give us any uneasiness. The Japanese, we fancied, were getting accustomed or resigned to the presence of foreigners amongst them; or our rough manners—at times somewhat frolicsome and boisterous—were seen to be harmless, and not intended to hurt or annoy them. But when the news of the murderous attack on H. B. M. Legation reached us, the scales fell at once from our eyes, and we saw we had been sitting in fancied security on the top of a mine which was liable to an explosion at any moment.

Various and contradictory accounts of the attack reached us at Kanagawa. As an authentic accotnt has however been sent home by Mr. Alcock to Earl Russell and presented to both Houses of

Parliament, I cannot do better than give an ex-
tract from it to the reader in Mr. Alcock's own
words :—

"Yedo, July 6, 1861.—Before another night
closes in, with its contingencies, which may well
prevent my addressing your Lordship again, I am
anxious to submit a simple statement of the events
which have marked the last; for, whether I sur-
vive or not, it is essential that Her Majesty's
Government should be well and duly informed
of all that has taken place. We have escaped a
massacre, but, seemingly, by the merest chance.

" I had only returned from Kanagawa four-and-
twenty hours, bringing Mr. Morrison and another
gentleman with me, on a visit to Yedo—the Legation being further augmented by Mr. Oliphant
and Mr. Russell—when the long-threatened on-
slaught roused us all from our beds a little before
midnight. Frequently as I had been warned that
such a deed was actually in contemplation, I confess I felt incredulous when Mr. Robertson, who,
previous to his retiring to rest, always takes the
duty of going through the premises, came to tell
me that there was a conflict going on outside,
and that men were forcing their way through the
gates. I had barely time to seize my revolver
and advance a few steps, when I heard blows and
cries, and the report of a pistol in the passage
which runs at the end of my apartment. The next
moment both Mr. Oliphant and Mr. Morrison
staggered forward, exclaiming that they were

wounded, and I saw the blood flowing profusely
from the former, whose left arm was disabled.
Mr. Russell, Mr. Robertson, and Mr. Lowder followed; the rest of the Legation were missing. Uncertain how many our assailants were, or from how
many quarters the attack might be effected (since
a Japanese house is open on all sides, and every
partition consists entirely of doors and windows
only, or sliding-panels offering no resistance), a
brief interval of intense anxiety followed, while I
stood in momentary expectation of seeing men
pour in from the passage in pursuit. After a
short lull, some of the band were heard outside the
apartment adjoining my bedroom breaking their
way through some glazed doors. Exposed to attack
from every side, with no sign of a yakoneen or
guard, several minutes were thus passed, two of
our number disabled, and the rest of us standing
at bay with such arms as had been hastily seized.
Our enemies had evidently mistaken their way,
and the increased distance of the shouts and yells
gave reason to hope they had at last been come up
with by the yakoneens, and had sought their safety
by leaving the house. To escape from a state of
intolerable suspense I went towards the principal
entrance for a moment, and to Mr. Macdonald's
room, to ascertain, if possible, what had become of
him. While on my way we thought they had
returned in force, seeing at the further end of the
passage a number of armed men advancing, who
would not answer our challenge. A shot was

fired by Mr. Lowder, and they disappeared. Still
the noise and clamour and conflict continued outside; and it seemed very long indeed before we
saw any of those (to the number of some 150)
Tycoon's and Daimio's men who had been held to
afford us such ample protection! At last, two or
three of the officers permanently on service appeared to say that they hoped the house was clear,
but begging us to keep together at one end while
they made further search.

"I had now a moment of respite to turn to
Messrs. Oliphant and Morrison and dress their
wounds, though amidst alarms of renewed attack,
which, I may add, recurred at frequent intervals
until daybreak. . . . Most providentially the
party, which seems to have been destined to penetrate the interior of the house and finish the work
there, mistook their way to the part occupied by
myself from the beginning, and where all who
remained after the first alarm were speedily collected, as the most defensible position. Had they
entered the grounds from that side (and nothing
was easier), steps and a path led directly to my
bedroom, and I should have most likely had no
time to seize a weapon, for there was nothing to
obstruct their entrance."

Fortunately for the little band in the Legation,
the yakoneen guard, when it arrived, fought
bravely, and the assailants were driven out of the
premises. It would seem, therefore, that, owing
to this on the one hand, and to the ignorance of

the locality on the part of the loönins on the other, a general massacre was happily prevented.

" The next morning the Legation looked as if it had been sacked after a serious conflict. Screens and mats were all spotted with blood, the former thrown down, broken, and torn; furniture and bedding all hacked, books even cut through by their sabres, and the marks of fury and violence everywhere. That our guards fought, there is no doubt whatever; but it is equally clear that they were, as I always asserted, utterly ineffective against a surprise; and, in truth, they left the Legation, notwithstanding their great superiority in numbers, at least ten minutes to its own resources, during which time the loönins were in possession trying to discover the inmates."

It does not appear that the loss of life was very great in this hand-to-hand encounter between the yakoneens and loönins, a circumstance which may possibly be accounted for by the attack taking place during the night. Of the Tycoon's and Daimio's men, two were killed and ten wounded; three of the loönins were nearly hacked to pieces, two wounded men were taken prisoners, and it was rumoured that two more committed the "harikari" next morning to avoid being arrested. The whole band of the attacking loönins was afterwards ascertained to have been fourteen in number.

" After such a night," writes Mr. Alcock, " comes a Governor of Foreign Affairs, deputed

from the Ministers, gravely to felicitate me on my
escape and return to Yedo, praying me to accept
a basket of ducks and a jar of sugar in token of
amity! Your Lordship will, I am sure, not blame
me, that I desired the messenger to take his presents back with him, and tell his principal I
desired justice and redress, not ducks or sugar, at
the hands of his Government."

When the news of this attempted assassination
reached us at Kanagawa and Yokuhama, the sensation created, both amongst natives and foreigners, was very great. Who were the loönins, and
who or what had induced them to attempt the
commission of such a fearful crime? Mr. Alcock
and M. de Wit had just come overland from Osaca,
although the Government had begged them not
to do so, and warned them of the danger of such a
proceeding at the present time. Great offence
had been given, it was said, by their visit to one
of Prince Fizin's coal-mines, although the road to
it had been blocked up by a bamboo fence with a
guard of soldiers behind it. It was also rumoured
that a dispute for precedence had occurred on the
road with a Daimio, who happened to be met
travelling in a contrary direction, although it now
appears from Mr. Alcock's despatch that he had
given way to the great man, and for his politeness
had been almost pushed into the ditch! As these
reports were spread about, it was the opinion of
many that this overland journey, in some way or
other, had been the cause of the attack which had

just taken place. On the other hand, it was argued, and with some reason, that, had the Government or offended Prince been the authors or instigators of the crime, it might have been much more easily and effectually accomplished on the journey than in the British Legation at Yedo.

In connection with this question there was a document found on one of the band who was wounded and made prisoner, to which a considerable amount of importance is due. Four translations of this document were made; one being official, while the other three were obtained from private sources. In the official copy the writer says,— " He is a man of low degree, moved by the desire to do a great deed in honour of the sovereign—to expel the foreigner, as it is intolerable to stand by and see the sacred empire violated by the barbarians. To achieve honour for himself, as a devoted patriot, making the empire to sparkle in foreign regions by a great deed, while tranquillizing the Imperial mind, and benefiting the country by ridding it of the presence of the foreigner"—for these objects this worthy is willing to risk his life.

The translations furnished by private individuals are similar to the above; but one or two important things come out which would appear to have been suppressed in the official copy. Thus the writer does not say that he is " moved by the desire to do a great deed in honour of the sovereign," but " to follow out my master's will." In two of the

private translations he takes it for granted that, if
he can massacre the officers of the British Legation,
" *all foreigners will abandon Japan*," or, " the land
of the gods," and so procure him the favour of
millions of his countrymen.

This paper appears to have been considered a
genuine document by the Japanese authorities,
and not, as some supposed, put into the man's
pocket as a blind to mislead investigation as to
the instigators of the deed.   In one of their letters
to Mr. Alcock they say—" Although your Excellency suggested that the attack was not made
spontaneously on the part of the assailants, but
that there was a secret director of it; yet, as we
have always communicated to you, it was known
that, in the early period of the opening of the
ports, there were, among the persons of rank,
some who disapproved of the conclusion of the
treaties with foreign powers."   Then they go on
to state that, owing to the arrangements made
from time to time by the Government, this prejudice amongst the higher ranks has entirely disappeared—an assertion which, I fear, is not " founded
on fact"—and that " the occurrence is only ascrib-
able to the acts of persons of low standing, who,
from obstinate adhesion to the old custom of
excluding foreign powers, persist in their feelings
of partiality.   The alteration in their nature will
therefore be difficult, without allowing a long
lapse of months and years."   The Japanese
Ministers remind Mr. Alcock that they had pro-

posed to him in the beginning, when officers for
his protection were appointed, their wish that a
guard should be stationed, not only in the en-
virons of the Legation, but even in the interior.
"But your Excellency was altogether dissatisfied
with it; so we left it to your will: hence the
danger which has just happened." And thus
these worthies prove three things, apparently to
their own satisfaction—1st, that persons of high
rank were not the instigators of the deed; 2nd, that
it was the work of prejudiced enthusiasts of low
degree; and 3rd, that, had the English Minister
taken their advice, the thing would not have
happened.

Mr. Alcock, "after three weeks consumed in
anxious inquiries as to the quarter from whence
the blow had come and any future danger might
be looked for," believes he has at last got at the
real facts. In a despatch to Earl Russell he says—
" It has come to me from divers sources that the
Prince of Tsusima, hearing that a great chief of
the foreigners was at Nagasaki on his way to Yedo
overland, immediately despatched emissaries to
slay this chief on the road, and bring his head.
. . . But I think the more recent versions [of
the story] are also the more probable. These tell
me that the Prince only sent a single emissary to
follow me to Yedo, and there to find the fit instruments for his purpose (never far to seek, it seems),
and bring him my head, after the massacre of
every one about me. A plot to attack the Lega-

tions, the Consulates, or Yokuhama, together or successively, having long been a favourite plan among Mito's disbanded followers and other desperate characters, it required but a signal from any chief immediately to get together the men necessary for an attack; and so it was suddenly resolved upon and carried into execution at the instigation of the Prince's emissary."

The true version of this story, whatever it may be, will probably never be known to foreigners, but that this is something near it there can be little doubt. I firmly believe the real instigator of the crime was some feudal prince, who was still hostile to foreigners, or perhaps was not unwilling to embroil his own Government in a quarrel which he supposed would in some way advance his interests. A feudal system exists in Japan at the present day not unlike that of our own Scottish Highlands a hundred years ago; and any chief can easily excite the passions of his retainers, and engage them in the most desperate enterprises. These retainers are very much like the MacIvors in Sir Walter Scott's ' Waverley :'—

"The MacIvors, sir," says Alick Polwarth, Waverley's servant, "hae gotten it into their heads that ye hae affronted their young leddy, Miss Flora; and I hae heard mae than ane say they wadna tak muckle to make a black-cock o' ye; and ye ken weel eneugh there's mony o' them wadna mind a bawbee the weising a ball through the Prince himsell, an the Chief gae them the wink—or whether he did or no, if they thought it a thing that would please him when it was dune."

In a country like Japan, where every one acts as a spy upon his neighbour, it seems absurd to suppose that the Government was unable to find out the instigator of the attack on H. B. Majesty's Legation. Whether it durst denounce and punish was a very different matter, and extremely doubtful. Instead of being at once united and powerful, as it was at one time supposed to be, it resembles that of the Scottish kings in the feudal ages, when a combination of the powerful clans could always embarrass or overturn the Government. In addition to this, some of the Daimios would seem to derive their honours and offices direct from the Mikado, or Spiritual Emperor, and to be, to a certain extent, independent of the Tycoon. These, by way of fomenting troubles, ply the Mikado's court with disturbing rumours to the disadvantage of the rival but confessedly subordinate court at Yedo; and keep up the smouldering embers of a still possible explosion in the renewal of the old struggles between the true sovereign and the usurping General-in-chief, each backed by their partizans amongst the Daimios.* This, therefore, is another element of weakness in the Government of Japan. We may, therefore, easily suppose that the Government well knew the insti-

---

* Mr. Alcock's despatch to Earl Russell.

gator of the attack on H. M. Legation, and yet
was afraid or unable to punish him.

With these difficulties to contend with, particularly in their relations with foreign powers and
their subjects, the task of the Ministers of the
Tycoon is not exactly an agreeable one. I believe
they are sincere in their endeavours to protect
foreigners from the dangers which surround them
on every side, owing to the hatred and fanaticism
of unfriendly Daimios and their retainers. Doubtless their suggestion to Mr. Alcock to have a
guard inside the Legation was well meant; and
their plan of surrounding the new settlement·of
Yokuhama, and placing guards on the different
approaches—which some people found so much
fault with—was intended for our protection. They
knew the dangers to which we were exposed much
better than we did ourselves, and took their own
mode of averting them.

But in the present state of Japan, with the
feudal system in full operation, with jealousies
existing amongst the nobles, with bands of idle
retainers roaming about the streets, always armed
and not over-friendly to foreigners, the task of
protecting us is no easy one. Those Ministers
who agreed to make treaties with foreign nations
did not foresee the difficulties and dangers they
had to encounter in opening up a country which
had been sealed to the rest of the world for nearly
three hundred years. The future is now enveloped
in thick darkness; but it is much to be feared that

war and all its horrors may, at no distant day, be the penalty which this happy and peaceful land will have to pay for a reintroduction to the great family of nations.

While these pages have been going through the press the overland mail has brought us an account of another brutal murder, which was perpetrated on the Imperial highway, within a few miles of Yedo, on the 14th of September last. The murderers in this case were the retainers of the father of the Prince of Satsuma, and he is stated personally to have given the atrocious order. The following narrative of this sad transaction is taken from the 'Japan Herald:'—

" Yesterday afternoon, about two o'clock, a party left Yokuhama for a country ride, intending to cross to Kanagawa in a boat, and proceed thence on horseback to Kawasaki, where there is a fine temple. The party was composed of Mrs. Borradaile, the wife of a merchant at Hongkong; Mr. Marshall, her brother-in-law, a merchant of Yokuhama; Mr. W. Clarke, of the house of Messrs. A. Heard and Co.; and Mr. Richardson, who had just retired from business in China, and was on a visit to Japan, prior to his return to England. The community, at about half-past three o'clock in the afternoon, were startled by the return of Mrs. Borradaile on horseback at Mr. Gower's house, in a fearful state of agitation and disorder, her hands, face, and clothes bespattered with blood, her hat gone, and in a fainting state. She informed Mr.

Gower that she had just ridden for her life over seven miles, and had escaped she knew not how from a most dastardly and murderous attack upon herself and her companions; that about four miles beyond Kanagawa, nearly half-way to Kawasaki, they had met part of a Daimio's train, consisting of a large body of two-sworded men, coming from Yedo, some of whom signed to them to move aside, which they did. They drew up their horses at the side of the road, but in consequence of continued signs to go back they turned their horses to return towards Kanagawa. Without a word, or the slightest further notice, some of the retainers drew their swords and fiercely attacked them. A cut was aimed at Mrs. Borradaile's head, which she fortunately avoided by quickly stooping, though her hat was cut away by the blow. The three gentlemen were badly wounded, and being entirely surrounded, and the road being for some distance lined by their assailants, and being themselves entirely unarmed, they had no course but to dash through them, and to endeavour thus to effect their escape. Mrs. Borradaile saw Mr. Richardson fall from his horse, as she supposed, dead, and the others were so badly wounded that Mr. Marshall told her to ride for her life and try to save herself, as he did not think they could keep up. She scarcely remembers what happened afterwards, but she recollects riding into the sea, preferring the risk of drowning to falling into the hands of these bloodthirsty miscreants. Her horse, however, re-

gained the road, and continued his headlong course
towards Yokuhama, twice falling under her. By
some means she regained her seat, and arrived,
fainting and exhausted, at the house mentioned.
Fortunately Dr. Jenkins and Mr. Gower's brother
entered the house at the moment, the former of
whom administered the needful restoratives; and
Mr. Gower's brother, at her earnest entreaties,
went at once to Captain Vyse to endeavour to
obtain assistance towards the recovery of the persons of her companions, all three of whom she
imagined were lying dead in the road. The report
at once flew round the settlement; and having
learnt from others coming from Kanagawa that
two of the party were lying dangerously wounded
at the American Consulate at that place, while the
third had been left weltering in his blood on the
road, some three miles beyond, a large body of
residents of all nationalities collected, and immediately started by water and by land for Kanagawa.
Among the first was Dr. Jenkins, of Her Majesty's
Legation, who had immediately procured his instruments to render what aid might lie in his
power. On arriving at the American Consulate
they found Mr. Marshall severely wounded in the
side and back, while Mr. Clarke's left arm at the
shoulder was nearly cut through, the sword having
penetrated half through the bone. Their wounds,
however, had been immediately attended to and
dressed by Dr Hepburn, of the American mission.
From what was gathered from Mr. Clarke, the few

who had arrived determined at once to proceed in
search of Mr. Richardson, who had been seen by
him also to fall from his horse exhausted. As
they reached the main road they perceived Captain
Vyse, accompanied by several residents on horseback, together with the mounted guard, proceeding
on the same errand. . . . They continued on
the road till they arrived at the half-way house
between Kanagawa and Kawasaki, where they
were joined by the French mounted guard, who
had received orders from M. de Bellecourt, His
Imperial Majesty's Envoy, to act in concert with
Captain Vyse and those who accompanied him.
Here they made inquiries, but could get no information, the people affecting entire ignorance
upon the matter. A little boy, however, came
forward and volunteered to point out where the
body was lying; under his guidance they retraced
their steps about half a mile, and found the body
lying about ten yards off the road in a field, at the
side of a small cottage. It was covered over with
a couple of old mats, which, on being removed, re-
vealed a most ghastly and horrible spectacle. The
whole body was one mass of blood; one wound,
from which the bowels protruded, extended from
the abdomen to the back; another, on the left
shoulder, had severed all the bones into the chest;
there was a gaping spear-wound over the region
of the heart; the right wrist was completely divided, and the hand was hanging merely by a
strip of flesh; the back of the left hand was nearly

cut through; and on moving the head, the neck was found to be entirely cut through on the left side. The two first-mentioned wounds had evidently been the first he had received, and had been given while he was on horseback; the last four, or certainly two of them, had been inflicted after he had fallen from his horse, if not after death. A litter having been hastily constructed, the party returned to Kanagawa with the body."

Poor Mr. Richardson! I knew him well. He was a fine manly specimen of a young Englishman, of a mild and conciliatory disposition, and not at all likely to give any wanton offence to the Japanese people. Why then was the party attacked, and why this brutal murder? They were riding along the Imperial highway, within the limits of the settlement provided by treaty with the Government of the Tycoon, and were apparently infringing no law. Perhaps their great offence was this: they did not turn back or out of the way quick enough when they saw the *cortége* of the great man approaching. But although this was probably the pretext for attacking them, other causes, lying far deeper than this, were not wanting. These are an intense hatred to foreigners of Western nations, and a dread of those innovations and changes which are seen to be coming upon the country, and which will eventually destroy the feudal power.

It is becoming clearer every day that the Government of the Tycoon, with whom we have made

our treaties, is powerless to enforce those treaty
rights.   The feudal princes, with that curious personage the Mikado, or "Spiritual Emperor," are
stronger than the Government at Yedo; and until
a change takes place, resulting in the formation of
a powerful Government either at Miaco or Yedo,
and the destruction of the feudal system, there
will, I fear, be little security for the lives of our
countrymen in this part of the world.   How this is
to be accomplished, whether by civil war or by the
interference of foreign powers, is at present uncertain.   •

It would seem that a kind of revolution has
already taken place in Yedo.   The 'Japan Herald'
of October 25th says, " It was with no small surprise and dismay that the populace of Yedo learned
this week that henceforth the highest Daimios are
only to visit Yedo once in seven years, and then
only for a hundred days at a time; the second
class, once in three years only, and then for a
hundred days; while the third are to remain as at
present; but in their case, as in all the others,
their wives and families are no longer to stay in
Yedo as hostages, but are to return and to remain
in the provinces.   This change, it will be seen at a
glance, is a great diminution of the splendour of
the Tycoon's position.   That these highest Daimios,
seven years hence, will think of visiting Yedo for
a hundred days, no one will be simple enough to
believe, or that the second class will return is exceedingly doubtful.   Thus shorn of its jewels, the

crown of the Tycoonship becomes that of head of
the lower Daimios only. The seat of power will
probably, in no long time, be removed to Miaco."

A correspondent of the 'Times' (December 29)
gives another and different version of the same
story :—

" The Government of His Majesty the Tycoon of
Japan issued a notification at Yedo on the 19th of
October, to the effect that all Daimios or Princes
(excepting only those of the blood Royal, and also
those intrusted with the direction of affairs) should
respectively withdraw to their principalities.

" Henceforth the Government make it no longer
compulsory on them to reside at Yedo; they will
be called up once in three years to the metropolis
for the space of a hundred days.

" The Princes of Awarri, Mito, and Kishni,
being of the blood Royal, they will reside at Yedo
by turns of one year each, one remaining while
the other two are permitted to withdraw to their
ancestral territories.

" A further notification has been issued imposing
sumptuary restrictions, and recommending eco-
nomy, both in clothing and living, to the people
of Japan, high and low.

" A brother of the late Tycoon has been appointed Prince Regent since the demise of the late
Emperor up to the present crisis. He belonged to
the priesthood, but, owing to his high consan-
guinity, coupled with his great talents, he has
been summoned to this important post.

" N.B. It is impossible to assign the true motives for such sudden and radical changes, but it does appear as though the Government of the Tycoon was much stronger than has hitherto been conceded. It is thought possible that greater liberality to foreigners may follow these events, and that a variety of restrictions hitherto imposed upon native traders may be gradually removed."

If the latter version of this strange story prove to be the correct one, better days may be in store for Japan than we had dared to hope for. It is very difficult for foreigners to understand the proceedings of this remarkable people, and future events alone can enable us to comprehend those of the present or of the past.

CHAPTER XVI.

Climate of Japan — Dr. Hepburn's tables — Hottest and coldest months — Monsoons — Gales of wind — The rainy season — Earthquakes — Agriculture — Rank of the farmer — Rocks and soil — Cultivation of winter crops — Seed-time and harvest — Curious mode of harvesting — Summer crops on dry land — Mode of planting — Manures — Crops requiring irrigation — Cultivation of rice — Other crops — Animals few in number — Waste lands — Crops and seasons.

In the preceding chapters of this work I have noticed, from time to time, the operations of the Japanese husbandman. But the agriculture of Japan is a subject of considerable interest, and one which is worthy of more than a passing notice. In order that it may be better understood I shall first endeavour to give an account of the climate of the country.

The empire of Japan covers a space of about 15 degrees of latitude, and is placed between 30° and 45° north. It consists of four large islands, namely, Kiu-siu, Sikok, Nipon, and Yesso, and occupies a position on the eastern side of Asia not unlike that of the British Islands on the west of Europe, only considerably further to the south. Like China it is liable to extremes of temperature —to excessive heat in summer and great cold in

winter—such as are unknown on our side of the
world within the same degrees of latitude. But
the sea, surrounding and running between the
various islands, prevents the extremes of heat and
cold from being so great as they are on the mainland. Hence Japan is a much more healthy and
agreeable place of residence than China, at least
for the English and other inhabitants of the more
temperate parts of Europe.

My remarks on climate, and the tables of temperature, &c., which I shall bring forward, apply more
particularly to the island of Nipon, near the capital
and centre of the empire. At Nagasaki, on the
island of Kiu-siu, in the south, the winters are less
cold than at Yedo; while at Hakodadi, in Yesso,
they are longer and more severe. The Russian
traveller Golownin tells us that at Hakodadi the
first snow fell about the middle of October, but soon
melted; winter set in about the 15th of November,
with deep snow, which lasted until April. But
making these allowances for the differences of latitude, the information which I shall give of the
climate of Nipon will present a fair idea of that of
the country generally. I am indebted for the
following tables to Dr. Hepburn, an American
medical missionary in Kanagawa, and they may,
I am confident, be fully relied upon.

In looking at the annexed table it will be seen
that July and August are the two hottest months
in the year, having a maximum temperature of 92°
and a minimum of 63°. In January and February,

	Thermometer, Fahr.				Clear days.	Cloudy days.	Rainy days.	Rain, in inches.	Snowy days.	Snow, in inches.	No. of earthquakes.
	Average at Sunrise.	At 2 P.M.	Highest.	Lowest.							
1860.											
January . . .	30	47	59	18	19	9	3	..	..	..	1
February . .	32	47	58	19	14	12	2	$\frac{1}{2}$	1	2	1
March . . .	40	51	69	30	9	4	18	$6\frac{1}{4}$	3	$1\frac{1}{2}$	2
April	49	64	76	36	16	5	9	$3\frac{1}{4}$	..	..	..
May	58	69	80	44	18	..	13	$16\frac{1}{2}$	..	..	2
June	67	76	87	54	10	7	13	$18\frac{3}{4}$	..	..	11
July	75	82	92	63	17	1	13	$8\frac{1}{4}$	..	..	4
August . . .	75	87	92	69	21	4	6	$1\frac{1}{16}$	..	..	2
September . .	72	80	89	62	14	4	12	$2\frac{1}{4}$	..	..	2
October . . .	57	70	84	50	15	6	10	$7\frac{1}{2}$	..	..	2
November . .	45	58	68	36	18	7	5	5	..	..	4
December . .	38	50	71	22	19	5	7	$3\frac{1}{4}$	1	1	1

which are the two coldest months, the temperature ranges between 18° and 59°. In some seasons it probably sinks considerably lower than it did in 1860, and no doubt it may usually be marked much lower than this in the more northern island of Yesso.

The heat of the summer months tempered by sea breezes is easily endured, while the cold of mid-winter has a bracing effect upon the constitutions of both natives and foreigners. The latter seem peculiarly healthy in Japan, and instances are not rare in which invalids from China, who have visited the country on account of their health, have been speedily cured. In March, April, and up to the middle of May (the commencement of the rains), the climate is very delightful. The autumnal months are generally of the same description; although the sun is sometimes hot in the middle of the day, yet an umbrella is not required; the air is cool and agreeable, and the evenings are most enjoyable. At this time of the year the sun, for days, and sometimes for weeks together, rises in the morning, runs his course, and sets in the evening in a sky on which not a cloud has appeared.

The monsoons which blow steadily along the eastern coast of Asia are not so decided in their character in Japan as they are in China. Still, however, northerly and easterly winds prevail from September to April, and southerly and westerly during the remainder of the year. Like China this country is frequently visited by those fearful hurricanes or cyclones, commonly known as typhoons, which unroof houses, tear trees out of the ground, and wreck many a goodly vessel at sea. It is also remarkable, more than any country known to me, for the suddenness with which gales come on. The morning may be calm and beautiful, yet long before noon it may be blowing a furious gale of wind.

In Japan the rainy season is much more decided in its character than it is in China. The hearty way in which the rains come down reminded me more of the season in Upper India, amongst the southern ranges of the Himalayas, than of that in China. But the rainy season in Japan is short when compared with India. It usually commences about the middle of May and lasts to the middle or end of June; and a glance at the table will show that these two months are by far the wettest in the year. This is the time when the monsoon is changing from north to south. The southerly winds come up loaded with moisture which they have acquired in their passage over the sea through warm latitudes. This moisture is suddenly condensed into thick fogs as it comes in contact with the land, which has been cooled down to a low temperature by the long-continued northerly winds.*

In 1860 but little snow fell on the low lands, although it was plentiful upon the adjoining mountains. But if Dr. Hepburn's table shows little snow, it is most prolific in earthquakes. In June there were no less than eleven shocks, and during the year the total number felt was thirty-two! When we take into consideration the number that occurred during the hours of sleep, which were not felt and registered, we may have some idea of the activity of the volcanos which lie under this extraordinary country.

Having thus given some idea of the climate of Japan, of "its summer and winter, its seed-time and harvest," I shall now endeavour to give a description of its agriculture. As a profession agriculture does not hold the same rank in Japan as it does in China. The Tycoon does not here mark his sense of its importance by putting his hands to the plough and throwing the first grains of rice into the ground, as is done by the "Son of Heaven." In social rank the farmer is said to be below the Buddhist priest, the soldier, the mer-

* Sir John Davis's ' Chinese.'

chant, and even the petty shopkeeper. We are told that he is but the serf of the great landed proprietor, and that he is heavily taxed and kept in a state of complete degradation. I am not in a position to deny these statements, but I can affirm, from personal observation in many parts of the country, that the farmers and their families live in good comfortable-looking houses, are well clothed, well fed, and appear to be happy and contented. It is just possible, however, that they may be a wealthier class in the territory adjoining the Imperial cities, such as Nagasaki and Yedo, than in that of the vassal princes and feudal lords of the soil.

The geological formation of the country and the composition of the soil vary greatly in the different districts. In the island of Kiu-siu, in the south, and also in Sikok, the upper sides of the hills are generally barren, with rocks of clay-slate and granite protruding. On the lower sides of the hills and in the valleys, where cultivation is carried on, the soil consists of clay and sand mixed with vegetable matter. On the south side of Nipon, Mr. Alcock informs us, the hills are formed of " sandstone and sand, and the valleys and plains seem little else." About three days' journey to the south of Fusi-yama, " the dark rich soil of the volcanic regions first appeared." In the country round the capital the soil is of a blackish-brown colour, composed chiefly of vegetable matter, and bears some resemblance to that which is found in the peat-bogs of England. This description of soil, as I have already noticed, is not confined to the low valleys, but is also met with on the tops of the hills.

The agricultural productions of Japan may be divided into two great classes, namely, the winter and the summer crops. The *winter crops* consist of wheat, barley, cabbage oil-plant (*Brassica sinensis*), and other cabbage for the table, together with buckwheat, peas, beans, onions, and English potatoes. The three first-mentioned may be considered as the staple winter productions. All these crops are cultivated on land which is above the level of the rice valleys. The wheat and barley are sown in the end of October or beginning of November; these soon vegetate, and cover the hill-sides with lively green during the winter months. The seed is sown in rows, about two feet three inches apart, and is dropped in the drills by the hand in patches, each containing from twenty-five to thirty seeds, these patches being about a foot apart from each other in the drill. As the land has been carefully cleaned and prepared previously to sowing, scarcely any further labour is necessary during the winter and following spring.

Early in the month of April the hill-sides are yellow with the flowers of the cabbage oil-plant, and the air is filled with its fragrance. About the 10th of May the wheat and barley are in full ear, and the seed-pods of the cabbage are swelling and coming fast to maturity. The latter ripens near

Yedo about the end of the month, and the oil harvest begins. The plant is not cut like corn, but is pulled up by the root, and laid on the field where it has been growing. When it has lain for a few days to dry, a convenient space is cleared in the middle of the prostrate crop, upon which mats are laid, and the labourers (women chiefly) take the stalks, handful by handful, and tread out the seeds upon the mats. In the beginning of June fires are seen all over the country, and smoke fills the air. The rape-seed has been harvested, and the farmers are now engaged in burning the stalks and other refuse on the land, with the view of getting the ashes for the summer crops which are now being sown to take the place of the rape.

The barley harvest commences in the first days of June, and in 1861 was in full operation on the 5th of that month. The corn is cut with a small hook exactly like that which is used in China. A portion of this is carried home to the farm-houses at once, in order to be secure from the weather, which is rather moist at this period of the year. Here the heads of corn are separated from the stalks by beating them over a bamboo grating. The bamboo, being flinty and sharp, cuts off the heads at every stroke, and leaves them to fall through the grating to the ground. In the court-yard of every farmhouse there is a broad flooring of chunnam, hard and smooth, on which the corn is laid and thrashed out with a flail, in the same way as in the olden time in England.

Another portion of the crop was harvested in a most curious way, which I think must be peculiar to Japan, for I have neither seen it nor heard of it in any other country. On the 10th of June— so says my journal—fires were observed blazing all over the country, and dense masses of smoke were seen rising from every cornfield. This time it was not the burning of rape-stalks, for they had all disappeared, having been converted into their elements of earth and air, the former of which was already entering into another form and was supplying food for the summer crops. It was the bearded barley which was now going through the crucible, the object being to separate the heads of corn from the straw and awns. This was done in the following way :—The corn, having been tied up in small bundles or sheaves, is removed to a convenient spot on the edge of the field. When the burning is to begin the workman takes a sheaf in one hand, and with the other applies fire to the upper or corn end of the sheaf. It immediately ignites, the awns go off in a blaze, the heads of corn snap from the stalk and fall to the ground. Lighting another sheaf, the workman throws the first away in a blaze, regardless apparently of the value of the straw, and so the operation goes on. As the beardless heads fall to the ground the fire goes out, leaving them slightly browned by the operation, but with the grain unharmed.

Straw is largely used for the flooring of rooms, and is laid under the matting, but, judging from the quantity which is burned in this way, it cannot be so valuable to the Japanese as it is to us.   The object in thus burning the barley is, no doubt, to economise the space which is available for shelter, for, if the grain were left exposed to the rains which fall at this season, it would soon germinate and spoil: Every evening these heads of corn are packed up in baskets and carried home to the farmstead, where they are threshed out by the flail on the chunnam floor, as I have already described.

The wheat harvest is later than the barley, and became general about the 23rd of June.   The varieties of both wheat and barley did not appear to me to be first-rate, but probably they may be more suitable to the climate of Japan than those of the higher qualities cultivated in Europe.   There were two or three varieties of wheat, one of them a red kind, said to have been imported from the United States of America.   By the 1st of July both barley and wheat harvests were over in Nipon, and the summer crops were already progressing rapidly on what had formerly been cornfields.

The *summer crops* consist of two classes, one which is cultivated on the dry hill or corn land, and another which succeeds best in the valleys which can be irrigated.   The first of these consists of soy and other beans of that class, French beans, hill rice—a kind that does not require irrigation—cotton, oily grain (*Sesamum orientale*), the eggplant, turnips, radishes, carrots, onions, gobbo (*Arctium gobbo*), cucumbers and melons, ginger, yams, and sweet potatoes.

No time is lost in getting these crops into the ground. The corn, I have already observed, is grown in rows, and some time before it is ripe the spaces between the rows are carefully weeded, stirred up, and manured with burnt ashes. The summer crops are then sown or planted between the rows of the ripening corn, and have made considerable progress in their growth before it is harvested. In this way a longer season of growth is secured. When the corn has been cut, the stubble, after a short time, is hoed up and drawn to the side of the new crop, where it rots and forms manure.

The manures which are used for these crops consist chiefly of burnt ashes at the time of sowing, and of night-soil diluted with water during the period of growth. Night-soil and urine are carefully collected and deposited in large earthen jars, which are sunk on the sides of the fields.

Sweet potatoes are preserved during winter in a square plot of ground in the farm-yard. This is surrounded with a straw fence, and covered over with paddy husks and straw when the weather is cold. Early in May,—the winter covering having been removed,—the potatoes begin to grow rapidly, and send out numerous young shoots, which are made into "cuttings," and transplanted at once into the fields. This

transplanting commences about the end of May,
and continues all June. When these cuttings are
put into the ground, they seem to form roots and
grow as easily as couch grass. But then this
operation takes place during the rainy season,
when the sky is often cloudy, and when the air is
charged with moisture,—a circumstance which
fully accounts for its success.

The second class of summer crops are those
which grow chiefly in the low valleys, and require
irrigation during the period of their growth.
Rice, the staple food of the people, is one of the
principal of these, and by far the most important.
The variety in cultivation is, I think, superior to
the kinds met with in China and in India, and is
probably the best in Asia.

The rice-lands generally lie fallow all the
winter, and consequently yield only one crop in
the year. In the last days of April, or about the
first of May, little patches of land are prepared in
the corners of the fields as seed-beds for the young
paddy. Here the seed is sown thickly, sometimes
having been steeped in liquid manure previously
to its being sown. It vegetates in a wonderfully
short space of time—three or four days, if the
weather be warm and moist, as it generally is at
this season of the year. In the mean time, while
this is vegetating in the seed-beds, the labourers
are busily employed in preparing the land into
which it is to be transplanted.

In China the rice-land is usually prepared by the

plough and harrow, drawn by the bullock or the buffalo. These animals are rarely seen in Japan employed in this way ; at least, they did not come under my observation. The rice-lands are prepared almost entirely by manual labour. A strong three-pronged fork, having the prongs bent like a hoe, is used for this purpose. The land is then flooded, and manured with grass and weeds cut and brought from adjacent waste ground, and used in a *fresh state*, as I have already described. The surface of the fields is then made smooth, and is considered ready for the young rice in the seed-beds.

The transplanting of the young paddy commences about the 8th of June. About three inches of water cover the surface of the fields, and the planting goes on with the most astonishing rapidity. The work is performed exactly in the same way as it is in China. A labourer takes a load of plants under his left arm, and drops them in little bundles over the surface of the land about to be planted, knowing, almost to a plant, what number will be required. Others, both men and women, take up the bundles which are thus thrown down, and the planting commences. The proper number of plants are selected and planted in rows, by the hand, in the muddy soil. When the hand is drawn up, the water rushes in, carrying down with it a portion of the soil, and thus the roots are covered instantaneously. Cranes, or herons, follow the labourers in the fields, and pick up the worms. The planting season is at its height about the 21st of June, and is generally over by the 10th of July. On some lands the seed is sown thinly, broadcast, and here, of course, no transplanting is necessary; this sowing takes place from the 15th to the 20th of May.

As the rice valleys near Kanagawa are intersected and surrounded by hills from which streams of water are continually flowing, it is not necessary to irrigate the fields by water-wheels, as in China. The streams are led, in the first place, into the fields near the foot of the hills, where the land is highest. Little ridges of earth or grassy embankments surround the different fields, each having a small space for the ingress and egress of the water. In this manner the hill stream first floods one field to the desired depth, then flows into the next at the point of egress, and so on, until the whole valley is irrigated. Natural or artificial watercourses, with channels lower than the fields, run through these rice valleys, and when the water is no longer required it is led into these, and carried out to the sea. By this means the water is kept always under the most perfect control; and in the autumn, when the ripening crops no longer require its aid, the little points of ingress are closed up, and the stream is allowed to flow in its natural channel.

During the remainder of the summer and autumn the paddy requires little more than attention to the irrigation, and now and then loosening and stirring up the soil between the rows, and removing any weeds. It is ripe and is harvested in November.

Amongst other agricultural productions which grow in the valleys of Japan, may be mentioned, *Arum esculentum, Scirpus tuberosus,* and *Juncus effusus,* the latter being used in the manufacture of mats which are so common in the country. In the lakes and ponds large quantities of nelumbium-roots are grown, and are used as a vegetable and also in the production of a kind of arrowroot.·

Such is a short account of Japanese farming as it presented itself to me in the autumn and winter of 1860, and spring and summer of 1861. The farms are small in extent when compared with those in western countries, and the homesteads also present a very different appearance to ours. They have no "lowing of oxen or bleating of sheep;" a stray pack-horse, or a solitary ox, may sometimes be seen, but these are only used as beasts of burden. Pigs may sometimes be met with, but they are generally kept in the background out of view; pork, however, is abundant in the butchers' shops. Goats and sheep do not appear to be indigenous; some of the latter have been imported from China, but the experiment of acclimatising them has not yet succeeded. They invariably become diseased, and die off. Cows or oxen are little used in agriculture, and it is probable that the Japanese, like their neighbours in China, have religious scruples as to using such animals for food.

It has been frequently repeated, by writers on Japan, that "hardly a foot of ground, to the very tops of the mountains, is left uncultivated." I have already shown in a previous chapter that such is not the case; that thousands of acres of fertile land are lying uncultivated, and covered with trees planted by nature, and brushwood, of little value. One naturally asks why these lands, which are capable of cultivation, should be allowed to lie in this unproductive condition. Is it because there is more than enough to supply the wants of a people that, for ages past, have been shut out from the rest of the world, and have therefore, while they have not contributed to the wants of others, been accustomed to rely entirely upon themselves for food and clothing ? *

I cannot conclude this description of Japanese agriculture without noticing the remarkable connection which exists between the climate and the productions of the country, and how well they are suited to each other. The rainy season does not come on until the dry winter and spring crops are ripe, and ready to be harvested. When the rice-planting begins, and when the cuttings of the sweet potato are being put out, the air becomes loaded with moisture, and the rain comes down in

* The land in question is suitable for the *dry* crops only—not rice-land. Rice in considerable quantities is brought from the Loo-choo islands to Nipon.

torrents. Every hill stream is filled with water,
and thus the means of irrigating the rice-fields are
ready to the hands of the husbandman. Such
excessive moisture would have been fatal to the
wheat and barley and rape, but it gives life and
vigour to the paddy and sweet potatoes, and is
necessary for their health and luxuriance. The
tea-plant, too, which, at this season, has had its
first leaves plucked, is revived by the moist air
and frequent showers, and is enabled to push forth
with renewed vigour, and to yield fresh supplies.
And when excessive moisture is no longer necessary to these summer products, the rain ceases, the
sky becomes clear, and the air comparatively dry.
Then the process of ripening begins, and a sunny
autumn enables the husbandman to gather into his
barns the fruits of his anxious labours.

CHAPTER XVII

Other productions of Japan — Silk, tea, &c. — Silk country — Value
of silk — Tea districts — Curious statements on tea cultivation —
Value of exports from Kanagawa in 1860-61 — Means of increasing
the supplies of silk and tea — Prospects on the opening of the new
ports — Japanese objections to the opening — The Tycoon's letter to
the Queen — Ministers' letter to Mr. Alcock — Their recommenda-
tions considered — Danger of opening Yedo at present — Remarks
on the other ports — Trade probably overrated — Japanese merchants compared with Chinese — Prejudices against traders in
Japan — Foreign officials and these prejudices — War with Japan
not improbable.

IN addition to the agricultural productions which
I have just described, there are many other articles
in the country "pleasant to the sight and good
for food," which are worthy of attention now that
the Japanese have entered into the great family
of nations. Perhaps no country in the world is
more independent of other countries than Japan.
She has, within herself, enough to supply all the
wants and luxuries of life. The productions of
the tropics, as well as those of temperate regions,
are found in her fields and gathered into her
barns. Wherever there are mountain ranges,
coal, lead, iron, and copper are found, and not
unfrequently the precious metals. Tea, silk,
cotton, vegetable wax, and oils are produced in
abundance all over the country. Ginseng and

other medicines, with salt fish and seaweed, are largely exported to China.

Silk and tea are, at present, the most important and valuable articles of export to Europe and America. I am indebted to Mr. Keswick, of the well-known house of Messrs. Jardine, Matheson, and Co., one of the earliest settlers at Yokuhama, for the following information regarding these articles of export. As Mr. Keswick was daily in communication with merchants from all parts of the country, and as he had considerable knowledge of the language, his means of acquiring information of this kind were greatly superior to my own. " Silk is more or less produced in almost every province of the island of Nipon north of Osaca, but the four districts in which it is found in the greatest abundance are Oshue, Joeshue, Koshue, and Sinshue. Oshue produces the largest quantity, but the silk does not equal in quality and fineness of size that of the other districts. Joeshue and Sinshue are noted for the fine size of their silk ; and even in the London market, when the best China silk was selling at 25s., it brought as high a price as 30s. per lb." These districts are situated in the northern part of the island of Nipon, and I believe are nearer to the port of Hakodadi than to Yokuhama. Japanese silk is more carefully reeled than Chinese, and is generally of better quality. At present it is nearly all bought for the Continent, and much more would be consumed if it could be obtained.

" Tea is produced, or grows wild, in all the provinces of the island of Kiu-siu, and throughout the greater part of Nipon. The finest qualities come from Ya-mu-si-ro, but the two largest producing districts are Isay and Owari. Suringa, Simosa, and Koshue are the provinces which supply the Kanagawa market with the earliest new tea; but as the season advances, large supplies arrive from the districts bordering on the Inland Sea."

The tea-plant is said to have been introduced into Japan from China about the beginning of the ninth century by a Buddhist priest named Yeitsin, who presented the first cup of the beverage to the reigning Mikado. It is now constantly observed on the sides of the roads, and in the gardens of the farmers and cottagers, who appear, in many instances, to cultivate only as much as will supply the wants of their families. I met with it in this way about Nagasaki and Kanagawa, and in larger quantities in the vicinity of the capital. There can be no doubt, I think, that the great tea districts of Japan are in the country near Osaca and Miaco, the residence of the Mikado. Should this prove correct, then the new port of Hiogo, in the Inland Sea, or some place in its vicinity, may, one day, prove of considerable value to our merchants.

Curious and almost romantic statements have been published regarding the mode of cultivating the tea-plant in Japan,—statements which, I am afraid, are more curious than truthful. Take the following as an example : " The plantations are situated remote from the habitations of man, and as much as may be from all other crops, lest the delicacy of the tea should suffer from smoke, impurity, or contamination of any kind. They are manured with dried anchovies and a liquor pressed out of mustard-seed. They must enjoy the unobstructed beams of the morning sun, and thrive best upon well-watered hill-sides. The plant is pollarded to render it more branching, and therefore more productive, and must be five years old before the leaves are gathered." (!) How our worthy tea-farmers in Japan and China would laugh if they were told that such things were written about their mode of cultivating the tea-plant!

Such statements remind me of reading, in a book upon China, an account of rice cultivation, in which the writer cannot understand the practice of sowing the rice-seeds very thickly in highly-manured beds in the corners of the fields. He sagely concludes that it must be upon the principle of " the more the merrier " ! It never occurred to his mind that these are merely seed-beds, where the plants are being reared for the purpose of transplanting, and that he may see the same kind of practice in any cabbage-garden in England. And the readers of the remarks on tea-cultivation quoted above may rest assured that that useful plant may be cultivated successfully, although not remote from the habitations of man, or manured with dried anchovies and mustard-seed oil. I may perhaps be pardoned for referring those interested in the matter to my 'Three Years' Wanderings in China' and 'Journey to the Tea Countries,' where the cultivation and manufacture of tea have been fully described from personal observation.

From a return made out by Consul Vyse and presented to Parliament, it appears that the value of the raw silk and silk manufactures exported from Kanagawa during the year ending the 31st December, 1860, was 548,630*l*. 13*s*. 4*d*. The value of tea exported during the same period was 64,260*l*. 16*s*. 8*d*. The total value of the exports from this port in 1860 amounted to 865,200*l*., the principal articles besides silk and tea being copper, oil, and seeds, dried fish, seaweed, medicine, vegetable wax, and lacquer-ware.

One of the merchants, in a letter to H. B. Majesty's Consul, dated August 8th, 1861, remarks, " In point of value the business transacted at this port during the first six months of 1861 far exceeds what was transacted during the same period of 1860. * * * To show you that there has been a rapid development of the export trade, I need only state that from July, 1859, to July, 1860, the export of silk was about 5000 bales; from July, 1860, to July, 1861, it was 12,000 bales. Of tea, from July, 1859, to July, 1860, there are no statistics, but the export was a mere trifle; whereas, from July, 1860, to July, 1861, it amounted to near 5,000,000 lbs. Such figures as these place the growing nature of our trade, and its importance, beyond question, and require no comment."

From my own observations in different parts of the country, I am fully convinced that the Japanese have the means of producing an almost unlimited supply of both these staple articles of export, and more particularly of tea. Thousands of acres of valuable land, on which the tea-plant would yield an abundant crop of leaves, are now lying waste, or in an unproductive condition. We may, therefore, look forward with confidence to increased supplies of tea from Japan, and also, I hope, to an improvement in their manipulation, and consequently in their flavour.

When the other ports and cities named in the treaty are opened to foreign trade, there will be a large increase in the value of both exports and imports. But the Japanese authorities are making great exertions to put off, what appears to them to be, "the evil day." The Tycoon himself has written a letter to Her Majesty the Queen of Great Britain, in which he states, "there are various objections that the Article of the Treaty providing for the opening of the ports of Hiogo and Ne-egata, and for the carrying on of trade in the cities of Yedo and Osaca, should be brought into operation on the conditions stated therein;" and he desires, therefore, "to defer the opening

of these places for a time." The Ministers for
Foreign Affairs, also, have addressed Mr. Alcock
upon the same subject. They begin by stating
that nearly three hundred years have elapsed since
the empire discontinued its intercourse with
Foreign Powers; that recently, in consequence of
the urgent advice of the President of the United
States and of the King of the Netherlands, this
old-standing law was altered, and foreign vessels,
sailing near the coasts, were allowed to put in at
the ports of Simoda and Hakodadi for fuel, provisions, and water. Again, after the arrival of the
American Minister, the Government, having taken
into consideration " the existing posture of foreign
affairs," concluded the treaty of amity which lately
entered into operation, and established free-trade
in the same manner, first with Great Britain, &c.
But the actual result of this proceeding differed
considerably from what had been anticipated.
" No profit has yet been derived; but the lower
classes of the people have already suffered loss
thereby." The price of things is daily increasing,
in consequence of the large quantity of products
which are exported to foreign countries; and the
people, when deprived of the means of gaining
their livelihood, ascribe the cause to trade and are
discontented. Even the wealthier classes, it is
hinted, are likely to condemn the abrogation of
the previously existing prohibition, and may
desire the restitution of the former law. This
being the result of opening two or three ports to

foreign trade, every one is grieved when he reads the stipulations of the treaty, which state that the ports of Hiogo and Ne-egata are to be opened, and that foreign trade will also be carried on at the cities of Yedo and Osaca, by which the loss and the injury will be still further increased.

The Ministers further state that " the popular spirit having already arrived at such a pitch, it is very difficult even for the power and the authority of the Government so to manage that each one should clearly understand the future advantage, and to cause them to endure for a time the present grief." Should the Government use violence in carrying out the stipulations of the treaty, " it would be uncertain what mischief would result from such an act against the national spirit."

In order, therefore, not to press too heavily upon the people, and to give time to the ignorant to accustom themselves to free-trade, and to feel its benefits, the Ministers propose to defer the opening of the two ports * and two cities for the space of seven years, and to agree that they shall be opened in 1868.

The document, of which I have just given the substance, is an able one, and demands most careful attention from the Governments of foreign powers who have treaties with Japan. As a general rule it is bad policy to waive any treaty-right with Orientals, as, in the case of China and

---

* Ne-egata is found to be useless as a port, and another will be chosen.

the question of our being allowed to enter the city
of Canton, such a proceeding may plunge us into
future and expensive wars.   But the Japanese
question is a peculiar one.   The Government
evidently felt it had committed a mistake when it
agreed to the treaty, and would now gladly return
to the old state of things.   As its experience of
foreigners had been confined to the Dutch at
Desima, who had carried on their trade in one or
two ships a year, it had no idea that merchants
with large capitals would come in such numbers,
and that fleets of ships would arrive to carry off
the produce of the country.   And the statements
the Ministers now made were perfectly true; provisions had increased in price; the people were
getting discontented, attributing the rise in prices
to the presence and action of foreigners, and not
understanding or caring for free-trade and its
future benefits.   In this state of things it is not at
all unlikely that, if the opening of the new ports
were pressed, a rebellion might take place which
the Government would not have the power to put
down.

There may be a difference of opinion as to the
propriety of agreeing to defer the opening of
Hiogo and Osaca, with another port on the west
coast instead of Ne-egata, but, I think, all who
have studied the matter must agree as to the
necessity of not pressing, at present at least, the
opening of Yedo.   I believe, even if it were
agreed to by the Government, it would be attended

U

with the greatest danger. I have already shown
the character of the population that crowds the
streets of this city,—idle retainers from all parts
of the country, full of prejudice against foreigners,
always armed with sharp swords, and ready to use
them upon the slightest provocation, or with no
provocation at all. Against these men and their
masters the Government itself would seem to be
almost powerless. "Both the American treaties
were inaugurated by the death of the reigning
Tycoon who signed or sanctioned them, the first
by the sword and the second by poison. One of
the royal brothers was deposed and exiled, and
the Regent of the kingdom was slain in revenge
for this act by the Prince of Mito's followers." *

A city like this would, therefore, be a most
unsafe place for a number of foreigners, full of life
and high spirits, with customs and manners very
different from those of the Japanese, and which
the latter, oftentimes, can neither understand nor
appreciate. In such a place life and property
would always be insecure, and it is not unlikely
that, sooner or later, a general massacre might be
attempted. With these things before our eyes,—
believing the Government to be anxious for our
safety, but to be almost powerless, feeling its
weakness and dreading the future, are we prepared to incur the risk of opening Yedo, or to
punish the Government if it fails to protect us?
It seems idle to talk of holding the Government

* Mr. Alcock's despatch to Earl Russell.

responsible for our safety in a country where it is
so weak as not to be able to protect itself. Taking,
therefore, into consideration the dangers attending
the opening of Yedo to foreign merchants, and the
fact that we have already a port of trade within a
few miles of it to which its produce can be easily
brought, where we can reside and trade in comparative security, I think it will be wise to waive our
right to the opening of that city, at least for the
present.

It seems doubtful, however, whether we should also
give way to the proposal of deferring the opening
of Hiogo and Osaca, in the Inland Sea, as also of
a port on the west coast, should a suitable one be
found there, to take the place of Ne-egata. Although the ignorance and prejudices of the people
may be as great against us in these places as at
Yedo, yet the same dangers to life and property
are certainly not so apparent. And if it be worth
our while to have a footing in these places at all,
it is almost certain that the difficulties in our way
will be as great seven years hence as they are at
the present time. We might, therefore, meet the
Japanese Government half-way, by insisting that
the provisions of the treaty be carried out in so far
as these places are concerned, while we waived, for
the present, our right of residing and trading in
the capital itself.

But it seems doubtful whether the Tycoon's
Government has the power to ratify the treaties
made with foreign nations without the sanction of

the Mikado; and this high and mysterious personage, it is suspected, has not yet given such
sanction.   The following note on this subject has
just appeared in the ' China Mail,' and is worth
attentive perusal :—

   " It is well known now that the Mikado has not
yet given his formal consent to the treaties made
with the Foreign Powers, and it must be evident
that without his consent those treaties have no
legal value in the eyes of the Japanese princes and
people.   This, then, is the root of all the recent
troubles.   This is the reason why the Tycoon's
Government is not able to defend our Ministers
and us, and is hardly able to defend itself, from the
attacks of the malcontents who seek its embarrass-
ment or our expulsion.   This is why it does not
and dare not punish those assassins who from time
to time cut unoffending foreigners to pieces in the
open streets, or in the very teeth of the native
guard and at the door of the British Minister.
This is why it endeavours to restrict our trade and
to make its further pursuit uninviting.   This is
why it refused to open Yedo last January, and is
reluctant to open Osaca next January.   This is
why we are desired to retire to Nagasaki, where
foreign trade has long been established, and are
offered there the facilities denied us here (Yedo).
In short, this is why there is no peace or friendship for foreigners in this part of Japan, and
why neither our political nor our commercial
relations with this people are what they ought to

be. It is not pretended that the Tycoon's Government is implicated in the numerous crimes which have marked with tracks of blood the history of our three years' relations with Japan. Doubtless this Government deplores those crimes as sincerely as any one. But it is powerless to prevent them; and for this plain reason—that it has not yet been able to abolish one of the laws of Gongen-Sama, in virtue of which licence is given to slay foreigners wherever they may be found. It is, then, useless for us to wait here with our lives in our hands while the Tycoon slowly gathers from our trade, and from his own enterprises, the means and the power to overcome these laws, and to redeem his promises to us. Either we must leave the country, or we must obtain from the only ruler who is supreme in it the full ratification of the rights and privileges we came here to enjoy. There is no middle course. Compromises, postponements, concessions, all half-measures, are of no avail in this matter. I repeat, therefore, that the alternative is either to have the treaties recognised by the real Government of the empire, or to abandon them as worthless, and depart from a country where we are unwelcome and unsafe."

As a place of trade, Japan, with all its advantages, has been probably overrated, particularly as a mart for our manufactures. There is no doubt, however, that it can supply us with large quantities of silk and tea, and thus render us less dependent on China for those articles which have now become indispensable to our happiness and comfort. But as a customer to our manufacturing districts, Japan will never be equal to China.

As merchants, too, the Chinese appear to be far ahead of the Japanese. While a Japanese would be haggling for a few *cash* on a hank of silk or a pound of tea, a Chinaman would be quietly settling for a ship-load of the same articles. Experience has also shown that the Chinese trader is more to be depended upon than the Japanese. Indeed, as merchants of honour and talent, I doubt if the former are to be excelled in any part of the world. That pithy little sentence which concludes a bargain, "put-e-book," or "book it," is considered as binding as if it was registered by the Bank of England; and rarely indeed will a Chinaman recede from his bargain, even if its fulfilment should involve him in an unfortunate speculation. At present this cannot be said of the Japanese; but they may probably improve when they become better acquainted with foreigners, and when others, now in the background, come into the field.

Traders in Japan, however wealthy or intelligent, are looked down upon with disdain by the merest serf of the Daimios; and the merchants of foreign countries are treated much in the same way. This state of things will not surprise any one acquainted with the history of our own country in the feudal ages. Every one doubtless remembers the wrath of Rob Roy when Bailie Nicol Jarvie good-naturedly proposes to take his sons " for prentices at the loom, as I began mysel, and my father the deacon before me." " '*Ceade millia diaoul!* hundred thousand devils!' exclaimed Rob, rising and striding through the hut. ' My sons weavers! *Millia molligheart!* but I wad see every loom in Glasgow—beam, treddles, and shuttles—burnt in hell-fire sooner!' " The Japanese of the present day resemble, in many ways, the Scottish Highlanders in the days before the famous '45·

It is to be feared that foreign officials, desirous of not being confounded with the inferior orders of their countrymen, do not contribute in any way to lessen this feeling, but, on the contrary, oftentimes give it a kind of official sanction. This is unfortunate, but I fear it is too true. It will scarcely be credited· in a country like England, where our merchants and sons of merchants occupy some of the highest positions in the kingdom, and where any one who took it into his head to act in such a manner would only be laughed at for his pains. But things are done in a different way in Japan.

With all our care in opening up this trade, it is much to be feared that a time may come, and that it is not very distant, when Japan will have to pay dearly for her former exclusive policy. As a nation we have an abhorrence of war and all its attendant horrors, but somehow or other—owing, no doubt, partly to our wide-spread dominions and to our extensive commerce—we have war always forced upon us against our inclinations; and that this will be one of the results of our new treaty with Japan, there is, as I have already said, but too much reason to anticipate.

HAVING thus endeavoured to give some description of the climate, agriculture, productions, and
trade of Japan, I shall now resume my narrative.
It was now the middle of July, the rains were
over for the season, and the days were sometimes
oppressively hot. The thermometer ranged from
80° to 90° Fahrenheit. The foreign community
were still in a high state of excitement, and
rumours of fresh attacks from some source—no
one knew whence—were freely circulated in Yokuhama and Kanagawa. M. de Wit, the Minister of
the Netherlands, was residing in the house of his
Consul at Yokuhama, and had a guard of men
from a ship of war then in the harbour. One
morning we were told that an attack had been
made on his house during the night by an armed
band, who, luckily for him, had been observed and

beaten off by the guard. M. de Wit had been one
of the party who had come overland from Nagasaki with Mr. Alcock, and it was alleged that his
life was sought for on that account. Another
report stated that there had been no attack at all,
but that the guard had been indulging rather
freely in strong drinks, by which means it had
been enabled to see an attacking force which
existed only in an overheated imagination. Then
another Dutchman, who was sleeping at the hotel
of the town, was alarmed by a two-sworded man
entering his bedroom in the dead of the night, in
search, it was supposed, of the correspondent of
the 'Illustrated London News,' then staying at
the hotel, who had also been another of the offend-
ing overland party. The good Dutchman was
greatly alarmed, and did not appreciate the honour
of being killed in the place of "Our own Correspondent." There were sceptics amongst us who
did not credit these rumours, and I merely mention them to show the state of alarm which then
existed.

At this time I was still living alone in my large
temple at Kanagawa. One day, as I was sitting
in the verandah arranging my herbarium and
drying my paper, several two-sworded men made
their appearance at the end of the avenue. I
began to speculate on the chance of an attack,
when I was relieved from all apprehension by
seeing a number of others come upon the scene,
amongst whom there appeared to be some persons

of high rank.   An interpreter was sent forward to
inform me that the Governor himself was my
visitor, and that he had come to make an inspection of the paling and hedges which surrounded
the grounds, in order to see whether there were
any holes through which *loōnins* could crawl and
do me mortal injury.   If any such holes existed,
he was good enough to say, he would have them
repaired.   The idea was an amusing one, and calculated to excite a smile on my countenance.   If
any *loōnins* wanted me, they could have had no
difficulty in getting in even after the fence was
repaired; but being in Japan, I took the matter
very gravely, and asked the interpreter to express
my thanks to his Excellency the Governor for his
care for my safety.

The Governor and his attendants now made the
circuit of the fences, and examined all the weak
places, after which they returned to me in the
verandah of the temple.   It was now explained to
me that one or two little holes existed which
should be closed, and that the gate of the cemetery
which led into the ground would be nailed up.
I was then asked to what nation I belonged—was
I English, French, or American?   I replied I was
an Englishman.   "Was I a Government official
or a merchant?"   I was neither, but had visited
Japan for the purpose of making collections of
natural history.   I then showed them my stores of
living and dried plants, insects, shells, and books,
with which they appeared greatly pleased.   I ex-

plained to them that in England we had such
things introduced from all parts of the world, and
that I was now endeavouring to add to our collections all that was useful or beautiful in Japan.
They understood and apparently appreciated my
objects, and mentioned that they knew Dr. Siebold,
who was engaged in similar pursuits.   When my
collections had been inspected, the Governor in-
quired if I was living alone in the temple, and
seemed to be surprised when he was informed that
no one was with me except my servants.   I then
desired the linguist to ask him if he thought there
was any danger to be apprehended, and had the
following consolatory and cautious reply :—" The
Governor cannot say there is no danger, but he
will see that the fences are repaired."   This remark
was followed by a polite " good bye " as the party
took their leave, and left me alone to my medi-
tations.

All was now bustle and excitement in Kanagawa, and the carpenters in particular appeared to
be driving a brisk trade.   The fences of the different Consulates, and those of the few unofficial
foreign residents, were repaired, some of them
being doubled, heightened, and armed with spikes
and nails.   Guards were stationed both in the front
and in the rear of the different houses, and the
Government appeared to be taking every means
in its power for our safety.   I believed then, and
it is my opinion still, that the Japanese were
acting in good faith, and that they were really

doing everything in their power, in their own way, to protect us from the vengeance of the dreaded loönins.

This state of things was exciting enough, but I must confess that it was far from being agreeable. I did not care much for any attack which might be made upon us during the day-time, when one would have an opportunity of either fighting or running away; but the prospect of being murdered in bed, while one slept, was quite another thing; and as I was alone in a large rambling building, I might have fallen an easy victim during the night, without any one being aware of it until the following day. In these circumstances, going to bed at night was about the most unpleasant part of the day's operations. My work, however, was nearly finished; and after a few days of this excitement I was able to go over to Yokuhama, where the principal portion of the foreign community resided. Here I was kindly received by Mr. Aspinall, a gentleman whom I had formerly known in China, and who had established a firm in Japan.

It was now the end of July, and a great change had taken place in the appearance of the flora of the country. Flowers had nearly disappeared in the vegetation. With the exception of Hydrangeas, Hollyhocks, Hibiscus, and some few weeds on the roadsides, there was now nothing in bloom. The common Hydrangea grows to a great size in Japan, and forms a most remarkable and beautiful object when in flower.

I had now accomplished the object which I had in view in coming to Zipangu. I had carefully examined the country during autumn and winter, spring and summer, in search of new trees and other plants of an ornamental character which were likely to prove suitable to our English climate. Large collections of insects and land-shells had also been made; and my spare time had been employed in procuring examples of works of art, particularly of ancient lacquer, for which this country has long been famous in Europe. The agriculture of Japan—the productions of the hills and those of the plains, the wet crops and the dry ones—had been carefully examined at the different seasons, and fully described from time to time in my Journal. While engaged in work of this kind I came much in contact with various classes of the people, and had an opportunity of observing their habits and customs in daily life. The political state of the country, its relations with foreign powers, and the prospects of foreign trade, had all passed in review before me, and enabled me to draw my own conclusions. This was the work which I had proposed to myself to do, and thus far it had been brought to a successful termination.

My collections of living plants and other objects of natural history were now very large and valu-able, and the whole had to be arranged and packed. I determined to take them over to China under my own care, as the monsoon was still blowing strong from the south, and it was too early to ship them for home. A number of Ward's cases which had been made for me by Japanese carpenters were now filled with soil, and planted with many rare and beautiful examples of the trees and shrubs of Japan. During the operation of planting I was visited by many of the inhabitants of Kanagawa, who evidently watched my proceedings with a good deal of curiosity and interest. They had never seen such queer little greenhouses before, and made many inquiries regarding the treatment of the plants during their long voyage. When I told them that the plants would be four or five months at sea, and that during that long period they would never receive any water—that in fact the cases would never be opened from the time they left China until they reached England—they looked rather puzzled and incredulous; but this was not to be wondered at, as that little fact has puzzled wiser heads than theirs.

When I had got everything ready for shipment, Her Majesty's Consul, Captain F. Howard Vyse, to whom I was indebted for many acts of courtesy during my residence in Kanagawa, gave me a note to the customhouse authorities, who allowed me to ship my collections free of duty, and, what was of even more importance, without being opened and unpacked.

On the morning of the 29th of July, 1861, the 'Fiery Cross,' Captain Crockett, in which I was a passenger, got her steam up and stood out to sea. As we passed rapidly onwards towards the mouth of the bay, the towns of Yokuhama and Kanagawa, with the well-known headlands in their vicinity, gradually disappeared from our view, and I bade farewell to the green hills and lovely scenery of Japan.   We had a pleasant passage down the North Pacific Ocean, through Van Dieman's Strait, and across the Tung-Hai or Eastern Sea, and arrived at Shanghae in China on a hot morning on the 4th of August.   My plants, which had come over in excellent order, were now landed and placed in Mr. Webb's garden here, where they were to remain until the season arrived for shipping them to England.   In the mean time it was my intention to visit the scenes of the late war in the north, and if possible the city of Peking, and the mountains beyond it.

CHAPTER XIX.

ON the 11th of August I sailed from Shanghae
for Chefoo, in Her Majesty's despatch boat 'Atta-
lante,' and reached that port on the 16th. Chefoo,
or rather Yentae, for that is the name of the place,
is one of the ports which have been opened to trade
under Lord Elgin's treaty. It is in the province
of Shantung, on the south side of the Gulf of Pe-
chele. The town is a poor straggling place, and
does not seem to be of much value as a place of
trade. The harbour, however, is good, and is
much frequented by junks engaged in the coasting
trade. When I went on shore I was kindly received by H. B. M. Consul, M. C. Morrison, Esq.,
an old and valued friend whom I had known from
my first visit to China in 1844.

It may be remembered that Chefoo or Yentae

had been occupied by the French troops during the late war, and at the time of my visit there were two French ships of war in the harbour, and the town was still partially occupied by the French. It is certainly a healthy station, and has a fine beach for sea-bathing, but those who think it important as a place for foreign trade will, I fear, be disappointed. It may, however, be of some value as a mail station in the winter season when the approaches to the Pei-ho river are frozen up. Ships can always get to Yentae, and the mails can be brought overland from Peking and Tien-tsin and shipped at Yentae.

The soil of the surrounding country is very fertile in the valleys and low lands, but the hills are extremely barren. The cultivated lands produce large crops of beans (*Dolichos*), peas, and several kinds of millet, one of which is not met with in the more southern parts of the empire. It grows to the height of from twelve to fifteen feet, and is, I believe, the Sorghum, which has, of late years, been introduced to Europe, and is said to be a good substitute for the sugar-cane. When in a young, growing state its stem is sweet to the taste, but I doubt its containing sugar enough to compete with the sugar-cane of commerce. It may, however, prove useful as food for cattle.

On the hill-sides I observed two trees of an ornamental and useful description, and secured a portion of their seeds, which are now growing in this country. The one is a curious pine, which,

when old, becomes flat-headed, somewhat like the
cedar of Lebanon; the other is an arbor-vitæ, apparently distinct from the *Thuja orientalis* which
grows about Shanghae and other places in the
south. The barren hills are said to be covered
with wild flowers in the spring of the year, and
even in the autumn many pretty things of this
kind were in bloom. *Platycodon grandiflorus*
several species of Veronica, Potentilla, Pardanthus,
&c., were in bloom at the time of my visit.

As there was little to detain me at Yentae, I
determined to go onwards to the mouth of the
Pei-ho by the first opportunity. The French com-
modore on the station was good enough to give
me a passage in a steamer named the ' Fee-loong,'
which was under charter to convey the mails from
Shanghae to Taku once in each month, the other
bi-monthly mail being taken by an English vessel.
We left our anchorage on the afternoon of the 1st
of September, and on the following morning we
were nearing the far-famed Taku forts and the
mouth of the Pei-ho, the scene of our disasters and
subsequent triumphs a short time before. The
view on approaching the mouth of this river has
often been described by writers on China from
Lord Macartney's embassy downwards, and therefore I need say nothing about it here further than
it was the most unprepossessing one which it had
ever been my lot to look upon. As the ' Fee-loong '
was a small vessel and drew little water, we were
not obliged to lie outside the bar as ships generally

are, but steamed in at once and dropped anchor in the Pei-ho abreast of the forts. The next day I went up to the port of Tien-tsin in a gun-boat which was employed to take up the mails and stores for our troops, which still held possession of that city.

A wonderful change has come over the Pei-ho since the days of Lords Macartney and Amherst, and of Staunton and Davis. Steam has now invaded its quiet waters, and gun-boats and other vessels go puffing and snorting upon it all day long. Instead of thousands of curious natives lining the shores and covering the salt-heaps as in the days of yore, English and French soldiers and merchants were observed in considerable numbers as we approached the city, and our appearance seemed to be a matter of too common occurrence to be heeded by the natives.

The wonderful collection of salt-heaps noticed by former travellers were still here and at once attracted our attention. During my stay in Tien-tsin I paid a visit to these salt-heaps in order to get some idea of their extent. They are placed on a piece of level land on the left bank of the river, just below the town. Many millions of bags, filled with coarse salt, are here heaped up in the form of hay-stacks. These stacks are about thirty feet in height, twenty in width, and of various lengths. To give an idea of the enormous quantity of salt collected here, I may mention that these stacks cover a space of ground fully a mile in length, and in some places a quarter of a mile in width! The ground on which they are placed is raised a considerable height above high-water mark, and is perfectly level and smooth. The salt-heaps have their ends at right angles with the river, and between each range there is a small open drain for the purpose of carrying off the rain-water and to keep the bottom bags dry. The bags are made of split bamboo, and are consequently very strong, and mats are thrown over the whole to afford the protection of a roof and to carry off the rain. On looking at the enormous quantity of salt roughly stored in this manner, one is apt to imagine that a considerable portion must be wasted, particularly during the wet months of spring and autumn. But the Chinese are too economical in their habits to allow any great amount of waste to take place, and therefore I suppose the rough covering must be more efficient than it would appear at first sight. That a portion of the salt gets melted was apparent enough; the little drains between the heaps were full of it, either in the form of salt-water or of salt itself.

The view from the top of one of these salt-heaps was curious and novel. The whole place had a wintry aspect, the ground was whitened as if with hoar-frost, and as I walked over it a crisp crushing noise was heard as if one was walking on frosted snow. On these grounds not a blade of grass or green thing was visible, and, had it not been for the view of green trees and fields in the distance, and the warm autumnal air which was blowing, I might easily have fancied myself in the midst of dreary winter.

A dense suburb lines both banks of the Pei-ho. This suburb is fully five miles in length, and in a mercantile point of view forms the most import-ant part of Tien-tsin. The portion on the right bank of the river contains all the best shops and the principal mercantile establishments. About half-way up the suburb a river falls into the Pei-ho, which is said to be the upper end of the Grand Canal, which was formerly navigable for boats all the way from Tien-tsin to Hangchow-foo in the province of Chekiang. This is here crossed by a bridge of boats, made to open and shut in order to allow boats to pass up and down, as well as foot passengers to cross to either side. There are two or three bridges of the same kind on the Pei-ho near Tien-tsin.

The stranger on visiting Tien-tsin is struck with the apparent meanness of its buildings, and cer-tainly, if fine buildings are necessary to give it importance, it has no claim to our attention. Poor-looking houses, with mud walls, oftentimes in a ruinous condition, are continually seen. But on a nearer and closer inspection of the place, one finds large warehouses stored with goods from all parts of the world, and numerous indications of mercan-tile wealth which are not visible at first sight. Coolies, loaded with merchandise, crowd the nar-row streets, and everything presents the appear-

ance of a busy and thriving place such as is seen
only in extensive emporiums of trade.   The river
and Grand Canal are lined with junks, cargo-boats,
and small craft of every description, all engaged in
active business.   In short, many indications stamp
Tien-tsin as an important commercial station well
worth the attention of the merchants of foreign
countries.

The main street of the suburbs which extends
along the banks of the Pei-ho and Grand Canal is
a most curious and bustling place.   Here are all
the best shops.   All day long men are going along
this thoroughfare with huge wheelbarrows loaded
with all kinds of produce and merchandise.   The
noise these fellows make is absolutely appalling;
they actually bawl at the passengers to get out of
their way, and every one makes way for them.
The loads which these men wheel along are generally very heavy, and the slightest obstruction or
contact is a very serious matter.   This is understood and universally acknowledged by the people,
and every one gets out of the way of the wheelbarrows.   Old curiosity shops for the sale of ornaments in jade-stone, rock crystal, porcelain, bronzes,
&c., are numerous and well stocked.   Clay figures,
representing the people of the country, and illustrating all ranks, from the highest mandarin down
to the public executioner, are here met with, and
are remarkably well modelled.   In the autumn
and winter skins and furs are plentiful; and as
there is a great demand for these owing to the

intense cold of the latter season, there are large shops for their sale. The old-clothes shops and their inhabitants are perhaps the most curious of all that dwell in this busy thoroughfare. All day long the shopmen are engaged in turning over piles of secondhand clothing and holding a kind of auction upon it piece by piece. Surrounded by groups of persons, some of whom are there out of curiosity, while others are waiting for bargains, the vendors call out, or rather sing out, the prices of the various articles as they lift them up and pass them from one heap to another. Every now and then an article is purchased by one in the group, but by far the greatest number are allowed to pass unsold. As the shops of the different dealers are alongside of each other, sometimes a little rivalry will spring up between the salesmen, who then raise their voices to the highest pitch, and appear to the stranger to be actually shouting at each other!

In a street beyond the north gate of the city, and leading in the direction of the western suburbs, there are some large respectable-looking hongs or warehouses, and here would appear to be the head-quarters of the great native merchants. This street is crowded with native produce, such as dyes of various kinds, drugs used in medicine, seaweed, rattans, and large quantities of hemp or rather jute, which is largely grown in the surrounding country.

Shops for the sale of provisions of all kinds were

plentiful and well-stocked. One dubbed " Fortnum and Mason " was famous for all sorts of preserves, dried fruits, cakes, and buns. Doctors' shops were numerous, and one famous physician had a stand in the street ornamented with a drawing representing the common diseases of the country which he professed to cure. Street hawkers were numerous, bawling out the names and prices of their wares in tones which could scarcely be called musical. Sellers of fruit—pears, apples, dates* (so called), chesnuts, walnuts—and of cooked locusts, &c., were met at every step of the way. The natives, old and young, are most inveterate gamblers, and gamble for almost everything which they wish to procure from the hawkers. The hawker is invariably provided with a hollow bamboo tube in which are placed a number of little sticks marked at the lower end after the manner of dice. He rattles them in the tube, and the customer, having first put down his stake, draws out three and carefully examines the marks on their lower ends. If he is lucky he may get three or four times the value of his stake, and he takes his choice of the good things which are lotted and priced on the vendor's table. Of course in China, as in other countries, the table has the chance in its favour, and so the hawker gets a living; but the propensity to gamble is strong in the minds of the Chinese, and they would rather lose their money

---

* This is the fruit of a Rhamnus, not a palm.

than forego the excitement which attends the risking it.

The walled city of Tien-tsin is a very poor-looking place. It has four gates, east, west, north, and south, and is about a mile and a quarter in length from east to west, and less than half a mile wide from north to south. Its walls and ramparts are generally in a most ruinous condition. The streets are usually paved, or rather they have been originally paved, with large stone slabs, but these too are now in bad condition. The pavement is broken up in many places, and large holes are seen everywhere, which, in wet weather, get filled with water. The shops are poor, and apparently contain only the simple necessaries of life. As in other Chinese cities, the high authorities live and have their public offices within the walls of the city, but the wealth, activity, and life of Tien-tsin are all in its suburbs.

Chinese towns, as a rule, are not remarkable for cleanliness; on the contrary, they are generally famous for filth and foul smells. But in all my travels in the Chinese empire, or elsewhere, I never came upon a place so disgustingly dirty as Tien-tsin. The pavement of many of the streets is thickly covered with mud which seems to have been accumulating for ages. This is well enough in dry weather, but when it rains it is almost impossible to walk along the streets without getting over the shoes in mud, and perchance tumbling headlong into one of the holes already mentioned.

Manure is apparently not appreciated here as it is in the south, and the habits of the people are filthy in the extreme. On the tops of the ramparts, on waste ground, and even in some of the streets, the stench is almost intolerable.

It is difficult to account for this state of things. Here we see a large and flourishing trade, great wealth, good shops, and an active commercial people, and yet their city is everywhere in a most ruinous condition, and their streets are frequently almost impassable. It is true that this place had been taken by the Allied troops a short time before, and it was then in the hands of the English and French soldiers; but there were abundant proofs that this state of dilapidation and filth had existed long before the place had been occupied by our troops. The cause of this state of things may possibly be traced to the corruption of the Government and its officers, who may have been in the habit of embezzling the sums annually raised from the people, or possibly of using the money for other purposes.

The country around Tien-tsin is one vast plain nearly as flat as a table, and at one period was probably covered by the ocean. Vast tracts of land are even now perfectly barren, and salt, which is shining amongst the soil, gives the ground an appearance as if covered with hoar-frost. On the south side of the city there is not a vestige of cultivation, and the plain here formed an excellent parade-ground for our troops. It also

served another purpose. A cemetery stands in
its centre, which already contains a goodly number
of our brave soldiers, who found the climate a
much more formidable enemy than the Chinese.
Beyond these barren lines the country gradually
becomes more fertile, and yields fair crops of the
gigantic millet—the Kow-leang of the Chinese—
which I had already seen at Chefoo. It is curious
to notice barren spots in the midst of the more
fertile ones, and to observe the white salt covering
the soil, telling too surely that the land is "sowed
with salt."

In this plain trees are few and far between.
Willows occur here and there, with Sophora japonica, Diospyros Kaki, stunted examples of Rhamnus zizyphus, and a few others, generally about
gardens, which I may notice afterwards. In
winter, when these few trees have lost their leaves,
and when the tall millet has been gathered, this
plain must have a very dreary appearance indeed.
The wild plants met with in the barren parts of
the plain were such as Salsola, Statice, Tamarix,
Asclepias, Chenopodium, Malva, &c., plants which
flourish in a salt soil.

As soon as our troops had compelled the Chinese
Government to act up to the letter and spirit of its
treaty with Lord Elgin, almost all the great foreign
mercantile houses in China sent representatives,
and opened branch establishments at Tien-tsin. I
found an old friend, Mr. Hanssen, representing
Messrs. Dent and Co., who kindly offered me

quarters in his house during my stay in the place. As my principal object in visiting this part of China was to obtain new plants for introduction to Europe, I lost no time in making the usual inquiries regarding the nursery gardens. Mr. Wild, a neighbour of Mr. Hanssen, who had resided for some time in Tien-tsin, was good enough to tell me of an extensive nursery on the banks of the Grand Canal in the western suburbs, and offered to accompany me to it. I gladly availed myself of his offer, and we set out one afternoon to examine it. As I was now several degrees further north than I had ever been before in China, and as the climate was very different from that of the districts I had formerly explored, I was in great hopes of finding many trees and shrubs entirely new, and looked forward to my visit to this garden with much interest. On reaching it I observed large quantities of plants cultivated in pots, but, curious enough, they were nearly all southern species, such as I had formerly met with in the gardens of Canton and Foo-chow. The Mole-hwa (*Jasminum sambac*) seemed to be the greatest favourite; hundreds of this plant were arranged in rows, and raised a little from the ground by being placed on empty flower-pots. *Olea fragrans*, pomegranates, oranges, limes, and such well-known things, were numerous and well cultivated. The only representatives of a cold climate, such as that from Shangae northward, were *Jasminum nudiflorum, Weigela rosea,* honeysuckles, and some roses.

The proprietor received us very politely, and seemed somewhat surprised when he heard me call his plants by their native names. I told him I was rather disappointed at not finding more of the indigenous plants of the district in his possession; but he was evidently enthusiastically fond of his southern beauties, and could not understand my wish to see those which he did not think worthy of his patronage. Before leaving this garden I made inquiries about other nurseries near the town, and was informed that there were several a little further to the westward, at a place called Chea-yuen.

During my stay at Che-foo I was fortunate in making the acquaintance of Brigadier-General Staveley, commander of the army at Tien-tsin, and Dr. Gordon, C.B., Inspector-General of Hospitals, and was a fellow-passenger of these gentlemen from Che-foo to Tien-tsin. They were both well acquainted with this town and the surrounding country, and I was greatly indebted to them for much courtesy and information. Dr. Gordon was an ardent lover of botanical pursuits, and was well acquainted with all the gardens, public and private, and other objects of interest, in the vicinity of Tien-tsin. My first excursion with him was to the gardens of Chea-yuen, which had been already recommended to me by the Chinese nurseryman.

These gardens are situated on the banks of the Grand Canal, some two or three miles west from the city, and beyond the extensive suburb which extends for miles up the side of the Pei-ho river and Grand Canal. We found fields in their neighbourhood planted with China asters and herbaceous peonies, whose flowers were in much request amongst the ladies of Tien-tsin. The nursery gardens (properly so called) were more than a dozen in number, and were well stocked with plants, some of which were cultivated in pots and others planted out in the ground. As in the garden already noticed, by far the greater number of these plants had been obtained from the southern provinces, and are tender in this latitude.

In order to save these plants during the rigour of a Tien-tsin winter there are, in every garden, a number of winter-houses, in which the plants are stowed away. These houses have thick mud walls on the north, east, and west sides; they have also mud roofs, and in front, facing the south, there is a framework of wood. This framework is pasted over with paper, which admits light enough to keep the plants alive; and there is a thick mat and straw covering, which can be used when the cold is unusually severe. Sometimes the floors of such houses are furnished with hot-air chambers and furnaces, by which means artificial heat, in a rude way, can be applied. Owing to the severity of the winter, almost every plant in cultivation is protected, in some way or other, at that season of

the year. Even common junipers, which are
perfectly hardy in England, have to be protected
during the Tien-tsin winters. Out of doors I
noticed large holes in the ground in various places,
and was told that these were used for the protection of plants, which, after being put in, were
thatched over or covered up with straw.

The few plants which did not require protection were of deciduous kinds, which shed their
leaves in the autumn, and are leafless all winter.
Amongst them were the *Jasminum* and *Weigela*
already mentioned, and the now well-known
Prunus triloba. There was also what appeared
to be a new species of *Forsythia*, with thick, dark,
shining leaves. Although I had previously found
most of these plants in Chusan, Shanghae, Soo-
chow, and in the countries adjoining these places,
it is not improbable they may be natives of a more
northern latitude, and this would account for the
hardiness of their constitutions, which enables
them to withstand the cold of our English winters.
It is a fact worth noting, however, that, as a
general rule, all *deciduous* plants from the places
just mentioned are perfectly hardy in Europe and
America. What, for example, can be more hardy
with us than the beautiful *Glycine sinensis* when
trained over our houses or walls, or the pretty
Jasminum nudiflorum, which becomes covered with
yellow flowers in mid-winter, and oftentimes shows
itself peeping out from under a mantle of snow ?

Chrysanthemums are largely cultivated in most

of these gardens. Some of them are trained as
" standards," and somewhat resemble in form our
dwarf standard rose - trees. In order that they
may assume this appearance, they are grafted on
the stout stems of a species of *Artemesia* or wormwood. They grow with great vigour on this
stock, and appear rather curious objects to those
who have seen them only on their own stems.
The Chinese are extremely fond of grafting plants,
and of having several species or varieties growing
on one tree. In one of these gardens I observed
two species of Thuja and one Juniper, all growing
together on one stem.

Apples, pears, and Siberian crabs are cultivated
in pots in these gardens, and, apparently, with
great success, for the little trees were all loaded
with fruit. The Chinese have, probably, been
doing this for ages past, just as they have been
growing roses in pots, dwarf and covered with
bloom, while we have only found out very
recently that such things could be done. The
Tien-tsin apples are very beautiful to look upon—
the skin is thin and transparent, and the colour a
delicate pink red, but the taste is sweet, without
flavour, and almost insipid.

Grapes also are plentiful, and may be had in
perfection all the year round. There are a
number of large ice-houses in the town, where
whole cargoes of apples, pears, and grapes are
packed away in round tubs, and taken out as they
are required. The floors of these fruit ice-houses

are considerably below the level of the surrounding ground. When I visited one of them, in company with Dr. Gordon, we were rather puzzled at first in our endeavours to find out the .manner in which the ice-water was carried off. On our eyes becoming accustomed to the darkness of the huge building, we groped our way towards one of the corners pointed out to us by the proprietor, and found a deep well which received the drainage from the floor. The tubs of fruit are packed one above another, and the spaces between them are filled in with ice ; they are also covered over with the same material. In this way fruit of all kinds can be kept perfectly sound from one year to another.

The vineyards, where the greater part of the grapes brought to Tien-tsin are produced, are situated on the left bank of the Grand Canal, about three miles from the city. Having seen the mode of preserving the grapes, we set out one day to see the vineyards. Crossing the bridge of boats already noticed, we rode through an extensive suburb, and then reached the open country. In this part the land, being comparatively fertile, is all under cultivation. Large fields of cabbages, onions, and garlic were passed, indicating the vicinity of a populous town. Here and there thin patches of millet and oily grain were observed as we went along.

Some distance beyond the suburbs of the town we came to a line of fortifications known as San-go-lin-tsin's wall and ditch, an immense earthwork which encircles the city and suburbs of Tien-tsin. This work was intended by the Chinese commander to defend the place against the attacks of the Allied force, on its march through the country *en route* to Peking. It occupied two years in construction, and was of no use after all, as every one knows who is conversant with the movements of the French and English troops during the late war. It is now best known to foreigners as "San-go-lin-tsin's Folly."

Passing through an opening in this earthwork, we observed the vineyards we had come to visit a short distance ahead of us, and were soon in the midst of them. Narrow lanes, bounded on each side by fences, intersected the ground, and divided the different vineyards from each other. Inside of the fences the vines were trained on flat wooden trellis-work, about ten feet from the ground, and looked like so many bowers or arbours. At this season (Sept. 9th) the grapes were ripening, and the crop appeared to be a most abundant one. It did not strike me that the natives were good cultivators. The stems of the vines were too crowded and rambling, and, apparently, but little care was expended on their training. Yet the pretty lanes, the green trellises, and the hanging bunches of grapes, had a pleasing appearance, and well rewarded us for the trouble we had taken to visit the place. These vineyards covered a large tract of land in this part of the country, and looked like a little oasis in the wide plain. The vines seemed to be nearly all of one and the same variety, and produced large berries of a greenish colour, getting darker as they ripened, and covered with bloom.*

Near these vineyards, and sometimes amongst them, there were a number of large nursery gardens, where annuals and herbaceous plants were cultivated in enormous quantities. These consisted chiefly of balsams, coxcombs, African marygolds, China asters, tuberoses, and chrysanthemums. Here, as elsewhere, the pomegranate seemed an especial favourite, and it was largely grown. In addition to the trees already mentioned as growing in this part of the country, I observed a poplar in these gardens, which grows to a large size, and is a tree of considerable beauty. Whether it be indigenous or introduced from some other country is at present unknown.

From this description of the gardens, fruit-trees, vineyards, and ice-houses of Tien-tsin, it will be gathered that, with all its crumbling mud walls and filthy streets, there must be many wealthy people in it, to whom the luxuries of life are indispensable. In my experience as regards Chinese towns, I have always observed a curious connection between nursery gardens and a thriving trade which produces wealth. Where the one is found, the other is generally not far off. In proof

---

* Another variety, with large thick-skinned oval berries, was common in the market of Tien-tsin.

of this I may instance Canton, Shanghae, and Soo-chow, and I have no doubt, when Tien-tsin is better known, we may add it to the list. The existence of this demand for the luxuries of life augurs well, therefore, for the future of this port as a great emporium for foreign trade.

On the approach of winter a wonderful change comes over these little gardens. Plants, flower-pots, and every green thing disappear as if by the stroke of some magician's wand, and the places which all summer long had been gay with flowers, then look like a desert waste. All the plants have been huddled together in the houses erected for their protection, and there they must remain until the severity of the winter has passed by. The vineyards I have described also disappear from the scene. The stems of the vines are taken down from the trellis-work, and buried in the earth at a depth sufficient to protect them from the frost. Here they remain in safety during the winter, and are disinterred in spring. The Tien-tsin plain, too, at this season is probably one of the most dreary-looking places on which the sun shines. As far as the eye can reach not a green bush or tree is visible in the horizon; all is cold and cheerless; and one is apt to fancy that at last he has reached " the ends of the earth."

CHAPTER XX.

The people of Tien-tsin — Visit to a gentleman's house — Reception —
Street beggars — Begging musicians — Civil hospital established
by the English — Dr. Lamprey's report — Chinese poorhouse —
Fat beggars — Climate and temperature — Dust-storms — Remarkable size of natural productions — Large men and horses — Shantung
fowls — Gigantic millet, oily grain, and egg-apples — Jute —
Vegetables in cultivation — Imperial granaries — Use of millet and
jute stems — Foreign trade — New settlement for foreign merchants
— The future of Tien-tsin as a centre of trade.

The people in Tien-tsin and in the country around
it are quiet and inoffensive, and particularly civil
and polite to foreigners. Our late intercourse with
them has been very different from that of former
days, when the dispute was about the performance
of the *ko-tou* to the Emperor, and when we were
only represented by an ambassador and his
attendants. This time we had visited them with
an army; we had driven the " Son of Heaven "
himself into Tartary, and had sacked and burned
his summer palace. Having received a good flog-
ging, these children had now become very good
boys; and if they did not love us, which we could
scarcely expect, we were certainly feared and
respected. But up to the present time they have
not the same confidence in us as their countrymen

in the more southern towns, with whom we have
been longer associated.   The women run into
their houses and shut their doors on the approach
of a foreigner, and the people generally are averse
to our entering their dwellings.

One day I observed, not far from the north gate
of the city, some high trees enclosed by a wall,
and, as the place looked somewhat like a garden, I
felt anxious to enter and examine it.   When the
inmates saw me approaching, an alarm was
instantly given, and the door, which had been
standing wide open, was unceremoniously shut in.
my face.   Nothing daunted by this proceeding, I
mildly remonstrated with those who stood behind
it, telling them they had nothing to fear from me ;
that I was, like themselves, fond of flowers, and
begged permission to examine the garden.   After
some consultation amongst them, the door was
opened, and ten or twelve of the male portion of
the establishment presented themselves.   I suppose I did not look as if I would do anything
wrong, so, after a little parleying, they consented
to admit me.   A message was sent in to warn the
ladies to get out of the way and hide themselves,
an order, by the bye, which was not obeyed very
strictly, and I was then led into the courts of the
mansion.   Here I found some pretty rockwork
and ponds, with a few flowering shrubs and trees
arranged and grouped according to Chinese taste,
and all very pretty and enjoyable.   Having had
much experience of Chinese manners and polite-

ness, I soon got into the good graces of the
gentlemen by whom I was accompanied; and, as
we discussed the merits of the different plants, the
fears which had taken possession of their minds at
first entirely disappeared. My knowledge of the
Chinese names of the different shrubs and trees,
which a long residence in the country had enabled
me to acquire, was most useful here, as it had often
been in other places. And as we talked of the
beauties of the "Mo-le-hwa," the "Cha-hwa," or
the "Tu-hwa," * I evidently rose many degrees in
their estimation, and was looked upon as a being
not so very *barbarous* after all. After drinking
sundry cups of tea, and getting the names of other
places where plants were cultivated, I expressed
my thanks and took my leave.

The beggars of Tien-tsin are rather prominent
objects. Here, as in the southern towns, they
appear to have a kind of organization, having a
chief, or "king of the beggars," who rules over
them and directs their proceedings. They are
most tyrannical in their conduct towards the more
respectable inhabitants of the town, particularly
the shopkeepers, whose business obliges them to
have their doors always open. These beggars will
assemble in companies, take possession of the
door, beat the counter with stones, sticks, or whatever they may have in their hands, and howl for
alms. It is an amusing sight to see the poor

---

* Jasmine, camellia, chrysanthemum.

shopkeepers, during an attack of this kind, sitting calm and quiet, and pretending not to see or hear what is going on.

Sturdy Beggars.—From a Photograph.

In Tien-tsin, as in other parts of the Chinese empire, the beggars divide themselves into three or four very distinct classes. There is, first, the able-bodied, without any apparent physical deformity, who could work if they liked, but who prefer to gain a livelihood by begging. These have a proverb which says, " The finest rice has not charms equal to a roving liberty."

Many of these appear to be very low in the scale of humanity, very cunning, weak-minded, or almost insane. They are not at all particular in their efforts to gain a living, and, when they have an opportunity, are quite as ready to thieve as to beg. They associate in gangs, and not unfrequently end their days on the scaffold.

The aged, diseased, lame, and blind, form another large class, many of whom are really objects of pity. Some of these are like Lazarus of old, "covered with sores" of the most loathsome kind, in many instances artificial, in others natural, but brought on by their peculiar mode of life. Story-tellers, singers of poetry beating time on sticks or bones, and blind musicians playing on a kind of guitar, are all common objects in the streets.

Street Musicians — From a Photograph.

The latter are generally better dressed and have a cleaner appearance than the other classes of mendicants.

The "widow and her fatherless children" is not an uncommon group, and is often met with at the corners of streets "begging for alms." As in other countries nearer home, the parentage of the youthful members of the family is not quite as certain as the mother would have us believe.

The above groups were photographed by Dr. Lamprey, of the 67th Regiment, who had charge of an hospital for the poor of Tien-tsin, established and supported by the British Army of Occupation.   All honour to the British army! this was a noble example to set before the natives of a heathen land.   The hospital was evidently appreciated by the Chinese, and did a great amount of good.   Dr. Lamprey, in a printed report which he was good enough to give me, tells some amusing stories of these Tien-tsin beggars.   "A beggar presented himself at the hospital, with his arm in a bent position, and drawn up to his head through the contraction of a cicatrix, caused by a burn he had received when a child.   A very simple operation would have sufficed to release the limb, and give him as good use of it as he needed to enable him to work, but he would not submit to it; it was not the pain of the operation he feared, but it was that he should lose so good a sympathy exciter!   In short, to be

cured of this deformity would have been utter ruin
to the man." On expressing some anxiety as to
the future of a poor lad who had had his thigh
amputated, and asking a Chinese " What was the
best thing for him to do to get his living ? " he
replied, " That the lad could not be a pedler or
keep a tradesman's shop, as he could neither read
nor write ; but, oh ! he is all right, he can make a
very good beggar-man," alluding to the absence
of his leg as a good exciter of charity. Dr. Lamprey adds his testimony to that of others regarding the coolness and patience with which the
Chinese submit to severe surgical operations.
When it is necessary to amputate an arm or a leg
the patient would say, " Good, cut it off ; but
give me the medicine to smell "—meaning chlo-
roform.

How these beggars can live through a Tien-tsin
winter it is difficult to imagine. The authorities
have a kind of poorhouse, where five hundred
human beings were located during the winter of
1860-61. Each inmate is allowed a small quantity
of the commonest kind of grain daily, but he is
obliged to provide his own fuel, which he begs,
steals, or picks up in some way or other ; he is
not particular so that he gets it. No doubt the
severity of the winter carries off many of these
poor wretches to their long homes ; indeed, their
bodies are frequently seen on the road-sides and
in the streets, lying where they died. Dr. Lamprey remarks, however, that their powers of

endurance, notwithstanding the low temperature of the climate and of the poorhouse, are rather remarkable. During the coldest days of winter, many were seen in the streets in a state of nudity, excepting a small rag round their loins. Such beggars were noticed to be remarkably fat; and it was supposed by some that this was owing to the quantity of carbonic acid gas inhaled in their close, ill-ventilated sleeping-places. Others rather attributed it to a provision of nature, which corresponded with what was observed in birds and other animals at this time of the year.

The climate of this part of China is very cold in winter and warm in summer. It is subject to those excesses of cold and heat which are experienced on the eastern side of large continents,— a fact noticed long ago by the immortal Humboldt. The following table, for which I am indebted to Dr. Lamprey, gives the maximum and minimum as shown by a registering thermometer during twelve months :—

1861.	Thermometer (Fahr.).	
	Maximum.	Minimum.
January	38	−0·8
February	46	−1·5
March	68	18
April	87	35
May	94	41
June	107	53
July	108	61
August	100	60·5
September	92	40
October	77	40
November	42	17·5
December	50	8

From this table, February appears to be the coldest month in the year. The thermometer in this month registered one degree and a half below zero, or upwards of 33 degrees of frost. January appears to be nearly as cold, and the lowest, in December, was only three degrees above zero. In places less sheltered, and away from buildings, a thermometer stood four or five degrees lower than it did in Tien-tsin, where the above observations were made. But the cold as indicated by the thermometer does not give an idea of that which is actually felt by those who are exposed to that cutting and piercing wind which sweeps along the dreary level plain.

The rivers and canals are usually frozen over by the end of November, and continue in this state until the middle of March. In 1861 the ice began to move on the the 12th of March, and in the short space of three days it had entirely disappeared. This is remarkable, when we remember that it is usually sixteen inches in thickness.

June, July, and August are the hottest months in the year. The highest point (108°) was registered in July. This heat, with the sun's rays streaming through an atmosphere which is generally clear and cloudless, was found to be very trying to the constitutions of our soldiers and the foreign residents who had settled down in Tientsin. During the months of April and May hot winds are not unfrequent. In the southern provinces of China the heat of summer is often

tempered by the rains which fall copiously at that
season, particularly in May and June, and sometimes as late as July. Judging from our experience in 1861, the rainy season does not extend
so far north as Tien-tsin. That the difference
is most marked will be seen by the following
table, in which Macao and Tien-tsin are compared :—

Average fall of rain in inches in Macao.		Average fall of rain in inches in Tien tsin.	
May . .	11·850	May . .	2·585
June . .	11·100	June . .	1·795
July . .	7·750	July . .	1·035
August .	9·900	August .	6·75
September	10·925	September	2·52

It is just possible that the year 1861 may have
been one of unusual dryness, and that future
observations may record a larger fall of rain
during the months just quoted.

Dust-storms of a very remarkable character
frequently occur in this part of China. They
come on suddenly, and a thick darkness covers the
land for many hours together. On the 26th of
March in the present year (1862) one of a very
extraordinary kind was experienced, which is
thus described in the ' North China Herald ' by
Dr. Lamprey :—

"During the greater portion of the day the
wind was blowing from the south in rather strong
gusts, almost approaching to a gale. At 3h. 15m.
P.M. the wind suddenly shifted to N.N.W. in a
strange manner, when all at once the air was
filled with dust, and the sun and light became

obscured as if a total eclipse had suddenly occurred. The wind blowing a hurricane, the darkness had something appalling in it, it was so
sudden and so unusual. It was noticed that the
darkness would lighten somewhat, at intervals of
a quarter of an hour or twenty minutes, as if about
to abate, when it would suddenly increase again,
along with a slight change of wind to the N.N.E.
The wind, endeavouring to become more northerly, would suddenly turn again to this point, and
bring along with it an increase of the dust. This
state continued till about midnight, when there
was a slight calm, which lasted until about eight
o'clock the following morning.

"On the occurrence of this dust-storm there
was a rapid fall of the thermometer, and during
the night a hard frost set in. At the place where
I made these observations—about thirty miles
N.W. of Tien-tsin—I noticed a poor man of seventy
years of age in a very excited state, crying out
' What day is this?' and ' low-le,' the words corre-
sponding to 'Oh, Providence.' He would give
me little or no information on the subject; but
from others I learned that such heavy storms had
occurred before; and on my return to Tien-tsin
I ascertained that one happened thirty-six years
ago which lasted a fortnight, and that the light
during that time was somewhat like the dusk of
evening. I also learned that the Chinese desig-
nated this storm as a red one—their classification
being as follows : white, yellow, red, and black ;

depending on the amount of light, or, more properly speaking, the amount of dust in the atmosphere at the time. The quantity of dust that covered one's person was astonishing, and the clothes, &c., inside the coat were thickly covered with it. On drawing a feather through the fingers it became strongly electrified. .

"When I returned to Tien-tsin I learned that the dust-storm occurred there about the same time we experienced it thirty miles N.W., and that the electric conductor showed an extraordinary quantity of electricity—a large blue flame poured out of the end of the conductor without intermission. There being little or no light, this showed a beautiful appearance, while the sound of it was quite audible at some distance off, and the shock felt on touching the conductor was powerful. The quantity of dust that entered the house was very great. There was a recurrence of the dust-storm on the 27th, but not approaching in strength to the one on the 26th. It was also ascertained that it occurred at Peking, and at Taku, where the fury of the storm was greatest. Several country boats were wrecked in the river Peiho. Repeated observations have enabled me to come to the conclusion that these dust-storms are owing to the electric condition of the atmosphere."

The natural productions of these northern provinces, both in the animal and vegetable kingdoms, are, in many instances, remarkable for their great size. In former days the merchants who came

z

down from Shantung to Shanghae astonished the
natives of the latter place, and were greater objects
of attraction than even the foreign residents.
These Shantung merchants were large men, much
above the average size of Chinamen, and, as they
took an airing in the evenings on the ramparts of
Shanghae, they were followed by crowds of admiring natives. Peking horses, which happened
to come down at that time, were also much larger
than the southern kinds. The well-known Cochin
China fowls, some of which are nearly as large as
turkeys, are also originally from the province of
Shantung.

During the late war the size of the common
grain in the fields about Tien-tsin and Peking
astonished our soldiers, and the high, thick stubble
formed a serious impediment to the marching of
our cavalry. This is the millet already noticed,
which grows to a height of fifteen feet and upwards. It covers the plains of this part of China,
being the staple summer crop, and ripening about
the middle of September. Oily grain (*Sesamum
orientale*) is also extensively grown on the plain of
Tien-tsin, from the Gulf of Pechele to the mountains beyond Peking, and is fully twice as large
and productive as that grown in the south.
Amongst plants cultivated for the sake of their
fibre, the Jute (*Corchorus sp.*) is the most important. This, too, grows to a great height.

Amongst green crops I noticed Brinjals,
Gourds, Cucumbers, Vegetable Marrows, Yams,

various kinds of Cabbages, Onions, Carrots, Turnips, French Beans, Capsicums, Ginger, and common and sweet Potatoes. Amongst these, the Gourds and the Egg-apples, or Brinjals, grew to a very large size,—some of the latter measuring eighteen inches in circumference ! The Sunflower was also a giant here, and attained a height of fourteen feet.

The greater part of the rice used in these districts is brought up in junks from the south. Large Imperial granaries have been built in different parts of the country, where the rice is laid up in store. I visited one of these at a place named Pae-tsang, situated on the left bank of the Pei-ho, some six miles from Tien-tsin. It consisted of sixteen large buildings or barns, each fifty feet wide, three hundred feet in length, and about forty or fifty feet high. At the upper end I observed a small temple, which contained a figure of Tsang-shin, the god who is supposed to protect the granaries. At the time of my visit the barns were all empty, and their doors were nailed up. In these troubled times the grain-junks could not pass through the country. At Peking I afterwards saw a number of Imperial granaries built upon the same plan, and presenting the same appearance.

It has been already observed that there are few trees in the Tien-tsin plain. Fuel from this source is therefore almost unknown; but bountiful nature here steps in and supplies the want from another source. The tall stout stems of the millet, and those of the jute-plant, from which the bark has been removed for its fibre, are saved and stacked up for this purpose, and thus take the place of branches of trees and brushwood. In other parts of China, where trees are plentiful, millet of this kind, and jute, are not met with.

Foreign merchants and traders at Tien-tsin have as yet met with few articles for export, except the precious metals. Here there is no silk or tea—articles which form the most valuable of our exports from the ports of the south. Peas and beans are sent to the south in large quantities, but chiefly from Shantung, on the southern shores of the Gulf of Pe-chele, and Newchwang in the north—the latter being the most northerly of the trading ports. It is to be hoped that, as we get better acquainted with the trade of Tien-tsin, some valuable articles for export may present themselves to the notice of foreign merchants, for at present their ships have generally to go away in ballast.

The import trade at this port is already one of considerable importance, but is confined chiefly to our cotton goods and opium. As the winters are cold, we may expect a demand, in the course of time, for our woollen manufactures, and doubtless for other articles of European and American comfort and luxury; and it is very likely that foreign merchants will take the coasting trade out of the hands of the junkmen, and bring up the supplies of medicine, dyes, and other articles of Straits produce formerly carried in the junks from Canton,

Singapore, and the other ports of the Straits of Malacca, &c.

On the right bank of the Pei-ho, below the suburbs of Tien-tsin, and near an old dilapidated fort, a large tract of land has been set apart for the houses and godowns of foreigners, and for the Consulates of those foreign Powers that have treaties with China. This land, at the time of my visit, was covered with vegetable gardens, a few miserable mud huts, and a good sprinkling of tombs. At one portion of the ground a granite stone, with Chinese characters, informed the traveller that this had been set apart for the merchants of the "Great English Nation." The French settlement adjoined the English, and the subjects of the other treaty Powers will be located in the same quarter. The ground is low, and I believe liable to be flooded by the river at high tides or after heavy rains. It will therefore require to be raised above the highest high-water mark. As in Shanghae, the dead will have to "move on" to some quieter locality, in order to give room for the living. When choosing their graves, these good people little thought that the "barbarians" or "white devils" from the West would one day turn them out of the quarters which they had selected with so much care.

When I last visited the site of the settlement (October, 1861) its purchase had been arranged, the money had been paid, and some of the merchants were about to commence raising the land.

It was curious to remark the effect of all this upon
the Chinese labourers, who had probably been all
their lives located upon the spot. They evidently
could not realize the idea that they were really to
move off to other quarters. In many instances I
observed them busily engaged in putting in fresh
crops for the following year! They could not
comprehend the justice or propriety of being
turned out of their houses and lands for the
benefit of the public, and that public the foreigner!
As the purchase-money had been paid into the
hands of the Chinese Government, it had doubtless
to submit to a "squeeze" before it reached the
pockets of the owners of the land.

In drawing to a close my remarks upon the port
of Tien-tsin and the country around it, I may state
my belief that ultimately this place will prove of
great importance as a mart for our manufactures.
Next to the opening of the Yang-tze-kiang, it will
probably prove the most valuable concession obtained from the Chinese in Lord Elgin's treaty.
When the rebellion, which has been raging for
years in this unhappy country, has either died out
or has been put down, the rivers and canals will
once more swarm with boats engaged in active
trade. The Grand Canal, which leads through some
of the richest and most populous districts of the
empire, and which is now choked up in many places
with mud, or rendered unsafe by bands of rebels
and robbers, will then become the busy highway it
once was, and foreigners as well as natives will be

allowed to visit the numerous cities and towns which line its banks. The river which leads from Tien-tsin to Pow-ting-foo, one of the chief towns of the province, will take a large quantity of our manufactures, and the caravans which come to that place will convey them all over the western interior. In addition to all this there is the capital itself, teeming with its many thousands of human beings, all requiring food and clothing, and carrying on an extensive trade with Western China and Tartary by means of camels, droves of which are daily arriving and departing from the city.

Taking all these facts together, we may venture to look forward to Tien-tsin becoming, at no very distant time, a most important mart for our manufactures. Already English houses begin to rise on the new settlement, and ere the world grows many years older a handsome foreign town will be seen on the land which was lately covered with cabbage-gardens, mud huts, and tombs. The Rev. Mr. Edkins and other Christian missionaries have also entered this field; and by their knowledge of the Chinese language, their inoffensive manners, and their blameless lives, do much to remove many prejudices which exist in the minds of the people against those who have come to reside amongst them.

CHAPTER XXI.

HAVING received permission to visit Peking from
his Excellency the Hon. F. W. A. Bruce, Her
Majesty's Minister at the Chinese Court, I left
Tien-tsin for that place on the 17th of September.
A passport, written in Chinese and English, and
signed by Her Majesty's Consul, was necessary
before I could set out on this journey. As the
passport system in China is something new, here
is the English portion of the one with which I
was furnished :—

Passport No. 53.
                              BRITISH CONSULATE, 16th Sept. 1861.
    The undersigned, Her Britannic Majesty's Consul at
Tien-tsin, requests the Civil and Military Authorities of the
Emperor of China, in conformity with the ninth article of the
Treaty of Tien-tsin, to allow   , a British subject,
to travel freely, and without hindrance or molestation, in the
Chinese Empire, and to give him protection and aid in case of
necessity.

Mr.   being a person of known respectability,
is desirous of proceeding to   , and this passport is
given him on condition of his not visiting the cities or towns
occupied by the Insurgents.

H. B. M.'s Consul.

This passport will remain in force for a year from the date thereof.

Signature of the bearer :

This passport was countersigned by the Chinese
authority of the place.

There are two modes of travelling from Tien-
tsin to the capital—by boat up the Pei-ho as far as
Tong-chow, and then on by land, or by cart on
the common highway. In going up I chose the
latter, in order to save time, and also to enable me
to see more of the country and its productions.
The carts used by travellers are strongly made,
and covered over so as to afford protection from
sun and rain. They look in the distance like little
oblong boxes on wheels, and are generally drawn
by two mules.

The Peking road starts from the north gate of
the city of Tien-tsin, crosses the Grand Canal by a
bridge of boats, and enters a dense suburb which
extends across towards the Pei-ho. My troubles
now began. The road was one of the worst I had
ever travelled upon. It was full of deep holes at
every step of our way; now one of my wheels
plunged into one of these up to the axle, and
it was scarcely up when down went the other.
Although I had before starting packed my cart
carefully with bedding and pillows, I was every

now and then jolted against its sides with great
violence. These carts are not furnished with
springs of any kind; indeed the strongest
springs, if subjected to such jolting, would soon
get broken.

On our way through the suburb I observed a
great number of large hotels for the accommodation of travellers in going to or returning from
the capital. Travelling onwards in a northerly
direction, we soon reached the banks of the Pei-ho,
near a point where another river falls into it.
This river is called the " Small Pei-ho," and is the
one I have already mentioned as leading up to the
important town of Pow-ting-foo, the chief town of
the district. Having crossed the river by a bridge
of boats, we found that we had left Tien-tsin and
its suburbs entirely behind us, and were now in
the open country. For many miles the country
around was perfectly flat, and covered in all directions with *Kow-leang*, the tall millet already
noticed. Now and then, during the journey, we
got glimpses of the Pei-ho as it wound, snake-like,
through the plain; and the tall masts and sails of
boats showed themselves here and there, in the
distance, above the tops of the millet.

During the day we passed through the towns of
Puh-kow and Yang-tsoun, and arrived at Tsai-
tsoun in the evening, having come a distance of
eighty-five le, or somewhere about twenty-eight
English miles. There are two large inns in this
place, and in one of these I determined on putting

up for the night.   The town in which I had taken up my quarters, as well as the others passed through during the day, was chiefly built of mud; and I must say all of them had a poor, dirty, and uninviting appearance, very different from those I had been in the habit of visiting in the provinces further south.

The inn which I had chosen was entered by a covered way; and in the courtyard I found fifteen other carts like my own, some going to the capital and others returning from it.   The courtyard was a square, with bedrooms on three sides, and the kitchen occupied the greater part of the fourth. Each traveller had his cart drawn up in front of his room.   Mine host presented himself on my arrival, and wished to know what it was my pleasure to order for the evening meal.   I made it an invariable rule, when placed in circumstances of this kind, to live upon the simplest food, and to abstain from mixtures and made dishes.   I therefore replied that I wished to dine on rice and eggs, two articles which I had generally found plentiful in the country, as well as clean and wholesome; but, to my surprise, mine host informed me that he had no rice in his house, and he did not think there was any to be had in the town.   "What! no rice in China!"   I could scarcely credit the man until I began to reflect that this was not a rice-producing district, and that the empty granaries I had visited showed too plainly that the rebellion and foreign wars had

prevented the arrival of the usual supplies from
the south. However, I obtained a mutton chop,
hard-boiled eggs, and soft bread made of millet,
and with these I made up a dinner. Animal food
appears to be consumed by these northern Chinese
to a far greater extent than by their countrymen
in the south. Butchers' shops are met with in all
the towns, and both beef and mutton can be had
anywhere. This is probably owing to the circumstance that a large number of the people
are Mahomedans, whose prejudices, as regards
the use of animal food, are not like those of the
Buddhists.

Nearly shaken to pieces, and thoroughly tired
with the day's journey, I retired early to rest.
The bed-place in these inns is a raised mud platform erected at one end of the room, beneath
which there is a chamber which can be heated
during the winter months when the weather is
cold. A mat is spread out on the top of this platform, and this is all that is furnished by the innkeeper; the traveller in China always carries his
own bedding with him. As the Chinese are early
in their habits—going early to bed, and rising
early in the morning—the inn was soon perfectly
quiet, and nothing disturbed our slumbers, except
perhaps the occasional bark of a dog or the neigh-
ing of a horse in the courtyard.

At daylight next morning we resumed our
journey. The country through which we passed
was still flat, but rather better wooded than what

we had passed through the day before. The trees were chiefly weeping willows, elms, and *Sophora japonica*, the latter yielding a yellow dye called by the Chinese *whi-hwa*. The first town we passed to-day was Hoose-woo, now well known as the head-quarters of the English army when on its way to Peking. About six miles further on a place called Nan-ping was reached, and here I found a large and comfortable hotel, where I stopped to breakfast, and then went on to Matao, another town occupied by the English and French troops when on their way to the capital. Every now and then the road brought us near the banks of the Pei-ho; and sometimes mud dykes or embankments were seen stretching across the country, evidently as a preventive against floods.

The main road was at some places impassable, being several feet deep with mud and water. The carters, however, did not seem very particular; and temporary roads were made through the fields in every direction. The tall millet-stems, towering above our heads on each side, oftentimes prevented us from seeing anything of the country around us, and there appeared no landmarks to guide us on our way. The carters themselves had frequently to halt, not knowing where they were; and on more than one occasion we had to retrace our steps and get into another by-road.

In the evening we reached the town of Chan-chow-wan, and took up quarters at a hotel

similar in all respects to the one I had stopped
at the night before.   The accommodation at these
Chinese hotels is certainly not of a very high
order, but the charges are moderate enough.
Dinner and rooms for myself and servant
amounted to the large sum of two hundred and
fifty "cash," or little more than one shilling of
English money.   It will be observed, therefore,
that poor accommodation and high charges did
not go hand in hand as they are sometimes said
to do in more civilized countries.

At grey dawn on the following morning we
left our inn, and, with many other travellers, went
rumbling along the old rough streets of Chan-
chow-wan.   When we reached the open country
it was found to be less flat and of an undulating
character, and more trees were also observed.
That the country was higher was evident from
the kinds of productions which were now met with
in the fields.   Large quantities of Indian corn,
buckwheat, sweet potatoes, and soy - beans were
here under cultivation.   The gigantic egg-apples
were very luxuriant here; and the oily grain
grew to a height of five feet and seemed to be
very productive.

The mountains which had been seen, now and
then, during the journey from Tien-tsin, appeared
but a short distance to the north and westward,
and the situation of the capital was pointed out by
the drivers of our carts.   By noon of this day the
high walls and ramparts of Peking were distinctly

visible, and shortly afterwards my cart rattled
through the gate of the Chinese city, and I found
myself for the first time in the capital of China.
As I approached the gate one of the guard rushed
out to inquire who I was and whence I came.
When my servant informed him that I was an
Englishman, and that I was on my way to Her
Majesty's Legation, he appeared perfectly satisfied,
and did not even ask me for my passport.

The paved streets through which we now passed
were in a most dilapidated condition, and the
jolting of my cart was so great that I was glad to
get out and walk. After we had gone about a
mile in a northerly direction we came to the wall
which divides the Chinese city from the Tartar
one, and entered the latter through a huge and
massive gateway, crowned with a guard-house
loopholed for guns, many of which are said
to be wooden ones and only for show! On
my arrival at the residence of the English Ambassador, I was kindly received by His Excellency
Mr. Bruce.

The British, French, and Russian Legations are
located in the Tartar city, near the south wall,
and close to the palace of the Emperor. The
residence of the English Minister is a most
gorgeous place. It belongs or belonged at one
time to a Duke Leang, and is called Leang-kung-
foo, or the Palace of Leang. It covers many
acres of land, and consists of a series of large and
lofty halls, four or five in number, rising one behind

the other by flights of broad stone steps, and
separated from each other by paved courts. The
wood carving in these halls is of the most elaborate
kind; and as the whole place has been put into
admirable order, it is a fitting residence for the
Minister of Great Britain, and one in which he
can worthily receive the high officials of the Court
of the Emperor.

At right angles with these halls, and ranged
along each side, are numerous buildings of a less
pretending kind, which are used as rooms for the
officers of the Legation, and for visitors. In one
of these rooms I found my old friend Dr. Lockhart, of the Medical Missionary Society, who had
come to establish an hospital in the capital, similar
to that which he had carried on so successfully
for many years in Shanghae. Before I left the
city he had obtained, through the influence of
Mr. Bruce and the assistance of Mr. Wade, possession of an adjoining building, which he intended
to fit up as a residence and as an hospital. This
is a matter of no slight importance, and will
doubtless be productive of a great amount of good.
I believe no religious efforts in China are likely to
be crowned with so much success as those of the
medical missionary. The Chinese, cold and un-
impressible as they are, can understand and
appreciate his labours. Skilful, disinterested,
" healing all manner of diseases " without " money
and without price," he can make an impression
on their " stony hearts," and thus prepare a soil

for the reception of the good seed which may be sown either by himself or by those who come after him.

In the afternoon I went, in company with Dr. Lockhart, to visit the Observatory, a place famous for its collection of astronomical instruments, and for the fine view of the city which can be obtained from its summit. It is placed inside the Tartar city, and close to the eastern wall. On entering its precincts we presented our cards and were politely received by the keepers. In their room they showed us a map of the world, prepared under the direction of Father Ricci upwards of two hundred years ago. We then ascended a flight of steps leading to the top of the Observatory, which is fully sixty feet above the level of the ground. Here we found a number of large astronomical instruments beautifully cast. Large celestial globes, quadrants, and other instruments, particularly attracted our attention. These were evidently the work of foreign missionaries, and had probably been imported from Europe. If cast in China during Father Ricci's time, they are well calculated to excite our wonder, but this I think can hardly have been the case. An iron rail of beautiful workmanship surrounded the whole.

The view from the top of the Observatory on a clear day is exceedingly fine. Looking southwards the Chinese city was seen to stretch for miles away in that direction. To the west and north the Tartar city lay spread out before us, having the Imperial city and its palaces, with their yellow-tiled roofs, in its centre. *King-shan,* a charming little hill, called by foreigners "Prospect Hill," with its temples and summer-houses, presented a very pretty object. This hill is said to be artificial, and formed almost entirely of coal, which had been stored up to be used in case of a siege. As we looked over the immense city we observed that, as in other Chinese towns, the houses were all about one uniform height, and the whole place was green with trees. The tree most common here is the *Sophora japonica* already named as one which grows on the plain of Tien-tsin. We could trace the walls and ramparts on all sides of the city, and discern the different gates, marked as they were by the huge guard-houses erected over each of them. Far away to the westward appeared some pagodas and minarets; and in the Chinese city, to the south, we could see the tower of the temple sacred to the God of Agriculture, to which the Emperor is said to repair once in every year to worship and to hold the plough.

The Tartar city has nine gates, is oblong in form, and is about three miles from east to west and four miles from north to south. The Imperial city, situated inside the Tartar city, is of a square or rather oblong form, and encloses the palaces and gardens of the Emperor, and the pretty little "Prospect Hill" already noticed. It is situated in the centre of the Tartar city, and is about one-third of its width from east to west, and one-half of its length from north to south.   Here reside the Emperor and the ladies of the court; the eunuchs in waiting, who amounted in Father Ripa's time to six thousand; and the family of the Emperor, some of whom have, when of age, separate establishments.   This is the only part of Peking which foreigners are not allowed to visit.

The Chinese city is situated on the south side of the Tartar one.   It is of a different form, being broader from east to west than from north to south. From the east to the west wall the distance is about four miles, while from the north to the south it is only about two miles, or perhaps rather less.   It has seven gates, in addition to three which lead through the wall dividing it from the Tartar city, so that, taking the two cities together, the number of gates is sixteen in all.

We lingered long on the top of the Observatory, and certainly the view we had was no common one, and was well worth coming a long way to enjoy.   This view was bounded on the west and north by a range of mountains of considerable height, while on the south and east lay the vast plain through which I had been travelling for three days, and in which, as far as the eye could reach, there was no sign of either mountain or hill—like the ocean, it stretched far away to the distant horizon.

2 A 2

There is no place in Peking whence a better idea of the size of the city and the positions of its various objects of interest can be obtained than from the top of the Observatory. Having marked well the different objects and places most worthy of closer inspection, I determined to visit them in order during the following days of my stay in the capital.

CHAPTER XXII.

HAVING obtained a bird's-eye view of Peking from
the top of the Observatory, we set out on the following day to visit the Imperial city, the outside
of·the palaces, the little hill named King-shan, and
other objects of interest to the westward. The
streets of the capital differ much from those of the
other towns in China which I have visited. They
are very wide, straight, and generally run at right
angles with each other, so that a stranger has little
difficulty in finding his way from one point to
another; but they are, for the most part, in
wretched condition. When the weather is wet
they are full of puddles and almost impassable,
and when it is dry and windy the dust is blinding
and intolerable.

Our way led us along the eastern walls of the palace, and we soon reached one of the gates which led into the Imperial city.   Entering this gate, we found ourselves close upon the Royal palace, which was surrounded by an inner wall and had its gate strictly guarded by soldiers.   Into this *sanctum sanctorum* we did not attempt to penetrate.   Passing onwards, we soon reached the northern end of the palace, and were then close upon King-shan or " Prospect Hill."   And very pretty this little hill looked, crowned as it is with temples, summer-houses, and trees.   Rounding it, we turned to the south and went along the outside of the western wall of the palace.   This is perhaps the most interesting part of Peking, and is well worth a visit. The roofs of the different palaces and temples, with their quaint forms and yellow tiles glittering in the sun, were particularly striking and interesting. Here we also found the Lama Mosque, surrounded by trees, and giving an Indian character to the scenery.   Although we could not enter the sacred enclosures, we got glimpses of pretty gardens with rock-work and artistic bridges, which gave us very favourable impressions of its internal beauties and made us long for a nearer view.   But, as already stated, although foreigners have liberty to wander all over the Imperial city, they cannot enter the grounds of the palace, nor King-shan, nor the enclosures in which the Lama temples and mosques are situated.

Leaving the walls of the Emperor's palace be-

hind us, we took a westerly course, and, passing
over a broad bridge, were soon out of the Imperial
city and again in the Tartar one. Here were
some wide streets with shops crowded inside and
out with all sorts of wares, and looking somewhat
like a bazaar. Passing out of the city by the Fow-
ching gate, we rode on in a northerly direction to
pay a visit to the Portuguese cemetery. This very
ancient place is in the form of a parallelogram, and
is surrounded with walls. A broad, straight, paved
walk leads up its centre. It is divided into two
parts by a cross wall with a gateway in the middle
of it. The outer department is used as a garden, and
has rows of pillars on each side of the centre walk
for the cultivation of vines. Passing up between
these and through the gate in the cross wall, we
found ourselves in the place of burial, in which lie
the remains of some hundred of the early Catholic
missionaries and their followers. Two marble
tablets of massive size, beautifully carved and surmounted by the cross, stand on each side of this
inner gateway. As we walked up the centre path-
way we observed rows of tombs at right angles with
the walk, one row behind the other in succession, all
the way up to the further end of the cemetery. In
front of each tomb there is a square slab of marble,
carved with dragons on the top in high relief, and
below this carving there are inscriptions in Chinese
and Latin giving the name of the occupant of the
tomb and the year in which he died. At the upper
end of the walk there is a row of carved stones, in

imitation of vases, and behind them, on a raised platform, a stone cross completes the arrangement.

The high state of preservation in which these tombstones are at the present day is very remarkable. Many of them, from the dates carved on them, must have been placed there more than two centuries and a half ago, and they show no signs of decay. I noted that of the well-known Father Ricci, with "P. Matthew Ricci, A.D. 1610," carved upon it. The tomb of the celebrated P. Fernandez Verries, who taught the Chinese the art of casting cannon, is also here. Some of these marble stones rest upon the back of a tortoise carved in the same material. This form of stone denotes that it was a gift from the Emperor of the time, who took this mode of showing his esteem for the deceased and his desire to honour his memory.

Pines, junipers, and other trees grow all over the cemetery, and throw a pleasing shade over the last resting-places of the ancient fathers. The Chinese seem to have charged themselves with the duty of keeping the place in order, and they have performed it well. When we left the cemetery we rode southwards along the side of the western wall until we came to the Chinese city. There was nothing in this part to attract our attention except the high walls and ramparts of the city and pleasant gardens in the suburbs. In our way from this point to the English Legation we passed the Roman Catholic cathedral, in which there are some foreign priests, who dress in the costume of the country, and are, no doubt, worthy successors of old Father Ripa.

My next excursion was through the Chinese city to some gardens which I had been informed were to be found in its southern suburbs. I passed out of the Tartar city by the Ching-wang-mun, the centre gate of its south wall. Inside and outside of this gate I observed carts in great numbers waiting to be hired, just as we see the cabs in London. Like them, the carts of Peking have their stands in the public thoroughfare. The noise and bustle about this gate was perfectly deafening. Carts were going to and fro, rumbling along on the rough stone road, and now and then sinking deeply into the broken pavement. Donkeys, horses, and long trains of camels laden with the productions of the country, were toiling along; a perfect Babel of noisy tongues was heard in all directions; and the dust was flying in clouds and literally filling the air. Stalls of fruit, hawkers of all kinds of wares, beggars ragged, filthy, and in many instances apparently insane, crowded the approaches to this gate.

When I had passed through I entered a straight and wide street which led through the centre of the Chinese city from north to south. The northern portion appeared to be densely populated. Each side of the main street was lined with shops and stalls, and a much more active trade was carried on here than in the Tartar city. The shop-fronts in Peking are rather striking, and differ in style from those observed in the more southern cities. Three or four long poles divide the front of the shop into equal parts. At a convenient height from the ground a signboard fills up the space between the poles, and has large letters upon it giving the name and calling of the owner. The tops of the poles are much higher than the roof of the shop, and each is surmounted or crowned by an ornamental carving.

As the fronts of these shops are moveable and always taken out during the day-time, their contents are fully exposed to the public. Articles of food and clothing, and all the common necessaries of life, are the principal wares which are dealt in by the Peking shopkeepers in the main streets of the city. Here there are no silk and tea for exportation such as one sees in the south, and everything stamps Peking as a consuming city rather than a producing one. Silk and cotton clothing, old clothes, skins, furs, and padded bed-covers to protect the wearer from the cold of a Peking winter, together with hats and shoes, are all plentiful. Substances used as food, such as pork, salt fish, beef and mutton, ducks and fowls, beans, peas, rice, various kinds of millet and other grains, are met with in all the market-places, as also oils of various kinds, dried fruits, and dyes. Vegetables and fruits are abundant, and are generally exposed for sale on open stalls lining each side of the street. At the time of my visit the large white Shantung cabbage, which is yearly sent to the south in junks, was very plentiful in Peking. I observed also a large white carrot, and the red turnip-radish, which is sent south every winter and made to flower in pots or flat saucers amongst pebbles and water at the time of the Chinese new year. Grapes and peaches were plentiful and fair in quality, but I did not meet with the latter weighing two pounds each, as they are stated to do in the works of earlier travellers. Pears are perhaps the most abundant amongst all the autumnal fruits in Peking. They are exposed for sale in every direction, in shops, in stalls, on the pavement, as well as in the basket of the hawker. There were two or three kinds, and one of them was high-flavoured and melting. This is the first instance of a pear of this kind having been found in China, and it is a most welcome addition to the tables of the foreign residents of Peking. Curiously enough, this fruit, excellent though it is, is as yet unknown at Tien-tsin, a place only about 70 miles distant !

On the right-hand side of this main street in the Chinese city there are numerous cross streets, some of which contained articles of a different kind from those I have just been describing One named Loo-le-chang appeared to be the "Paternoster Row" of Peking. This street is nearly a mile in length, and almost every shop in it is a bookseller's. There are, no doubt, an immense number of rare and curious books and maps in this place worthy of the inspection of our sinalogues. Here are also a number of shops having for sale carvings in jade-

stone, ancient porcelain, bronzes, and other works
of an early period. One old man, in particular,
had some beautiful examples, which it was impossible for a lover of Oriental porcelain to resist, and
although he asked high prices for them I was
obliged to submit. These pieces are now in my
collection, and, as I sometimes look at them, they
bring vividly back to my memory my old friend
in Loo-le-chang.

A street in the same quarter of the city, and
named Ta-sha-lar, is also famous for its collections
of works of art both ancient and modern. Specimens of carved jade-stone and rock crystal are
plentiful in this street, and not unfrequently very
fine examples may be purchased at a moderate
price. The greater part of the porcelain is of the
Kein-lung period, and although not ancient is very
far superior to the porcelain made in China at the
present day. According to the Chinese, that
Emperor was a great patron of the arts, and tried
to copy and imitate the productions of the ancients.
But beautiful as the productions in his reign un-
doubtedly were, they were far inferior to those
manufactured during the dynasty of the Mings.
The wonderful and lovely colours in turquoise,
ruby, apple green, and red found in the ancient
specimens are still unrivalled by anything which
has been produced in more modern times, either in
China or amongst the civilised nations of the West.
Some of the foreign residents in Peking and Tien-
tsin had, from time to time, picked up some beau

tiful examples of Ming porcelain.   His Excellency
Mr. Bruce, Colonel Neale, the Secretary of Legation, and Dr. Rennie, had each secured many specimens of great beauty.   Brigadier-General Stavely
had a large collection, amongst which were some of
the finest little pieces I have ever met with.

But to return to the main street, out of which I
have been wandering in order to examine the book-
shops, jade-stones, ancient porcelain, bronzes, and
other articles of taste and luxury.   After proceeding about half a mile, more or less, up this street,
I was surprised to find myself apparently out of
town.   Here the broad paved street runs through
a large uncultivated plain, which, from its appearance, must be frequently covered with water.   I
then saw, for the first time, that but a small portion of this Chinese city (so called) is covered with
houses.   At some distance on my right and left I
observed large parks enclosed with high walls.
The enclosure on my left, or to the eastward, contained the temple of Tein-tin, sacred to the god
of agriculture, to which the Emperor repairs once
in every year to worship Heaven.   Here, it is said,
he devotes three days to solemn fasting and prayer,
and then proceeds to a field near the temple, where
with his own hands he holds the plough and throws
a portion of rice-grain into the ground to show the
importance which the Government attaches to the
cultivation of the soil.   At the time of my visit to
Peking the Chinese had some objections to this
place, and that on the opposite side, named Tee-tin,

being visited by foreigners, so that I merely saw the outside of them.

The south wall of the Chinese city, which I was now approaching, has three gates—one in the centre and one near each end. I passed out by the centre gate and through a mean-looking suburb into the open country. Here I found myself amongst fields and vegetable gardens; and tombs innumerable were scattered over the surface of the country. My object now was to reach the south-western suburbs, where I had been told there were a number of gardens in which plants were culti-vated for sale. I had no difficulty in finding the south-west gate, as, for this purpose, I had only to follow the line of wall. But when I got there I was informed that the gardens I had come in search of were some two or three miles in the country to the southward. Nothing daunted, I set off in the direction indicated by my informant, determining to make inquiries as I went along. Many were the contradictory statements and direc-tions I received on the way. Sometimes I was assured that I was on the right road and only a short distance from the object of my search, and then, when I made sure that that distance had been gone over, the next person I met would coolly inform me that nothing of the kind I was in quest of existed in that part of the country.

At last, however, the place I was in search of was found, and I presented myself to Mr. Jow, or Jow-sing, as he was called, the proprietor of one of the principal gardens in the village. He received me with great politeness, and showed me all over his extensive nursery garden. He had a large collection of plants cultivated in pots, but they were nearly all southerners, such as those I have already noticed in describing the gardens of Tien-tsin. Sweet-scented Jasmines, Pomegranates, Olea fragrans, Oranges, Citrons, Apples, and Pears, cultivated in pots, were the chief objects of Mr. Jôw's care. As I looked eagerly into every hole and corner for something new, something indigenous to that part of the country, the good Chinaman was evidently much puzzled. "Had I not come for flowers? Well, here were plenty of the finest which could be had; why did I not take some of them?" When I asked him whether there were any other gardens in the neighbourhood, he replied that there were plenty, but that none of them had any plants different from those he had shown me.

Leaving Jow-sing's garden, I proceeded to look out for the others. I soon found that the whole of this part of the country was covered with them. Here, as at Tien-tsin, Canton, and other parts of China, as well as Japan, it seems the fashion for nurserymen to form themselves into little communities at stated places; and the custom, I think, must be considered a good one, and convenient to the purchasers of flowers. There were some ten or twelve of these nurseries in this place, but, strange to say, they did not contain a single new plant. The few species of a hardy kind, and

probably indigenous to this part of China, were
all well known, and had been already introduced
to England from the gardens farther south than
Peking. These were *Jasminum nudiflorum*, *Prunus
triloba*, the Judas tree, *Weigela rosea*, Honeysuckles, and Roses, amongst which I observed the
Banksian rose.

As this part of the country had probably not
been visited by foreigners, my appearance created
considerable sensation amongst the natives.
Every living thing in the villages—men, women,
children, babies in arms, and dogs—turned out
to see me. All seemed in good circumstances;
they were well clothed, and apparently well fed.
Although the crowd which gathered round me
was rather noisy, all were good-humoured, and
much more polite than such a crowd would have
been in some countries nearer home. When I
had gone over all the gardens in this neighbourhood I bade adieu to the crowds by which I had
been attended, and rode back in the direction of
the city, which I entered by the Nan-see-mun, or
south-west gate.

There are few houses in the south-west and
western part of the Chinese city. A large portion of the land looks a dreary waste; much of
the ground is lying uncultivated or covered with
reeds, while other parts are occupied as vegetable
gardens, and here and there are some wretched
mud hovels. It will be observed, therefore, that
although the walls of the Chinese city enclose a

large tract of land, by far the greatest portion of
the enclosure is either lying waste or is used as
garden ground. When we hear of the vast size
of the Chinese and Tartar cities of Peking, we
must therefore keep in view such facts as I have
pointed out, which will moderate our ideas with
regard to the extent of the population.

As I approached the wall of the Tartar city,
the evening began to close in, and it was necessary to ride sharply onwards to get through before
the gates were shut for the night. These are
invariably closed soon after sunset.

Next day I had arranged with Mr. Wyndham,
of Her Majesty's Legation, to explore the northern
part of the Tartar city, the Russian cemetery, and
the Lama temple outside the northern walls.
Early in the morning, however, a message came
from the Chinese authorities, requesting foreign
residents not to go in that direction during the
day, as the ladies of the Court were expected
on their return from their flight into Tartary. Of
course we were too polite to intrude in any way
upon the privacy of these distinguished personages,
and gave up the intended excursion until a message came telling us that the ladies had passed in,
and that the road was clear.

It was now the end of September, and the
mornings in Peking were very enjoyable. That
on which we started for the excursion which had
been put off was clear and calm, and the air was
cool and bracing. We were early astir, and the

2 B

traffic with carts, horses, and camels, which stirs
up the dust at a later period of the day and
renders the streets almost impassable, had not yet
commenced. Turning into one of the long wide
streets which stretch from south to north, we rode
slowly onwards in a northerly direction towards
the Yan-ting or An-ting gate. At some little
distance on our left was the Imperial city, with
the yellow roofs of its palaces and temples glittering in the morning sun. A curious building,
known as the Drum Tower, was also on our left.
Shops and stalls lined the wide street, but there
appeared little of interest in either to attract our
notice as we went along.

Passing through the An-ting gate, we were soon
in the open country. This part is well known to
those of our troops who took a part in the late
Chinese war. Here the troops were posted ready
to take the city at a moment's notice. A little
distance beyond the gate we came to the Russian
cemetery, in which lie buried the bodies of poor
Bowlby, the special commissioner of the 'Times'
newspaper, and some other gentlemen who had
been treacherously murdered by the Chinese during
the late war. Their bodies lie side by side, and a
headstone records their names and their sad fate.
It is intended, I believe, to remove their remains
to an English cemetery, as soon as a site has been
granted for this purpose. The Russian cemetery
is a small, unpretending spot, situated amongst
some high trees, and surrounded by a wall. At

its upper end there are a considerable number of foreign tombs.

The Lama temple, situated in these northern suburbs, is a very large establishment, and was occupied by the force under Sir Hope Grant when it marched on Peking. It appears to have been a kind of caravansera as well as a temple. I observed a number of priests lounging about, clothed in robes of the imperial yellow colour. The most remarkable object in the grounds is a · fine octagonal marble monument, richly carved with figures in high relief. Like the mosque I have already noticed, it is unlike anything one sees in China; it is quite Indian in form, and the characters and figures are probably Thibetian. Leaving the temple, we galloped along a grassy plain to the north-east corner of the city; then passing southward under the eastern walls, we entered the city again by one of the gates on this side, and went home by a different road from that by which we came out. Before we reached the English Legation all Peking was up and astir,—horsemen were galloping about, carts were jolting along the dusty streets, long trains of camels with bells jingling from their necks were toiling along, and clouds of dust were filling the air and rendering · locomotion far from pleasant.

After rambling over this great city in almost every direction, I may mention the following as being its peculiar and most striking features. As an eastern city it is remarkable for its great size, and for its high and massive walls, ramparts, and watch-towers. Its straight and wide streets are different from those of any other Chinese town which has come under my observation. Its imperial palaces, summer-houses, and temples, with their quaint roofs and yellow tiles, are very striking objects; and the number of private dwellings, situated amongst trees and gardens surrounded with high walls, give a country or park-like appearance to the great city. The trees and gardens of the palaces, with King-shan, or "Prospect Hill," are objects of considerable interest, as is also the Lama mosque, suggesting, as it does, some connexion in times long gone by with Thibet or India.

CHAPTER XXIII.

A journey to the mountains — Long trains of camels and donkeys — Pagoda at Pale-twang — Large cemetery — Curious fir-tree — Agricultural productions — Country people — Reach the foot of the hills — Temples of Pata-tshoo — Foreign writing on a wall — A noble oak-tree discovered — Ascend to the top of the mountains — Fine views — Visit from mandarins — Early morning view — Return to Peking — Descend the Pei-ho — Sail for Shanghae — Arrange and ship my collections — Arrive in Southampton.

ONE of the principal objects I had in view in coming thus far north was to get a peep at the capital of China. Another inducement, and perhaps a greater one, was the hope of being able to add some new plants of an ornamental kind to my former collections. And considering the cold winters which are experienced in this part of the world, anything of that kind would have been almost certain to prove hardy in our English climate. As the nursery-gardens I had visited both at Tien-tsin and Peking were filled with well-known southern species, and as the plain through which I had passed was nearly all under cultivation and contained few trees, I was anxious to visit the mountains which bound this plain on the north and west, where I hoped to find something new to reward me for my long journey.

Amongst these western mountains there are some celebrated Buddhist temples, well known to the inhabitants of Peking, and often visited by them. The Buddhist priests, in all parts of the East, preserve with the greatest care the trees which grow around their houses and temples. It was therefore probable that those at Pata-tshoo—the name of the place in question—would have the same tastes as their brethren in other parts of the empire, and I determined to visit them in their mountain home.

Having engaged a cart for the journey, I had it packed with my bedding in the usual way, and started one morning at daybreak. Atmospheric changes are very sudden in this part of the world. The temperature, since my arrival in Peking, and even when I went to bed the night before, had been mild and warm, although not oppressive in any way. This morning, however, a north-west wind had come suddenly down, and the summer seemed to change instantly into winter. The wind was bitterly cold. Sudden changes of temperature are common in every part of China, but I never experienced such a change as this was. Great-coats and blankets, which would have pained one to look upon a few days before, were now most welcome, and were eagerly sought after.

As I preferred walking to being jolted in a springless cart, this change of temperature was far from being disagreeable. Passing out by the Fow-ching-mun—a gate in the western wall of the Tartar city—and through an extensive suburb, I then found myself on a country road. It was evidently the great highway between Peking and the countries to the westward. Long trains of camels and donkeys were met and passed, loaded with various kinds of merchandise. These camels were very fine animals, and much larger and apparently much stronger than those met with in Egypt and Arabia. They were covered with long hair, which is, no doubt, intended by nature to preserve them from the extreme cold of these northern regions. The tuft of long hair on the hump had a peculiar appearance as the animals moved along in the distance. One of the camels in each drove had a bell suspended from its neck, which emitted a clear tinkling sound.

About nine o'clock in the morning I arrived at a long straggling town named Pale-twang, and halted to breakfast at an inn on the road-side. This place is remarkable for a pagoda about 150 feet in height, which can be seen from the ramparts of Peking, forming an excellent landmark to the traveller on this wide plain. This pagoda is octagonal, having eaves projecting on all sides, on which are hung many thousands of little bells, which are always tinkling in the wind. Its lower sides are covered with figures of ancient warriors, gods, and dragons, and heads of all sorts of animals appear to support the walls. Altogether it is one of the most remarkable specimens of Chinese architecture that have come under my

observation. Four small temples are placed round
its base, in two of which are some figures representing Buddhist deities, and in the other two
there are tablets with inscriptions. A large
temple in a ruinous condition is placed between
the tower and the main road.

A little further on I came to a large cemetery
surrounded with high walls. As I was making
some inquiries about this place, an old Chinese
gentleman kindly volunteered to accompany me
over it, and to explain anything I wished to know.
When we entered this cemetery I was very much
struck with its appearance. It covered many
acres of land, and was evidently a very ancient
place. Broad walks intersected it at right angles,
and lofty trees of Juniper, Cypress, and Pine were
growing in avenues or shading the tombs. Here
was an example of taste and civilization which
existed at a very early period,—probably two or
three hundred years ago. When the nations of
Europe were crowding their dead in the dismal
churchyards of populous towns, and polluting the
air, the Chinese, whom we have been accustomed
to look upon as only half-civilized, were forming
pleasant cemeteries in country places, and planting them with trees and flowers. They were
doing ages ago in China what we have been doing
only of late years.

At the upper end of the cemetery, and forming
a termination to the broad avenues, I observed
some large marble tablets, supported by the tor-

toise and another animal, which my guide informed me were placed there some two hundred
years ago, by order of the reigning emperor, over
the grave of one of his subjects, whom he " delighted to honour." I have remarked elsewhere
that a tombstone placed upon a carved representation of an animal of this kind is a sign of a royal
gift.

Near these royal tombstones I observed a species
of Pine-tree, having a peculiar habit and most
striking appearance. It had a thick trunk, which
rose from the ground to the height of three or
four feet only. At this point some eight or ten
branches sprang out, not branching or bending in
the usual way, but rising perpendicularly, as
straight as a larch, to the height of 80 or 100 feet.
The bark of the main-stem and the secondary
stems was of a milky-white colour, peeling like
that of the Arbutus, and the leaves, which were
chiefly on the top of the tree, were of a lighter
green than those of the common Pine. Altogether
this tree had a very curious appearance, very
symmetrical in form, and the different specimens
which evidently occupied the most honourable
places in the cemetery were as like one another
as they could possibly be.

In all my wanderings in India, China, or Japan,
I had never seen a pine-tree like this one. What
could it be ?—was it new ?—and had I at last found
something to reward me for my journey to the far
north ? I went up to a spot where two of these

trees were standing, like sentinels, one on each side of a grave. They were both covered with cones, and therefore were in a fit state for a critical examination of the species. But although almost unknown in Europe, the species is not new. It proved to be one already known under the name of *Pinus Bungeana*. I had formerly met with it in a young state in the country near Shanghae, and had already introduced it into England, although, until now, I had not the slightest idea of its extraordinary appearance when full grown. I would therefore advise those who have young plants of this curious tree in their collections to look carefully after them, as the species is doubtless perfectly hardy in our climate, and at some future day it will form a very remarkable object in our landscape. One of the trunks, which I measured at three feet from the ground, was 12 feet in circumference.

The country through which I was now passing, although comparatively flat, was gradually getting a little higher and more undulating in its general appearance. It was the harvest-time for the summer crops of millet, Indian corn, and oily grain, and the farmers were busy in all the fields gathering the crops into their barns. As I walked during the greater part of my journey, and did not always confine myself to the high road, many were the amusing adventures I met with by the way. Sometimes the simple villagers received me with a kind of vacant wondering

WHITE-BARKED PINE (*Pinus Bungeana*).

stare, or scarcely condescended to look up from
the work with which they were engaged. At
other times they gathered round me, and, when
they found I was civilized enough to know a little
of their language, put all sorts of questions, com-
mencing, for politeness, with those in relation to
my name, my age, and my country. On one occasion, as I was passing through a village, a solitary
lady, rather past the middle age and not particularly fascinating, was engaged in rubbing out
some corn in front of her door. I gave her the
usual salutation. She looked up from her work,
and when she saw who stood before her she gave
me one long earnest stare, and whether she thought
I was really " a foreign devil " or a being from some
other world I cannot say, but after standing for
a second or two, without speaking or moving, she
suddenly turned round and fled across the fields.
I watched her for a little while; she never appeared to slacken her pace or to look back, and
for aught I know she may be still running away!

About noon I began to get near the foot of the
mountains, and I could see in the distance a group
of temples extending from the bottom to near the
top of a hill, and nestling amongst trees. This
looked like an oasis in the landscape, for all else
round about was wild and barren. Shortly afterwards we left the main road, and another mile of
a byway brought us to the bed of a mountain
stream, dry at this season, and covered with
boulders of granite, but no doubt filled with a

torrent during the rains. We had now reached
the famous Pata-tshoo, or eight temples, which,
with their houses and gardens, are scattered all
over the sides of these hills.

My carter, who seemed well acquainted with the
place, proceeded up the hill-side to the second
range of temples, named Ling-yang-sze, and halted
at its entrance. Here I was received by the head
priest, a clean, respectable-looking man, who
readily agreed to allow me quarters during my
stay. My bedding was removed from the cart
and placed in a large room, whose windows and
verandah looked over the plain in the direction of
Peking. The temples for Buddhist worship in
this place are small, but the rooms for the reception of travellers and devotees are numerous, and
in better order than I had ever met with before.
In one of these rooms a marble tablet was pointed
out, which had been presented by one of the
Emperors of the Ming dynasty, who had visited
the place. Between the various rooms and temples
were numerous small courtyards and gardens, ornamented with trees, flowers, and rockwork. Here
I noticed some fine old specimens of the " Maiden-
hair tree " (*Salisburia adiantifolia*), one of which
was covered all over with the well-known glycine.
The creeper had taken complete possession of this
forest king, and was no doubt a remarkable and
beautiful object in the months of April and May,
when covered with its long racemes of beautiful
lilac blossoms; but the Salisburia evidently did

not like its fond embraces, and was showing signs of rapid decay. A pretty pagoda stood on one side of these buildings, with numerous little bells hanging suspended from its spreading eaves, which made a plaintive tinkling noise as they were shaken by the wind.

When I had rested for a little while in these pleasant quarters I informed my host that I was desirous of visiting the other temples on the hill-side, and begged him to procure me the services of a guide for this purpose. A very intelligent young priest volunteered to accompany me, and our party was soon joined by eight or ten more. The different temples were like so many terraces on the hill-side, and were connected with each other by narrow walks sometimes cut out of the hill, or, where the place was steeper than usual, flights of stone steps had been made. In one of these temples, named Ta-pae-sze, I observed some writing on the wall, evidently by a foreign hand. It was dated " 1832."

The largest of these temples, named Shung-jay-sze, has been honoured with a mark of royal favour in the shape of a tablet resting on a carved tortoise. Here too is pointed out, with no little pride, a room in which the favourite Emperor of the present dynasty, Kein-lung, slept when he visited the temple. Fine views of the plain are obtained from the front rooms; and a large bridge, named Loo-co-jou, was pointed out to me in the distance.

On the sides of these hills I met with a new oak-tree (*Quercus sinensis*) of great interest and beauty. It grows to a goodly size—sixty to eighty feet, and probably higher—has large glossy leaves, and its bark is rough, somewhat resembling the cork-tree of the south of Europe. Its acorns were just ripe, and were lying in heaps in all the temple-courts. They are eagerly bought up by traders, and are used in the manufacture of some kind of dye. I secured a large quantity of these acorns; and they are now growing luxuriantly in Mr. Standish's nursery at Bagshot. As this fine tree is almost certain to prove perfectly hardy in Europe, it will probably turn out to be one of the most valuable things I have brought away from Northern China. A species of maple and an arbor-vitæ of gigantic size were also met with on these hills, apparently distinct from the species found in the more southern provinces of the Chinese empire, and walnut-trees were observed covered with fruit in some of the temple-gardens. Amongst wild plants on these hill-sides there was a pretty species of *Vitex* resembling *V. agnus-castus*, and a neat little fern (*Pteris argentea*) was growing on some old walls. Amongst the plants cultivated for their flowers by the priests, I observed oleanders, moutans, pomegranates, and such things as I had already noticed in the gardens of Peking. A marble bridge of great age spanned the bed of a mountain stream, which was dry at this season; and examples of nature's rockwork, looking almost

as fantastic as if it had been artificial, were met
with in many places.

High above all the other temples, and· nearly at
the top of these hills, was a small one named Pou-
choo-ting.   The most charming views were obtained from this situation, not only over the vast
plain which lay beneath us, but also of the summer
palace of Yuen-ming-yuen, rendered famous by the
scenes enacted there during the late war.   Passing
out of the grounds of this place, I now commenced
the ascent of the hills behind it, and kept on until
I reached the highest point of their summits.
Here I sat down upon a cairn of stones to enjoy
the scene which lay spread out before me.

It was a lovely autumnal day, the air was cold
and bracing, and the atmosphere so clear that
objects at a very great distance were distinctly
visible.   Looking to the eastward I could see the
walls and watchtowers of Peking, and the roofs of
its yellow palaces.   On my left hand I looked
down upon the ruins of the palace of Yuen-ming-
yuen.   A little hill in the vicinity of the Summer
Palace, and the lake of Koo-nu-hoo, were distinctly
visible from where I was stationed.   On my right,
to the westward, a small stream appeared winding
its way amongst the hills in the direction of the
plain, where it was spanned by a bridge of many
arches—the Loo-co-jou I have already mentioned.
In front, to the south, the mighty plain of Tien-
tsin extended far away to the distant horizon,
dotted here and there with pagodas, but without

a mountain or a hill on any part of its surface.
Behind me, to the north, were hills and mountains
of every size and form, separated by valleys in
which I observed, in some places, little farm-houses
and patches of cultivated land.   The tops of these
mountains, and by far the greater portion of their
sides, were bleak and barren, yielding only some
wiry· grasses, a species of stunted thorny *Rhamnus*
(? *R. zizyphus*) ; and here and there, at this season,
a little *Campanula*, not unlike the Blue Bells of
Scotland, showed itself amongst the clay-slate rocks
which were cropping out over all the hills.   In
the spring there are no doubt many other kinds of
flowers which blossom unseen amongst these wild
and barren mountains.

This map of nature which lay before me was
one of no common kind.   It reminded me of the
views from the outer ranges of the Himalayas over
the plains of Hindostan, with this difference, that
these Chinese mountains rival in barren wildness
many parts of the Scottish Highlands.   When I
was in full enjoyment of the scenery around and
beneath me, my companions pointed to the setting
sun, and suggested that it was time to go down to
the temples.   Night was already settling down
upon the vast plain, and objects were becoming
gradually indistinct there, while the last rays of
the setting sun still illuminated the peaks of the
western mountains.

When we got back to the temple the good priest
pretended to have been greatly alarmed on account

of our long absence and the darkness of the night. We might have lost our way or missed our footing amongst the mountains and ravines. However, an excellent Chinese dinner was soon smoking on the table; and although chopsticks had to supply the places of knives and forks, the air of the mountains had furnished me with a tolerable appetite, and made me quite indifferent to the deprivation. After dinner I was honoured with the company of some high officials of the district, who came to inquire what my objects were in visiting this part of the country; but as my servant had already informed them that I had come from the Yamun of the great English Minister, they were easily satisfied, and did not even ask for a sight of my passport. Sundry cigars and a glass or two of wine put them in capital humour, and we parted very good friends.

When the mandarins left me the priests and others in the temple retired to rest, and shortly afterwards the only sounds which fell upon my ear were caused by the wind rustling among the leaves of the surrounding trees and the tinkling of the bells which hung from the eaves of the pagoda. Fatigued with the exertion of the day I retired early to rest, and nothing occurred during the night to disturb my slumbers.

Next morning I was up before the sun, and enjoyed a view of the vast plain as it was gradually lighted up by the early rays. It was curious to see the light chasing away the darkness and exposing to view the pagodas, bridges, and towers which but a short time before had been invisible. During the day I visited some temples and gardens on the other side of a valley, and secured a supply of the plants of the district for the herbarium, and the seeds of several trees of an ornamental and useful character worth introducing into Europe. The people amongst these hills seemed to be a quiet and inoffensive race, miserably poor, having only the bare necessaries of life and none of its luxuries. The Buddhist priests were apparently much better off, being, no doubt, upheld and supported by their devotees among the wealthier classes of the capital, who came to enjoy the scenery amongst the hills and to worship in the temples.

After a pleasant sojourn of two days in this part of the country I returned to Peking. As on the way out, long trains of donkeys and camels were met and passed on the road, many of them being laden with coal, which is found in abundance amongst these western hills. On the way back I paid another visit to the cemetery of Pale-twang, and obtained a fresh supply of the seeds of the curious fir-tree I have already described.

Having finished my work in Peking and packed up the collections I had formed there, I left that city on the 28th of September, and considered myself as once more "homeward bound." My friend Dr. Lockhart accompanied me several miles on my way. With many good wishes for a prosperous voyage home the worthy medical missionary bade me adieu, and returned to his arduous duties in the far-famed capital of Cathay. As it was my intention to return to Tien-tsin by boat down the Pei-ho river, I had taken the road which leads from Peking to the city of Tong-chow, at which place boats were to be procured for the voyage. A short distance on the north-west of Tong-chow I passed the now celebrated bridge and battle-field of Pali-kao. On arriving at Tong-chow I found no difficulty in engaging a boat, and we sailed rapidly and pleasantly down the stream.

As opportunities for leaving Tien-tsin for the south were few and uncertain, I had to remain some days there before I could get onwards. At last, owing to the kindness of the French commandant at Taku, I procured a passage in the despatch boat ' Contest,' and reached Shanghae on the 20th of October. Here I found my Japanese collections (which I had left in Mr. Webb's garden) in excellent condition, and I employed the next fortnight in preparing them for their long voyage home round the Cape of Good Hope. The collections were divided into two equal portions, and, as a precautionary measure, were put on board of two ships. These cases have now reached England, and nearly every plant of importance has been introduced alive. Long shelves filled with these rare and valuable trees and shrubs of Japan have been exhibited during the last two summers by Mr. Standish at the different botanical and horticultural exhibitions in the metropolis, and already many of the earlier introductions have been distributed all over Europe.

Some especial favourites, which I did not like to trust to the long sea journey round the Cape, were brought home by the overland route under my own care.   One of these is a charming little saxifrage, having its green leaves beautifully mottled and tinted with various colours of white, pink, and rose.   This will be invaluable for growing in hanging baskets in greenhouses or for window gardening.   I need not tell now how I managed my little favourites on the voyage home; how I guarded them from stormy seas, and took them on shore for fresh air at Hongkong, Ceylon, and Suez; how I brought them through the land of Egypt and onwards to Southampton.   More than one of my fellow-passengers by that mail will remember my movements with these two little hand greenhouses.   On the 2nd of January, 1862, the Peninsular and Oriental Company's ship 'Ceylon,' Captain Evans, steamed into the dock at Southampton, and thus ends the narrative of my visit to Zipangu and Cathay.

INDEX.

THE END.

LONDON: PRINTED BY W. CLOWES AND SONS, STAMFORD STREET, AND CHARING CROSS.

CPSIA information can be obtained
at www.ICGtesting.com
Printed in the USA
LVOW07s2242260617
539401LV00014B/158/P